D0824923

WITHOUT SURRENDER WITHOUT CONSENT

Daniel Raunet

WITHOUT SURRENDER WITHOUT CONSENT

A History of the Nishga Land Claims

Douglas & McIntyre
Vancouver/Toronto

© 1984 by Daniel Raunet

All rights reserved. No part of this book may be reproduced or transmitted in any form by any means without permission in writing from the publisher, except by a reviewer, who may quote brief passages in a review.

Douglas & McIntyre Ltd.
1615 Venables Street,
Vancouver, British Columbia
V5L 2H1

Canadian Cataloguing in Publication Data

Raunet, Daniel, 1946–
    Without surrender, without consent

    Bibliography: p.
    ISBN 0–88894–433–0

    1. Niska Indians – Land tenure. 2. Indians of North America – British Columbia – Land tenure. 3. Indians of North America – British Columbia – Claims. I. Title.
    E99.T8R38 1984   333.2   C84–091154–8

Design by Barbara Hodgson
Printed and bound in Canada by D. W. Friesen & Sons Ltd.

It's not like your papers. Sometimes your papers, people don't believe in them, some people read them and he says this is not true, somebody else is right. But in our traditions, once it's taught to the people and it passes on, it's just like History, you know: you write on a paper that goes on and on and never stops. And when the Great Spirit gave the chieftainship to our people, and it carries on and it's still carried on today. There had to be the leaders of the village. There's four head-chiefs of every tribe that are leaders of the village. And it's still like that today. And whoever is not wise, see, he is forgotten. He's just disappeared.

Chief Roy Azak, 1981

CONTENTS

ACKNOWLEDGEMENTS

This book represents solely the views of its author. However, it would not have been possible without the help and hospitality of the Nishga people and the Nishga Tribal Council. I want particularly to thank James Gosnell, Rod Robinson, Frank Calder, Harry and Deanna Nyce and their parents, Nelson Leeson, Morris and Ginette Squires, Chester Benson, and Percy Tait; many more names could be added. I will always have warm memories of the late Roy Azak. Bill Horswill of the Ayuukhl Nisga'a Project was generous with his extensive knowledge. In the course of my research I had invaluable assistance from a great number of people including Jim Aldridge, Thomas Berger, Cam Ford, Jim Fulton, David Garrick, Anthony Jenkinson, Geoff Meggs, Bud Mintz, Richard Overstall, Tony Pearse, Jean Rivard, Don Rosenbloom, Marie-Lucie Tarpent, and, in the United States, Don Aubertin, José Burrero, Edwin Dahle, Bruce Johansen, Winona LaDuke, Rich Nafviger, Chris Shuey, and Yvonne Swan. Special thanks are also due the Native Brotherhood of British Columbia, the historians of the Vancouver Public Library, the Provincial Archives of British Columbia, the archives of the Vancouver School of Theology, the Special Collections Division of the University of British Columbia Library, and their staffs. The manuscript was edited with great professionalism by Richard Howard, who on many occasions made me feel that I had never been as coherent in my life. Last but not least, credit should be given to my wife Aubin and to Jane Munro for weeding so many Frenglishisms out of the text.

Daniel Raunet
March 1984

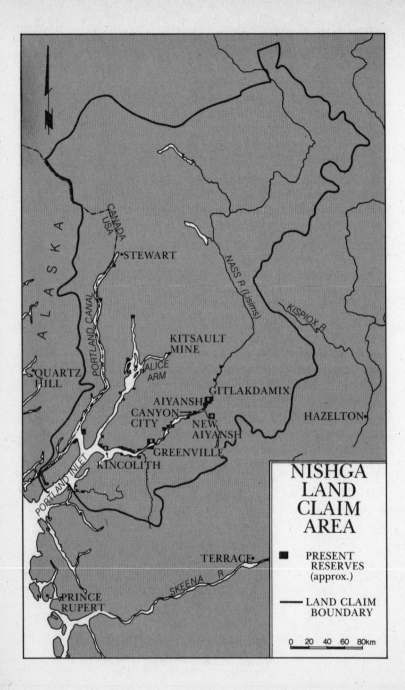

ALASKA

CANADA
USA

•STEWART

NASS R. (Lisims)

KISPIOX R.

PORTLAND CANAL

KITSAULT
MINE

ALICE
ARM

•QUARTZ
HILL

GITLAKDAMIX

AIYANSH
CANYON
CITY

NEW
AIYANSH

HAZELTON•

GREENVILLE

KINCOLITH

PORTLAND INLET

TERRACE•

SKEENA R.

PRINCE
RUPERT

NISHGA
LAND
CLAIM
AREA

■ PRESENT
    RESERVES
    (approx.)

—— LAND CLAIM
     BOUNDARY

0   20   40   60   80Km

INTRODUCTION

R oy Azak was not exactly a reckless driver; he knew every pothole and every hairpin turn in the dirt road by heart, but the savagely rough nature of the terrain was still unnerving. Twenty kilometres from the airport, we had left the smooth surface of Highway 16 to enter what looked like a private property, an immense marshalling yard littered with large pieces of machinery, scattered log piles, boxcars, and torn carcasses of bark. This was the territory of the Kitsumkalum. We had passed a few of them in downtown Terrace, but there was no human life to be seen here. The land of the Kitsumkalum was like an open wound after several decades of chain-saw massacring. Company signs proudly advertised ten- or fifteen-year-old reforestation projects that still looked like plantations of matchsticks to the untrained eye. Here was no totem-pole material, but every five minutes an eighteen-wheel monster would pass by with four or five giant logs fettered to its bed. There must be something more than this desolation beyond the clouds licking the slopes.

Roy Azak's cap displayed the name of a leading manufacturer of logging equipment. In spite of his age, somewhere around sixty, he was still working part time in a sawmill. A three-inch wooden cross on his chest proclaimed another facet of his life. As he explained, Canyon City had asked for a resident priest in the twenties, but the Anglican church refused. There was already a parish on the Aiyansh reserve twenty-five kilometres upstream, and the presence of two hundred or so worshippers could not justify the expense. The Canyon City people were incensed. In those days, a clergyman meant not just a church but a school as well. They advertised the position in Prince Rupert, letting it be known that they would all join the first denomination to send them a minister. The Salvation Army answered the call, and that was that.

Roy Azak described himself as a lay preacher. He was thankful to the Army for its struggle against loose morals and drunkenness, but his religious convictions ran deeper than a simple code of ethics. For him, the Bible and Nishga tradition were one and the same. Jonah, he pointed out, had been saved by a whale. Animals had taught Native folk the basic skills of survival. The Nishga were still calling each other "Wolves," "Killer whales," "Eagles," "Ravens." The people of the Bible survived the Flood on Noah's Ark; in the Nass Valley, the wise ones built a raft and clung to a cliff on the mountainside. He could still show the marks where the ropes had bitten into the rock.

His Christian faith, however, was not blind. He knew that the churches had been very wrong in the past. They had forbidden the old customs, asked for the removal of the totem poles. The Nishga had never knelt in front of the poles; they were not idols but family treasures. The white people had understood nothing.

After a couple of hours Roy Azak announced that we had entered Nishga country. A very long lake located behind a lava wall drew out another story. On the right side of the mountain there was an extinct volcano that had erupted four or five centuries earlier. Young people were cruel and stuck burning sticks in the dorsal fins of salmon just so they could watch the fish glow as they swam away. The elders warned against such foolishness, and that same night thousands of Nishga died in a powerful lava flow which buried several villages and invaded the middle of the Nass Valley. The river disappeared for several years; many more died, this time of starvation. Now, Roy Azak could see the same thing happening again. A mining company named AMAX had opened a plant on a Nishga fjord near the Alaska border, and it wanted to dump its tailings straight into the ocean. New catastrophes would happen if mankind kept tampering with nature.

The clouds lifted, and the beauty of the country was breathtaking. The broad lava plain where only moss and a few bushes could grow was encircled by tall forests, high mountains, and glaciers. Every place had a name, every site an owner. The trees, the berries, the fish, the game were still all-important to the people of the land: it had been given to the Nishga by the Creator. The government said that the country did not belong to the Nishga, but Roy Azak knew this was not so. The land had not been sold, it had not been ceded; it had been stolen. The tale of this theft was well preserved in tradition: how the first boat had arrived; how the commissioner had come, a hundred years or so ago, and created the reserves, without telling anybody; how the Nishga had protested, how they had stopped the surveyors; how they had gone to Victoria, Ottawa, even London.

The van pulled up at the edge of the cliff. There was no road to Canyon City. Cars were parked on the lava bed and villagers had to cross the Nass River on a narrow suspension bridge swinging fifteen metres above the fast-moving water. There was a lot of mud and no sidewalk, no real street, no fire engine, no ambulance, no landscaped garden in front of the band office. This was the spring of 1981; this was an Indian reserve. Yet the sorry state of its public amenities was not owing to lack of initiative on the part of the population. Canyon City had a chapter of the Lions Club and a number of organizations devoted to charitable, sports, youth, religious, feminine, musical, professional, and other interests. There was no evening, I was assured, without a meeting of some sort. The villagers were particularly afraid that the young people might leave the valley. With their own funds, they had just completed a large gymnasium at the top of the hill.

The organizers of the Nishga Tribal Council convention had "billeted" me in the house of a young couple. We talked with their relatives late into the night. One of my hosts took me out on the porch to listen to the wolves, so close and so alien, howling in the mountains above the village. I was told that their concert was a good omen for the annual convention. I did not doubt this for a single instant. In Canyon City, the Wolves are the leading clan.

The following evening, several hundred people attended the opening banquet in the new gymnasium. The master of ceremonies, the executive council, distinguished guests, a small delegation from the Terrace Lions Club, the Salvation Army captain and his spouse, the dignitaries of the Anglican church, representatives of the major native organizations of British Columbia were all in place, but Roy Azak was nowhere to be seen. . . . An eerie sound, coming from just outside the door, halted the speechmaking. I immediately recognized the wolves of the night before. This time, however, the animals were on two legs. A handful of young people entered the hall howling with great skill followed by a herald carrying the "talking stick" and shouting a solemn message in Nishga at the top of his voice. Behind him, a little man dressed in full regalia and covered with a magnificent wolf pelt walked with immense dignity. Roy Azak the preaching woodworker also turned out to be Chief Baxkap, head of the House of Luxanuulhkw, and, by protocol, the most important person in the village. After the speeches were done, he removed his wolf fur to go behind the head table and take his place with the rest of the Canyon City Brass Band, where he played Victorian hymns during the rest of the meal.

Roy Azak died in June 1983. To the outsider that I was, his blend of tradition and new values, protocol and simplicity, was at first disconcerting. Like many Natives of his generation he was a living history book, a wise man who had kept alive the ideals of his nation, the deep sense of solidarity, the longing for the lost lands. I discovered later that much of what Roy Azak said to me, his vision of his people's future, kept recurring word for word, or almost, in century-old records as well as contemporary speeches and presentations to parliaments. Regardless of time, an uncanny pattern emerged from everything the Nishga had ever put on the record — a central message transmitted by those who, like the old Chief Skadeen of 1886, told white trespassers, "Saayeen! Saayeen!" — "Get off my land!"

Those newcomers did not move into a void. All the land save for the frozen mountain tops was already stamped with purpose. The first inhabitants had very precise concepts of ownership, law, and political structure. They knew what was theirs and they saw it seized without consent and without compensation. The most competent jurists have always been baffled by this fact, unable to reconcile the blatant denial of justice with the self-proclaimed principles of a British-derived legal system.

The history of Native people in Canada, as well as in such colonies of settlement as the United States, Australia, and South Africa, is the story of an "apartheid," that is to say of a "setting apart." The original inhabitants of these countries were set aside because they were obstacles barring free access to the wealth of the land for those who coveted it. Adventurers, missionaries, soldiers, merchants, racist officials, dishonest politicians, foreign colonists, multinational big businesses — the faces of the exploiters have changed often enough, but exploitation's pattern has remained the same: the theft of land, the plunder of resources, the destruction of a way of life and a culture that are incompatible with the rule of profit.

Aboriginal people are by no means the sole victims of coercion in our midst, but in their case the myths of North American society have never really applied. For the non-immigrant, this has never been the land of freedom, of democracy, of opportunity, that it was supposed to be. The physical, cultural, and economic genocides of the last century have been followed by poverty and slow despair on the reserves and social deprivation among those who have left for the cities. The fate of the Natives is not the result of a "mistake" of history, it is not the product of a want of generosity on the part of the rulers that could be alleviated by a few well-crafted legislative measures.

The failure of the reserve system, the failure of Canadian apartheid, is now acknowledged by most. The sad litany of statistics must convince even the most stubborn skeptic. In Canada, Native infant mortality is 60 per cent above the national average. After age one, life expectancy is ten years shorter. The death rate is two to four times higher, the suicide rate three times. Native people are three times more likely to be unemployed, and their average income is 50 to 66 per cent lower. Some 80 per cent of Native children are not reaching Grade 12 when the national rate of school failure is only 25 per cent. About 40 per cent of status Indians live more than one family to a house, and in 1977, 60 per cent of Native dwellings had no running water, sewage facilities, or indoor plumbing. In Manitoba, Saskatchewan, and the two territories, 40 per cent of prison inmates are Natives. And so on, and so on.

There was a time, before the fifties, when the mere mention of the land issue was unlawful. The wind of reform has now been blowing, however fitfully, for several decades. In the early seventies, land claims became acceptable for discussion in official circles. The rapid development of the North had made settlements politically necessary. By the end of the decade, the Department of Indian Affairs was speaking of "Indian band government." In September 1983, a committee of the Canadian Parliament finally used the term, "first nations," and called for recognition of "Indian self-government." These are clear signs that the Native question is on the verge of entering a "decolonization" process. But as with other "decolonizations," this process will not necessarily lead to improvement.

The Native movement and our governments do not speak the same language. The first inhabitants' original goals of cultural and economic survival, respect for the environment, local control, are now expressed with increasing frequency in nationalist terms. And despite the recent recommendations of the Commons Committee on Indian Self-Government, there is as yet no proof that Canada will accept the principle of self-determination. Even if this issue were resolved, moreover, the question of the land base, central to the survival debate, would still remain. There is ample evidence in recent land-claim negotiations that Canada has not renounced its historical goal of "extinguishment of native title," that is to say the assimilation of Native nationalities.

By insisting on direct rule on the reserves, Canadian authorities have placed Native people in a unique situation. Not because of some revolutionary calling, but because they have been left with no other choice, they have come more rapidly than other groups to realize a basic fact of North American life: the state does not represent all segments of society, it serves the interests of powerful minorities.

The convergence of radicalism, traditionalism, and nationalism is not, however, the only trend in the Native movement. The official move towards devolution of some powers to the reserves, though without any concession on the land question or the issue of real control, has resulted in the emergence of a new breed of "valid interlocutors." In their haste to gain access to untapped natural resources, governments have actively encouraged a class of Native collaborators who would be ready to sign new surrenders, abandon their elders' communal values, and open the gates to corporate invasion.

This book is not an attempt to pay tribute to the folklore of the far west or the nostalgia of the last of the Mohicans; rather, it tries to confront modern problems directly. With more than a century of resistance to encroachment, the Nishga of British Columbia offer one of the most vivid examples of tenacity in the Canadian Native community. They leave us with a message that reaches far deeper than an exotic anecdote pulled out of the foggy past of the "land of the totem pole." Their struggle is the struggle of all those who refuse to submit to a future they have not chosen; it is the struggle of those who have tried to remain, faced with the dehumanizing momentum of state and money, masters in their own houses, and on their own lands.

"MAMAHUIT," THE ONES WHO LOST THEIR WAY

They did not know if these people were human beings or not. Because they were different people, different type of people. Don't forget that our people had not seen the white man. They didn't even know there was a white man on the earth prior to that time. They did their own quick research on the spot to see if they were human beings, and they discovered that they were human beings.

This is not a funny story. This is a fact. They really did not know there were these people, or some type of beings, or whatever. They researched their ship without the white men knowing about it while they were sleeping. They found out that their ways were entirely different from our ways; language, mainly there were sign languages in those days. The main part of it was that they discovered that these people were human beings.

Now I guess if you look at it from the other direction, as the white people, I think, thought that our people were not really human beings. They classified us as animals for many years. I think history will tell you that. So I guess if you meet different people, like supposing, for example, that somebody came from outer space at this moment, we would want to know what is there, a human being or not.

So to begin with, our people did respect the white man right at the outset. Because if they didn't, and this is the story passed on to us, if they didn't, none of those white men that came on that ship at the mouth of the river would have survived. Not one of them. The ship would have been totally destroyed. They had the man-power to do it.

They pointed this — when I say, "they," I'm referring to our grandfathers — they pointed it out that we never did have any cause of violence or being violent, because no one prior to that time had threatened our existence. And they did not realize that was the beginning of the threat to our existence, when they met the white man. And looking back now, as I see it, they didn't realize it, they thought these people were there for a visit and then go. They didn't, you know.

Chief James Gosnell, President of the Nishga Tribal Council

The year was 1778: George Washington had not yet ousted the British; the French kings had lost Quebec, but they still owned Louisiana. On the Pacific coast of America, between Spanish California and Russian Alaska, lay a vast territory inhabited by free nations of fishermen completely unknown to white men. In many ways, they were as rich in culture as the ancient civilizations of Europe. Like the Vikings, they traded, travelled, and made war over thousands of kilometres. Like the Greeks, they had elaborated a mythology into sophisticated art forms — sculpture, theatre, and music. Like the Romans, they had precise concepts of law and property that formed the basis of a solid social system.

In 1778, the first white men landed on the west coast of Van-couver Island. The local Mohachat people called Capt. James Cook and his storm-battered crew "Mamahuit," the ones who lost their way in the fog. More Mamahuit came, from London, from Boston, from Cadiz. Their attitude was always the same: as far as these white men were concerned, the Coast Natives were living in barbarous heathenism. This basic misjudgement was described with remarkable lucidity by the Mexican creole Jose Mariano Moziño, a botanist who spent some time among the Mohachat with the 1792 expedition of Capt. Juan Francisco de la Bodega y Quadra.

It astonishes me inexpressibly to hear the kinds of sour comment passed about the reputation of these Natives, of whose perversity not one act is cited that could serve as proof. In the five months that we were among them, we experienced not a single offence on their part. . . .

The occasions were rare that any petty larcenies came to light, notwithstanding the many articles around which they could quite easily have had. Many of our officers went alone, and without arms, to visit some of the *rancherias* in the savages' own canoes, and they always came back taken by the kindness and gentleness observed in all of them.

What a pity that they cannot say the same of us, for the sailors, either because of their near-brutish upbringing or resentful of the humane treatment the Commander and most officers always gave the Natives, did them injury in various ways, crippling some and wounding others, and managed to kill a number of them. Humaneness is civilization's finest quality. All the sciences and arts are worth nothing if they serve only to make us cruel and proud.

Whites were drawn to the area by its rich lode of lucrative furs. Sea otter, mink, and other pelts from the Pacific Northwest were rapidly becoming fashionable in China, and traders found the Natives eager to exchange these for European goods. Spaniards, British, and New Englanders were becoming very active along the shores of what is now British Columbia, but as the eighteenth century's final decade opened, no outside nation had yet established sovereignty in any decisive manner. The newcomers had only a vague idea of areas beyond the west coast of Vancouver Island, and they knew nothing of the Nishga, a people living near the present border between Alaska and Canada. In 1777, the Spanish navigator Juan Pérez had spotted the archipelago of the Queen Charlottes. Their inhabitants, the Haida, proved to be trading partners of some interest, having a good supply of sea otter and acting as middlemen between the white merchants and the unknown nations of the continent. Connections were growing closer.

Who were the first white traders to establish direct contact with the Nishga? A "Boston ship," according to a group of chiefs writing to the Victoria *Weekly Colonist* in March 1888. If this was the case, the most likely candidate would be Capt. Robert Gray's expedition of July–August 1781 aboard the *Columbia Rediviva*. A century afterwards, in fact, the historian Hubert Bancroft was led to speculate that these New England traders did reach the present Alaska-Canada border, exploring "many of the inlets and passages between the 54th and the 56th parallels, in one of which — most probably the same afterwards called by Vancouver the Portland Canal — he penetrated from its entrance, in the latitude of 54 degrees 33 minutes, to the distance of a hundred miles northeastward, without reaching its termination." Bancroft based his version on the journal of the expedition's chief officer Robert Haswell, but another document, Pilot Boit's log, indicates that the *Columbia* was actually sailing inside the Alaskan archipelago, past Tlingit country.

The first European known to have seen the shores of northern British Columbia was an Englishman, Capt. James Colnett. Exploring with two vessels, the *Prince of Wales* and the *Princess Royal,* he sighted the approaches of the Nishga fjords in 1787. However, the map of three years later based on his voyage shows that he had not understood the region's geography. Navigators of that time were still looking for an "inland passage" which would lead them miraculously through to the Atlantic Ocean and shorten the trip from Europe to the Far East. Colnett had dutifully noted several possible entrances to this mythical waterway, one being a "Stevens Sound" at the edge of Nishga territory.

When Colnett returned to Nootka, the Mohachat harbour on the west coast of Vancouver Island, his papers were seized by the Spaniards, who were disputing possession of the area with the British. Five years later, representatives of His Most Catholic Majesty decided to follow this lead in an attempt to solve the mystery of the inland shortcut. Like Colnett, Don Jacinto Caamaño did not venture off his poop deck; nor, according to his journal, did he see any Natives. In July 1792, he sighted the entrances to two fjords at the present border of Alaska, Pearse and Portland canals, and confirmed the presence of a major waterway inside the Alaskan archipelago. Heading south again, he spotted the islands off the northern British Columbia coast for which he chose the devout name, "Archipelago of the 11,000 Virgins." Favoured by excellent winds, the whole voyage had not lasted more than four days.

The first documented contact between the Nishga and the white man occurred the following year. It was a time when traders were experiencing increasing difficulty gathering their furs. The bargains of the first years were no more. The Natives had become price-wise. Europeans and Yankees from New England were in hot competition, and often had to spend full seasons on the coast before they could hoist sail for China.

The 1792–93 expedition of Capt. William Brown reflected this changing situation. Brown was sent to the Pacific by a company of London merchants with three vessels, the *Buttersworth*, a French frigate captured by the British, and two sloops, *Jackal* and *Prince Lee Boo*. In August 1792, his men distinguished themselves by murdering a Clayoquot man on the west coast of Vancouver Island in an incident which, according to another trader, Joseph Ingraham, stemmed from the theft of some furs by the *Buttersworth*'s crew. In 1793, after a disappointing season, Brown decided to look for better supplies along the northern coast of British Columbia. At the same time, a major expedition left England for the Pacific Northwest under Capt. George Vancouver to look for the elusive passage through to the Atlantic. On the evening of 20 July 1793, Vancouver's two ships, *Discovery* and *Chatham*, found themselves in a bad storm in Hecate Strait, south of the modern city of Prince Rupert. His party was rescued by white men in a rowboat, who guided them through the reefs to the safety of a cove on Banks Island where the *Buttersworth* was already moored. Vancouver reported the meeting in his journal:

> Mr. Brown informed me that he had spent some time in this immediate neighbourhood, and on coming out of a harbour that lies to the NNW of this station, about three leagues distant, his ship had struck upon a rock. . . . Whilst the *Buttersworth* had remained stationary, Mr. Brown had been employed in his small vessels in various directions, and to some extent, about this coast, particularly to the northwestward, in procuring furs. . . . He had understood from the natives that there was in this neighbourhood a very extensive inland navigation, communicating with a sea to the northward, that employed the inhabitants nearly three months in reaching its extent. . . . This inland navigation Mr. Brown supposed to be in an extensive arm, lying from hence about nine leagues distant; the entrance of which he had visited, and found it spacious and large, but had not penetrated any distance into it. . . . They anchored before a village of the natives, whose improper conduct made it necessary to fire upon them from the vessels, which was attended with some slaughter.

On 21 July, Vancouver decided to investigate Brown's report and found a "spacious" opening that he hoped would lead him to the eastern sea. In fact he was at the entrance of Observatory Inlet and Portland Canal, the gate of Nishga territory.

If this is the same branch described by the natives, which is much
to be questioned, especially as some of Mr. Brown's gentlemen
considered the opening meant by those people to be further to the
westward, it is called by them Ewen-Nass. The word Ewen, we
understood to signify great, or powerful; as, Ewen Smoket, a great
chief; but the word Nass was completely unknown to Mr. Brown,
and all of his party.

The expedition met its first aboriginals in the afternoon.

A few of the natives visited the ship in five or six canoes; they
brought little to dispose of, yet appeared to be anxious that we
should remain in their neighbourhood. Several inquiries were
made for Ewen Nass, but these people seemed to be totally ignorant of the phrase, until it had been repeated several times, and
we had pointed in various directions; upon which, some of them
repeated the words, and imitated our motions, giving some
amongst us reason to imagine that they meant that the Ewen Nass
was up this identical branch of the inlet; though in all other
respects we remained totally ignorant of their language.

It took Vancouver a full month and 140 kilometres of rowing
along the present border of Alaska and Canada to discover that
his passage would not lead across the continent:

The shores of this inlet were nearly straight, and in general little
more than a mile asunder, composed mostly of high rocky cliffs,
covered with pine trees to a considerable height; but the more
interior country was a compact body of high barren mountains
covered with snow. As we pursued this branch, salmon in great
plenty were leaping in all directions. Seals and sea otters were also
seen in great numbers, even where the water was nearly fresh, and
which was the case upwards of twenty miles from its termination.
    Mortified with having devoted so much time to so little purpose,
we made the best of our way back.

This chimerical quest — the fantasy that had never been absent
from the minds of European explorers of America — would not
have been savoured by his down-to-earth hosts. Far from being
intimidated by the white men, they decided to treat them like
any other strangers in their waters. After all, it was not uncom-
mon for these coastal peoples to travel great distances for trade.

From the Gulf of Alaska to the mouth of the Columbia, the coast was a vast mart in which nations speaking entirely different languages had commercial and cultural patterns in common. To the Nishga, this new people, like the Haida, the Tlingit, or the Kwawkgeulth, would have come there only to trade.

This, George Vancouver did not understand. On 23 July, a group of Nishga exchanged some fish for "looking glasses and other trinkets." On the following day, however, they tried to get down to more serious business:

> We stopped to dine. ... Here we were visited by seven of the natives, who approached us in a canoe with much caution, and landed some of their party at a little distance, whilst the others advanced, seemingly with no small suspicion of our friendly intentions; this, however, was soon removed by the distribution of some trivial presents amongst them; and their reception being made known to their companions who had landed, these without the least hesitation joined our party also. They were well prepared with arms, consisting of long spears, bows and arrows, together with an iron dagger, that each man wore about his neck or wrist.

Others joined this group; "on finding however that we did not return for the purpose of trading, they all retired to the village." On 27 July, another attempt was made, but when the English persisted in not getting the idea, the Nishga made it clear that the refusal was not appreciated:

> As we advanced, we were joined by a party of fifteen natives in two canoes. ... These people approached us without much hesitation, and in their countenances was expressed a degree of savage ferocity infinitely surpassing any thing of the sort I had before observed in the various tribes that had fallen under my notice. Many of those we had before seen had their faces painted in various modes; but these had contrived so to dispose of the red, white, and black, as to render the natural ugliness of their countenances more horribly hideous.

Worried by this time, Captain Vancouver discovered that these people were not interested in beads and trinkets: "They were rejected by some with disdain, whilst the few who deigned to accept any thing, received our gifts with a stern and cool indifference." They then lowered their spears and pulled out their daggers, gestures read by Vancouver as an invitation not to try an attack.

> They frequently made use of the words, "Winnee watter," signifying to stop and trade, producing at the same time some very indifferent sea-otter skins. Recollecting the avidity with which all the inhabitants of these parts enter into commercial intercourse, I thought their uncourteous behaviour might have arisen from our backwardness in following the same pursuit; and hoped, by offering to trade with them, we should be able to obtain their friendship. But neither cloth, iron, copper, nor any thing we had, was in their opinions sufficient in quantity, or equal in quality to the value of their skins.

The Englishmen decided to follow the Nishga to the shore, where they discovered to their surprise that the goods previously rejected with contempt were now suddenly acceptable. Far from plotting an ambush, the Natives had displayed one of their master skills: the art of driving a good bargain.

A similar incident occurred on 31 July. This time, the whites' refusal to do business was greeted by derision:

> The natives, who had visited us at dinner time, made their appearance again, accompanied by a large canoe, in which was the chief of their party. I directed them to land at a small distance from our boats, with which they readily complied. The chief received some presents, and, in return, gave me two or three sea-otters' tails. . . . On a promise of entering further into trade the next morning, they retired to a small cove about half a mile from us, with every appearance of being perfectly satisfied; but, about an hour afterwards, one of their canoes was seen paddling towards us. On this a pistol was fired in the air, which had the good effect of shewing that we were upon our guard, and prevented their giving us any further disturbance.
>
> As soon as it was day-light the next morning, these people, accompanied by another canoe, were with us according to appointment the preceding evening. They offered for sale the skins of the sea otter, and a large black bear, that seemed to have been killed by a spear in the course of the night. I was not backward in complying with our part of the agreement; but, like those whom we had seen on Saturday, these rejected every article we

had with us for the purpose of barter; and, excepting fire-arms and ammunition, which were not offered to them, we could not discover on what their inclinations were placed. They followed however for two miles, persisting in desiring we would "Winnee watter," until, at length, finding no other articles were tendered them than those they had before declined, they retired, exclaiming, "Pusee," and, "Peshack"; which could not be misunderstood as terms of disapprobation.

It had been a long way to sail for a ranking officer in the Royal Navy — and one, let us not forget, who "discovered" that Vancouver Island is an island — only to be treated as a common huckster. The sovereign Nishga saw no other use for him; they had divined him human, but did not know what he thought he was for. By the time they found out, the trap was sprung.

2

"ALU-GIGIAT," A PUBLIC PEOPLE

The first Europeans to come into contact with the indigenous groups of the Pacific shore wrote little about the folk they met. The newcomers were seeking furs, gold, and land. They had no reason to show any interest in Native history, culture, or social organization. And even if the whites had made a genuine effort to reach out and understand their new contacts, there is no proof that the locals would have been moved to impart their ways and thoughts, so many of their customs being reserved to the initiated. The two solitudes so remained until Europeans decided to remodel these aboriginals in their own image, and convert them to Christianity. Missionaries, of course, lived with their clients, and spent many years trying to fathom societies like the Nishga. Though their descriptions are marked by strong prejudice against a culture they saw as fundamentally inferior to their own, they are invaluable as the only existing first-hand accounts of the old Native ways that were current at the time of contact.

The Nishga like to say that they have lived in the valley of the Nass "since time immemorial." According to one of the first missionaries, the Reverend William Henry Collison, the river's name means "food depot" in the language of the Tlingit, the immediate neighbours of the Nishga to the north. The mountains, fjords, and streams of the Nass country are indeed a food depot. When the salmon swim upstream from the sea to spawn and die, rivers turn red with fish. For the old Nishga, the salmon were the ancestors of the people, committing the sacrifice of their flesh every year to feed their children. Their bones had to be returned to the water with respect in order to regenerate and complete the cycle of life.

Every spring at the mouth of the Nass River, they also caught a little oily smelt, the oolichan (*thaleichthys pacificus*), a morsel as fine as the smoked eel of the Baltic Sea. The oil extracted from this fish was an important source of wealth. Natives came to the Nass along the "Grease Trail" from the interior to trade beaver, mink, rabbit, and groundhog furs for the precious substance. The Nishga exchanged the pelts with the Haida of the Queen Charlotte Islands for their famous carved canoes. Salmon and oolichan, but also halibut, seal, sea lion, herring roe, kelp, mussels, cockles, clams — the inhabitants of the Nass depended on the sea's bounty for their survival. On land, they hunted bear and mountain goat. In the clearings of the forest and the crevasses of the lava beds, they collected an amazing number of berries and edible plants, most of them unknown to the white man.

The March oolichan run drew entire Nishga villages to the river's mouth, along with representatives of other nations from hundreds of kilometres away. In 1887, the Methodist missionary Alfred Green set down a vivid description of the event:

> In the spring, when the small fish come into the river, the gulls are so numerous as to resemble a heavy fall of snow. The eagles soar high above the myriads of gulls, seeking their chance. In the water are seals and larger fish after the small fish, all under intense excitement. We have Indians from the interior, from Skeena River, Alaska, Port Simpson, Metlakatlah, and other places, making in all about five thousand people, some Christians and many not. Those who are heathen are known by their faces — some red, some black. They are dressed in all kinds of strange, fantastic costumes and present a wonderful sight as they move about on the ice. We have man life, fish life, and bird life, all seeking to destroy the delicious fish. In former years the people used to offer sacrifice to the Great Spirit for giving them the fish, and the one who caught the first fish would put it in his bosom and run about, crying, "Oh, you, salvation fish, you salvation fish."

The Anglican William Collison explained the oolichan's importance:

Their dried salmon and halibut are eaten with this grease. The herring spawn and seaweed when boiled are mixed with a portion; and even the berries, crab-apples, and cranberries are mixed freely with the olachan grease when cooked and stored away for winter use. The olachan, because of its richness in oil, was formerly known as the "candle fish," as when partly dried the Indians used it as a torch by night . . .

Each household will thus have from five to ten tons of fish, and more, from which to extract the oil or grease after they have salted sufficient for future use, and also a quantity to be sun-dried or smoked. Formerly the grease was extracted from the fish by stones made red hot in large fires. These heated stones were cast into large boxes filled with fish and water, and the process was repeated until the grease floated freely on the surface, when it was skimmed off into chests made of red cedar.

The missionary disapproved of the process. Instead of extracting the oil as soon as the oolichan were caught, the Natives preferred to wait for several days until it had disintegrated in the brine. No matter: oolichan grease is a delicacy equal to the best fish sauces of Southeast Asia.

Nishga daily life was vividly recorded by the Methodist missionary William Pierce, who knew the west-coast cultures intimately as he was himself a Tsimshian through his mother — his father was a Scot. He spoke the local languages and understood the old ways better than his white colleagues did. In summer, according to Pierce, Natives of higher rank went about in blankets of mountain-sheep wool tied at the waist with a belt; the other classes wore skins of deer or mountain goat sewn together in the shape of a banket. Winter robes were made of fur: deer, mountain sheep, or groundhog for commoners, lynx or marten for the upper classes, and for the higher chiefs, sea otter or fox. Everyone had two suits of clothing for each season, one for daily wear and the other for festive occasions. Like the other nations of the coast, the Nishga wore weatherproof coats, woven of the fibres of red-cedar bark, to protect them from head to toe against snow and rain. The roots of the spruce were also woven to make perfectly waterproof conical hats. In lieu of socks, the Nishga wrapped their feet in dried grass and wore mocassins and fur leggings.

The Nishga moved frequently during the year, making temporary settlements near fishing or hunting grounds, shellfish beds or berry patches, but families still kept their main residences in the village. These were often impressive structures, "long houses" made of logs and roofed with planks that could be spaced apart to let the smoke escape. The Anglican missionary Robert Tomlinson visited the upper Nass in August 1870:

> I will try and give you a picture of a scene which is indelibly printed in my mind. A shed about thirty feet by ninety feet, with a passage down the centre, and a row of fires on each side. Overhead, and about five feet from the ground, were thin poles, on which were hanging salmon, some freshly caught, some half-way and some quite dry. Around each fire a knot of people, and here, there, and every where, mats, pillows, boxes of food, and such like.

The basic social unit of the Nishga was the "wilp" or "house," a matrilineal group that included several households and carried the name of its most prestigious chief. Depending on the number of relatives, a wilp could own one or several buildings in front of which the prominent families often raised totem poles. These poles, with their intricately carved figures of mythical men and animals, did not represent idols, as many missionaries assumed; they were simply the crests of the wilp, not unlike the coats of arms of European aristocratic houses. The various wilps were grouped into four distinct clans. The Anglican missionary James McCullagh recorded them as Wolf, Frog, Eagle, and Cannabis, while the anthropologist Franz Boas found them as the Raven, Wolf, Eagle, and Bear. Modern Nishga reject these early accounts. McCullagh, Boas, and others were confused by the fact that each clan has more than one totemic symbol. The main crests of the Nass Valley are grouped in sets: Wolf and Bear, Killer Whale and Owl, Eagle and Beaver, Raven and Frog. McCullagh's "Cannabis," coincidentally the Latin word for "hemp," may refer to the fireweed, a crest used by the Skeena River Gitksan, though never by the people of the Nass.

Clan membership was transmitted through the mother. The children of a woman from the Raven clan were automatically Raven like their maternal uncle, a very important figure in the Nishga family, but their father could never have been a Raven. By the Nishga, marriage inside a clan was viewed as incest. The system was common to all the villages and all neighbouring nations: a Nishga Eagle, for instance, could consider himself related to an Eagle from another tribe even if they did not speak the same language. The entire society was a web of hierarchies. Each name carried with it a precise title of property — the right to a certain trapline, fishing spot, or berry patch.

The Nishga held frequent ceremonies and feasts at which everyone's position within the system was confirmed. Whites called them "potlatches" after a word from the Chinook jargon, a lingua franca used from Alaska to the mouth of the Columbia. The missionary James McCullagh interpreted this crucial expression of the Nishga culture in these words:

> No better description could be given of the Indian people than that supplied by the name they give themselves — "Alu-gigiat." Truly they are a "Public-people," for they have no private business, no private rights, and no domestic privacy. Every right is "holden" (that is the meaning of the word YUQU, which the White-man, judging from outward appearance, calls Potlatch, i.e., "giving"), and every matter regulated by a public manifestation of assent on the part of the united clans. And this public expression of assent, made by the clans and acknowledged by the individual, is what we call Potlatch.

He reported that the potlatch, or "yuqu," was held for the following events: after the birth of a child; when the ears of a boy were pierced, or the under-lip of a girl; when a child reached the age of eight, then again at twelve; when a girl reached puberty; at the tattooing of a totemic symbol; at the "O'sk" ceremony, when a man assumed the right to wear some important crest; at the "Oiag," when a Nishga was allowed to apply for membership in one of the secret societies of the nation; at the "Llin," a legal formality that recorded a change of status, for instance a divorce; at the funeral of a chief, one of the most sacred ceremonies of the Nishga; and at the "Hooks," a feast given by a chief for the members of his clan.

To fulfil the duties of his rank, the "potlatcher" had to distribute appropriate gifts, often emptying his house of goods. By accepting the gifts, the guests gave official recognition to his claims and guaranteed the legitimacy of the titles he assumed. White observers of the potlatch believed that the organizer of the ceremony was condemning himself to the most abject poverty. They saw the custom as an obstacle in the way of Native economic progress. This was a complete misunderstanding. The potlatch was not a private endeavour, but a collective one, as reported by missionary Pierce: "As a rule, the potlatch must be carried on by one crest. For instance, a wolf crest will give a potlatch to all the other crests of the different villages excepting that of the wolf, but all the wolves of the village where the potlatch is held will help the wolf who is the giver of the potlatch. The same is true of the eagle, blackfish, and crow." Moreover, one potlatch was always followed by another, and the figure who had organized the first event was bound to receive gifts in later ceremonies. The Anglican Robert Tomlinson even held that "by Indian law, he is entitled to receive back all that he gave away." And at all events, most of the goods distributed were not for use on a daily basis. Such was the case with the piles of blankets that the Nishga exchanged during potlatches and did not seem to have any special function between ceremonies.

The favourite season for festivities was winter, when the rivers were frozen and there was very little fishing or hunting to be done. Reverend McCullagh was present at such a feast, a banquet given in his honour by Skaden, the pagan chief of the village of Gitlakdamix, on 21 December 1893. The Christians arrived at five in the afternoon:

> On reaching Skaden's, we found a large crowd assembled, who were lustily hishdilautqushing, i.e., shouting loudly in our honour, and showing many signs of joy. As we entered, those of us who were chiefs were thus ushered to our seats. "O chief, great chief, real chief, here it is, here it is, sit in your ancestors' house until the dawn!" I was conducted to the place of honour. We all sat facing inwards, in the form of three sides of a square, a huge fire being built up in the centre, the fourth side of the square being towards the door, where our entertainers stood in a motley group. Skaden went around and shook hands with us all.

A young chief holding a "talking stick" then made a speech in honour of the guests. Basins and soap were taken around and people washed their hands. An elderly man made another oration, announcing that the food would soon be served, and oolichan oil thrown on the fire

> to make our ancestors' house as bright as the sun for us until morning. The pile of fuel, which was in an energetic state of combustion in our midst, was about four feet long, three feet high,

and three feet wide, around which now sat eight or ten young men, holding up to the heat two dried salmon each. Each dried salmon covers a surface of two square feet, so that by holding one above the other they shielded themselves from the heat, and yet toasted the salmon. When these were toasted they were handed to the chief's wives, who, in the form of a crescent, squatted round an assortment of pots and pans, into which they shred the salmon, putting into each vessel portions for two or three people.

A chief sampled every dish, a procedure taken by the missionary as proof that his food was not being poisoned. During the meal there were more speeches by hosts and Christians, and the Natives gave the missionary the product of a collection they had taken up among themselves— two pounds and seven shillings. The second course, mashed berries, was served with horn spoons. Meanwhile, several boxes of oolichan oil had been shovelled into the fire. This meant that the missionary was an important guest and his host a man of prestige who did not hesitate to indulge in such luxury.

It was very hot in our "ancestors' house" part of the time; I sat about twelve feet away from the fire, but every time they threw in a shovel full of fish grease the flames shot up and on through the large opening in the roof to the height of thirty feet! At these times Skaden was careful to send his slave, or adopted son, a deaf and dumb man, to stand between me and the fire as a screen. Several times the house caught fire, but there seemed to be a small fire brigade on the roof, for every time a beam became ignited a hand was seen applying snow to the burning spot. We did not quite stay in our "ancestors' house" until the morning for many reasons, but we had three hours of it.

The Nishga certainly knew how to do things with style.

Winter was also the time for meetings and ceremonies of the secret societies. Admittance to one of these was one of the greatest honours any Nishga could hope for. According to Reverend McCullagh, there were four such societies, the "Mitla," which he described simply as a "dance," the "Lu'lim" or dog-eaters' society, the "Ulala" or "cannibal degree," and the "Unana," whose rituals, he said, involved the wholesale destruction of household goods. For his part, Franz Boas identified six societies which he named as the "Semhalai't," "Meitla," "Lotle'm," "Olala,"

"Nanesta't," and "Honana'tl." The anthropologist attributed his information to interviews with a number of Nishga, among them the great Chief Mountain. In the opinion of modern descendants of this chief, there are significant errors in Boas's report, but since the secret societies and especially the Olala were systematically maligned by the missionaries, his serener testimony, even if shaky, is still extremely valuable.

According to Boas's rendition of the myth of the Cannibal, one Sagaitla'ben, a hunter of the Bellabella nation to the south, became trapped following a bear. The animal hid in some rocks, and the hunter, entering a crevasse on the side of a cliff, heard the voices of the Olala. His soul made prisoner, he had to wear a bearskin and two red-cedar bark rings, one around his head and the other around his neck. The Olala commanded him to kill men and eat human flesh. For three years the Cannibal terrorized the region, devouring people in the woods. Finally, some of the Kitamaat people caught him and managed, after a series of ceremonies, to break the spell and reintegrate him into society.

The initiation of a new member of the Olala society followed closely and theatrically the sequence of the myth. The candidate was attacked by a group of friends but allowed to slip away discreetly while his assailants cut off the head of a dummy. His relatives organized a full-fledged funeral, giving a banquet, distributing gifts, and burning the "corpse." The candidate then had to spend several nights in a grave. Thereafter he was not to be seen for a full year except by the Olala society members. When the year was up, the ritual called for his nephew to organize a search party and his totem animal to carry him back to the village. Once captured, the "Cannibal" was given normal food, but he had to feign a relapse by biting several people. Finally, he was "tamed," and after another year's retreat inside his house, allowed to resume a normal life.

Boas reported with great skepticism the testimony of some Christian Nishga who told him that the ceremonies of the Olala involved the eating of human flesh and the sacrifice of slaves. The missionary James McCullagh also accused the Nishga of cannibalism and necrophagy shortly after his arrival in the area. The charge was not repeated, however, in his later diatribes against local tradition, which might suggest that he had been fooled at first by the acting talents of the villagers. The accusation was frequent at the time, but not one first-hand account of man-eating is to be found on the record.

Most of these customs were part of a system much larger than the Nishga nation alone. Kwawkgeulth, Bella Coola, Haisla, Tsimshian, Gitksan, Nishga, Haida, Tlingit — from the north of Vancouver Island to the 60th parallel there was a continuous chain of peoples speaking very different languages but sharing a common culture. Carried by canoe over thousands of kilometres, this civilization, which left the world the totem pole as its best-known monument, would collapse before the onslaught of the "ones who lost their way in the fog."

THEY CAME TO STAY

A s the nineteenth century opened, the Nishga and their neighbours were living their last years of freedom. The Spaniards and British had spent years in the previous century planting crosses and flags around the region in the names of their respective and august Majesties, but none of these symbolic actions had meant anything to the people living there. The argument between the two European powers over the ownership of Nootka Sound on Vancouver Island was the subject of great controversy in the chancelleries, but for Maquina, chief of the Mohachat, the Spaniards, Yankees, or British mooring in his harbour were no more than guests whose presence was sometimes cumbersome, but generally useful. The arrival of the white man had meant a sudden influx of goods unknown until then. Controlling this trade was crucially important for the villages; their strategic locations could win them political, economic, and social power over their competitors.

For the whites, competition was increasingly difficult. As Vancouver had discovered, Native suppliers were masters in the art of bargaining. They had no interest in beads or trinkets, preferring iron items that could help them improve a technology very poor in metals. In the beginning, foreign sailors found a quick and abundant supply of furs, but some species, such as the sea otter, soon became vanishingly scarce. The locals had learned how to wait for the best offer, stocking their pelts and playing

Briton against Spaniard, Yankee against Russian, in order to get the best price. For native societies, the maritime fur trade represented not a decline but rather a blooming of their cultures and a development of their commercial relations.

Yet the outside world was closing in on them. In 1819, a weakened Spain renounced the Oregon territory and recognized British sovereignty over that huge area. A few years later, in 1825, the Russians, who had never been very active along the coast, retreated officially to Alaska. The British traders plotted to monopolize the fur trade between America and China, but Yankee interlopers kept trading with the Natives behind British backs, and goods kept moving north and south, to and from Russian territory, following price trends.

The centre of gravity of the trade was no longer the west coast of Vancouver Island. The British had established a fort on the lower Fraser River, and from there they effectively controlled an important part of the southern network. The northern trade was still dominated by the Haida of the Queen Charlottes, and Yankee captains regularly visited the harbours of this powerful nation. On the mainland, the Tsimshian and Nishga acted as middlemen, controlling the movement of furs from the interior. The British had not yet tried to interfere in their affairs, and observers who ventured into the area were struck by the fierce independence of these Native nations. For the white people, convinced of the superiority of their own race, religion, and civilization, the Natives' lack of submissiveness was unacceptable, and writings of the period are marked by blatant racism.

This is certainly the case with the journal of Jonathan Green of the American Board of Commissioners for Foreign Missions, who spent some time in the north Pacific in 1829. Perched on the deck of his boat, the good pastor observed with horror the heathens who came to barter:

Before the Indians made their appearance, Capt. Taylor ordered the boarding nets to be put up, and he stationed watch on different parts of the deck. This net, made of strong cord, prevents the Indians from coming over the ship's sides. When they came to trade, they were admitted, a few at one time, through a port hole, and all their movements narrowly watched. The Nass men seem to combine the "man-brute" with the "man-devil." They appear more dirty and degraded, than any Indians whom I have yet seen, while, at the same time, they exhibit an intelligence strongly marked. This intellectual strength, without one softened feature, assumes the aspect of a desperate fierceness.

Stopping for the second time at the mouth of the Nass River, Green again showed his prejudices:

> The Indians are numerous, and inconceivably noisy. I have been astonished today to witness their savage manners, their efforts to make a good bargain, and their insolent requital of favors. Here is a people, whom I would recommend to the attention of those who talk of the efficacy of moral lectures to subdue the obduracy of the heart.

The mouth of the Nass was by that time one of the major centres of trade, at least as important as the Columbia more than a thousand kilometres to the south. John McLoughlin, the Hudson's Bay Company representative in the area, reported this to his superiors in 1826 after meeting with the captain of the Boston vessel *Owhyhee,* who related that

> a few days previous our people entering Observatory Inlet he had at Nass on the North side of the entrance, traded one thousand beaver and land otter skins. For this and the documents we have on the Coasting trade stating more furs are traded at Nass than at any other place along the Coast (at that time exceeding those traded at the entrance of the Columbia).

The Crown had granted the Bay company the official monopoly over trade along the coast, and the British traders wanted to eliminate foreign competition, especially ships from New England. This prompted George Simpson, Pacific coast governor for the company, to recommend to his London headquarters in 1828 the establishment of a new post at the mouth of the Nass:

> We have little doubt of acquiring the Command of the Trade; it may however cost in the first instance a considerable sacrifice of money but the prospect it holds out in point of returns, and the necessity which appears to exist of our being firmly established on a navigable communication between the Coast and the Interior we conceive fully to warrant the expense we propose entering into.

Simpson had another concern. The fur traders had only three possible routes through the mountains to the coast: the Columbia in the south, the Fraser in the middle, and the Skeena in the north. The young American republic was claiming the southern part of the Oregon territory and threatening to cut the Bay men out of the Columbia trade. Since the Fraser Canyon was thought at this time to be too hazardous for a permanent road, Simpson attached great importance to the northern route. Unfortunately, the governor was badly informed about the geography of the area, and he assumed wrongly that the main corridor between the interior and the coast was the Nass Valley, not the Skeena River: "It is therefore necessary for the Salvation of our interior Trade in the event of our being excluded from the Columbia, that we should have a Settlement on the Babine (or Simpsons River) situated Lat. 54 at the Port of Nass which is the grand mart of the Coast both for Sea Otters and Land Skins." But how would the independent Nishga accept a fort on their territory? Simpson feared trouble and recommended precautions:

> The establishing of this Post will be a Work of great danger, and great expense on account of the number and hostility of the Natives and of their powerful means of offence, indeed it cannot be attempted with a smaller force than One Hundred Officers and Men say 50 for the Establishment and 50 for the two Vessels to protect and act in concert with the Land Party while building.

In July 1830, the governor announced to his subordinate McLoughlin that the project had been approved by London:

> We are anxious that an establishment should be formed at Nass as early as circumstances admit, to act in concert with our shipping on the Coast; and if we could once get them in full operation, I have not the smallest doubt that the trade will fall entirely into our hands, and more especially so as it appears that the Russians do not mean to afford any further encouragement to the American adventurers.

Three ships were sent to the Nass to choose a suitable location. In his report, the expedition's leader, Lt. Aemilius Simpson, repeated his superiors' error in assuming that the Nass River was the main thoroughfare to the interior and led to the Babine, which is actually a tributary of the Skeena. He did venture to doubt, however, that the Nass would prove to be an easy waterway:

With respect to the size of this I must acknowledge I feel disappointed, as the body of water it discharges is considerable it has no comparison to Frazers River and its capacity for the navigation of Vessels extends but a short distance up and from its being bound by mountains of great elevation (even close down to our position) I much fear it will be found too rapid for boats or Canoes passing with goods to the Natives.

The lieutenant tried to find out more from the Natives themselves, but the Nishga did not seem anxious to tell him about the geography of their land:

Owing to our total ignorance of their language very little information could be acquired, indeed it appeared to me that they were not inclin'd to give any, their reason I ascribed to selfish motives, as it strikes me they enjoy a monopoly of the Trade with the Indians of the River which they feel apprehensive they will be deprived of in the event of our settling there.

Eventually, in April 1831, a Bay factory was established by Aemilius Simpson and Peter Ogden at the mouth of the Nass, near the modern village of Kincolith, and christened "Fort Simpson." A few months later Lieutenant Simpson died and was replaced by another factor, John Kennedy. For all the company's fears, the expected Native hostility did not materialize. By choosing their territory, the Hudson's Bay Company had given the Nishga an important trading advantage over their Tsimshian neighbours on the Skeena, making them the exclusive intermediaries of the British.

This explains the anger with which the Nishga learned three years later that the fort was to be moved fifty kilometres to the south, on the Tsimshian peninsula halfway between the Nass and the Skeena. The company had several reasons for the change: anchorage was very difficult in the Nass harbour, and winter winds turned out to be a major problem; the English had at last understood the strategic importance of the Skeena Valley to the south; and, last but not least, the Tsimshian had managed a diplomatic coup by marrying the daughter of their head-chief, Legaic, to Factor Kennedy. A company physician, William Fraser Tolmie, who had been called to the Nass to treat a fractured leg, witnessed the move:

On Saturday morning rum had been sold to the Indians and some of them getting intoxicated were very turbulent and from noon till sunset when we embarked we were all under arms and in momentary expectation of having to fight our way on board or being butchered on the spot. They attempted frequently to beat down the slight barricade raised on the site of the bastions, but were deterred on seeing us ready with firearms to send a volley among the intruders. About a dozen or twenty indians with muskets were posted on a hill immediately behind from whence they could fire with deadly effect into the Fort at any part. Outside the pickets they were numerous and armed with guns, boarding pikes and knives and endeavouring by their savage whoops and yells to intimidate us.

While trying to give the best review to the British, Dr. Tolmie recognized that the Nishga were keeping the situation under control:

Owing to a temporary lull in the clamor outside, ventured to send a few articles to the boats which were in waiting at the beach, one or two had passed down with wooden utensils unmolested — no indians appearing in sight — another man was proceeding with a barrel full of miscellaneous articles, and unheeded when at once several armed villains rushed out from amongst the bushes — and one more inebriated and thence more daring than the rest seized the barrel and with drawn dagger drove the man from his charge — he returned to the fort and first meeting me I went out but seeing the savage advancing with his knife aloft in a menacing attitude I stepped slowly to the gate and procured a cutlass from the door keeper. Thus armed I walked toward the Indian who was surrounded by his friends persuading him to desist and at the same time Kennedy issued and addressed the savages — the barrel was rolled to the beach in the meantime without molestation. Soon after a gun was fired from the woods at one of the people employed at the strand, the ball whizzing past his ear. Every thing of value having been already embarked, no further attempts were made to ship what remained. Red Shirt the Indian just mentioned, was, to prevent his doing mischief outside, admitted into the Fort and was immediately assailed by Caxetan the chief with a volley of abuse for his conduct. From words they soon came to blows. Red Shirt's dagger was prevented from doing mischief by two sober indians Jones and Couguele, but being a tough active fellow he still retained it in his grasp and managed with the other hand most cruelly to abuse Caxetan's visage who, in his part fought bravely tooth and nail, considerably damaging his opponent's visual organs.

Until then, Tolmie had given the impression that the scene was a confrontation between a small group of courageous white men and a vociferous crowd of drunken Indians, but the British were not to get off unscathed:

Mr. Ogden at length got Caxetan and Jones to accompany him on board and once there retained them as hostages for our safety. Now prepared to abandon the Fort and held a debate as to the propriety of leaving behind a cask containing 25 gallons Indian Rum. It was left, Kennedy being the only person who wished to take it along with us. Took the precaution of drawing the priming from all the superfluous muskets after each man had been provided with one. As soon as the gate was opened, the armed natives collected around. I went out first and stood at the threshold until the last person had issued. The natives then rushed in to pillage and we reached the boats unmolested. Soon after to our astonishment, Caxetan and Jones from the bank shouted to us, that they wished us to send the boat for the Rum and on our refusing, offered to bring it on board themselves and on this intelligence they brought the rum on board the vessel to be divided by us. This act proved them to be possessed of more prudence and foresight than we would have given them credit for.

Having conceded that the "savages" were more civilized than first thought, Tolmie regained his composure in the safety of his boat: "All night a constant hammering was kept up in the deserted fort and dawn revealed several gaps in the pickets made by those who were intent on procuring the iron spikes which attached the pickets to the bars. It blew a NE. We set sail soon after daybreak bidding adieu without regret to the inhospitable regions of Nass."

The impression must not be left by such events that the Bay company forts were in a permanent state of siege amid hostile Native nations. On the contrary, the Natives accepted their presence and turned it to their advantage. That the white traders would never have survived without local help emerges clearly in an 1836 comment by Factor Duncan Finlayson about life in the second Fort Simpson: "The resources in the way of living which Fort Simpson affords, are Deer, Halibut, and Salmon, which, however may be considered as precarious while our dependence is placed on the natives for providing them."

With Fort Simpson, the Nishga lost an obvious advantage in the fur trade. But the departure of the Hudson's Bay Company was a blessing in disguise. It sheltered their nation from direct contact with white people and political subjugation — a precious reprieve. Eager for the advantages of contact, their Tsimshian neighbours saw their culture and society irretrievably damaged by the company settlement and the missionary colonizers who came in its wake.

On the surface of it, the move to the Tsimshian peninsula did not seem to alter the Natives' position. The Europeans enforced their own laws within the walls of their establishment; outside it, the Tsimshian people were still the sole rulers of their territory. The Hudson's Bay Company had no intention of disturbing Native structures. Its sole objective was trade with the local population. White strangers were not welcome, and it took the fort more than twenty years to admit a missionary. James Douglas, who combined the functions of chief factor of the company and governor of the colony of Vancouver Island, feared that challenge by missionaries to Native beliefs could only foment political unrest which would necessarily have a negative effect on business.

In spite of this official non-interventionism, however, the presence of the British trading post had a deeply disturbing influence on Tsimshian society. Many of the Tsimshian people were lured by the abundance of new goods to leave their old villages and settle around the gate of the fort. The traditional balance between families and villages was destroyed; the whole Tsimshian political system was suddenly in jeopardy. In an attempt to define a new hierarchy of power, the Natives were caught up in a maelstrom of festivities and potlatches. And the abrupt and seemingly unlimited availability of foreign products changed the very nature of the potlatch by introducing an uncontrollable factor of inflation. It became harder and harder to put on a good show for the neighbours; in order to give potlatches befitting their claims, chieftains became the virtual slaves of an unending search for material goods.

This search took on unprecedented proportions when the Tsimshian started travelling the eight hundred kilometres south to Fort Victoria, capital of the colony of Vancouver Island. Shanty towns sprang up at the gates of the small white settlement, and contemporary observers leave little doubt as to the sordid conditions prevailing there. The Natives went to the capital to sell not only their furs but also in many instances their women of lower rank. They brought back staples and money, but they also brought firearms and even alcohol that had been smuggled across the American border. This seasonal pilgrimage occurred on a massive scale; in the year 1860, witnesses claimed that practically the whole Tsimshian nation moved down to Victoria.

The presence at Fort Victoria of Natives from a number of nations, in contact with the worst elements of colonial society, created a dire situation. Disease spread like lightning in a Native population that had not been exposed to many of the white man's germs. In 1836, a terrible smallpox epidemic was carried north and killed, two years after the founding of the post, one third of the Tsimshian of Fort Simpson. Plagued by alcoholism, drunken brawling, illness, and new social tensions, the Native society slowly disintegrated. Although still a majority with, in 1858, only four hundred whites on the whole British Columbia mainland, the Tsimshian had lost the reins of their own destiny.

Here was fertile ground for the churches. In 1857, Governor Douglas finally agreed to the appointment of a Church Missionary Society representative for Fort Simpson. Fresh from England, the young Anglican cleric William Duncan was shocked by the dissipation of the Tsimshian. Convinced, like most of his contemporaries, of the superiority of the industrial society he had left behind, Duncan quickly came to believe that the conversion of the Natives had to be accompanied by profound changes in their mode of life. True to the tradition of nineteenth-century English utopianism, he dreamed of creating a Christian community that would be kept isolated from the temptations of this world. Reporting to the government, he outlined his project in these terms:

1st. To place all the Indians, when they became wishful to be taught Christianity, out of the miasma of heathen life, and away from the deadening and enthralling influence of heathen customs.

2nd. To establish the Mission where we could effectively shut out intoxicating liquors, and keep liquor vendors at bay.

3rd. To enable us to raise a barrier against the Indians visiting Victoria, excepting on lawful business.

4th. That we might be able to assist the people thus gathered out to develop into a model community, and raise a Christian village, from which the Native evangelist might go forth, and Christian truth radiate to every tribe around.

5th. That we might gather such a community around us, whose moral and religious training and bent of life might render it safe and proper to impart secular instruction.

6th. That we might to able to break up all tribal distinctions and animosities, and cement all who came to us, from whatever tribe, into one common brotherhood.

7th. That we might place ourselves in a position to set up and establish the supremacy of the law, teach loyalty to the Queen, conserve the peace of the country around, and ultimately develop our settlement into a municipality with its Native corporation.

Duncan was a good strategist. Instead of imposing his views on the Tsimshian, he waited for them to adopt these as their own. He unveiled his plans in the summer of 1859, but did not attempt any move until three years later. For the Tsimshian, an exodus from Fort Simpson was not such a far-fetched idea. Facing similar problems of social decay after the arrival of the white man, such other aboriginal peoples as the New Zealand Maori had reacted by withdrawing to remote missions. At Fort Simpson, the wave of violence, drunkenness, and vice that came with the gold rush of 1858 spurred a small group of chiefs to adopt the missionary's suggestion. The Tsimshian themselves chose the location of the model settlement — the island of Metlakatla, where a village had been abandoned a few decades earlier.

On 27 May 1862, Duncan left Fort Simpson by canoe with a party of fifty Indians to found his Christian city. Confirmation of the experiment's success came within months, as Fort Simpson began to feel the effects of a new smallpox epidemic that would claim five hundred lives. Many Tsimshian tried to take refuge at the new mission. Duncan's conditions were draconian. Newcomers had to renounce the fundamental elements of their culture completely:

1. To give up their "Ahlied" or Indian devilry;
2. To cease calling in conjurers when sick;

3. To cease gambling;
4. To cease giving away their property for display;
5. To cease painting their faces;
6. To cease drinking intoxicating drink;
7. To rest on the Sabbath;
8. To attend religious instruction;
9. To send their children to school;
10. To be clean;
11. To be industrious;
12. To be peaceful;
13. To be liberal and honest in trade;
14. To build neat houses;
15. To pay the village tax.

The natives were not deterred by all this from moving to Metlakatla. The population increased to four hundred very rapidly, though most of the Tsimshian, some nineteen hundred souls, remained around Fort Simpson.

Duncan did not try to abolish all the Native customs. Chiefs kept some of their authority as they were included automatically in the village council, which also had ten councillors elected by male suffrage. Moreover the missionary, who in 1864 had been granted the powers of a justice of the peace, preferred to use Native rather than colonial law in the settlement of local disputes. Traditional ways were also fully respected in fishing, the villagers' main livelihood.

As far as daily life was concerned, however, Duncan imposed a punishing schedule, using the comfortable words that "this is the place for toil; heaven is the place for rest." Above all else, the Metlakatlans were busy people. Women spun wool; men built roads, houses, a thousand-seat church. The village was endowed with a sawmill, a brickyard, a soap factory, a smithy, a general store, a cannery, a museum, a library, and a jail. The inhabitants were housed in dwellings that resembled the working-class paradises projected by English Utopians.

The executive power was exercised by the village council with the help of ten "companies" overseeing the general population. Each company was made up of two councillors, two Native constables, and, after a few years, two Native teachers, two musicians, and eleven volunteer firemen, including their captain. The forty-man constabulary not only enforced public order but respect for morality as well; their mandate embraced the villagers' work habits, conjugal lives, and religious practice. Every evening there were catechism sessions for adults, and every week, prayer meetings in each company.

Duncan founded a boarding school that was open to the young people of neighbouring nations, thus abetting the spread of the Christian faith. Village girls entered the school at age sixteen and did not leave until marriage. The missionary rightly believed that by subjecting future Tsimshian couples to a few years of puritanical education, he could cut the younger generation off from the customs of their forefathers.

The basis of his system was control of all daily activity. He knew that the cold months were the ones when the old habits of the Tsimshian were most liable to resurface. Those were the traditional times of the potlatch, the secret societies, and the midwinter celebrations. Therefore he offered new festivities. Christmas and, even more, the New Year, became solemn occasions when village notables, hereditary chiefs, councillors, constables, and firemen had a chance to show off their medals and uniforms, make speeches, and reaffirm their ranks, surrounded by the pompous magnificence of the church choir and the Metlakatla brass band.

This Christian utopia would serve as a model for the first missionaries venturing into Nishga territory. The Tsimshian had accepted William Duncan's protection to escape the ignominy of life at Fort Simpson, but the Nass Valley inhabitants would resist the coming of the white man's religion, and, when finally converted, impose a compromise between ancient and modern that is still their strength today.

4

ONWARD, CHRISTIAN SOLDIERS

The Native nations of the Pacific Northwest differed from one another as much as European nations did, but amid the linguistic diversity of the coastal peoples the Tsimshian and Nishga could be considered as "cousins." They understood each other with some difficulty, not unlike Italians and Frenchmen. Their clans shared the same totemic symbols and recognized a certain kinship that reached across linguistic boundaries. From the economic point of view, the two nations had common interests, particularly during the oolichan fishing season at the mouth of the Nass River.

This closeness between the two peoples explains why missionaries trying to convert the Tsimshian were led naturally to the Nishga. William Duncan made his first trip to the Nass in 1860, even before the founding of Metlakatla. As his report to the Church Missionary Society shows, the Nass folk did not go out of their way to make him feel at ease:

I had heard Kadonah say that they intended to perform me their "Ahlied," but I requested him to have no playing, as I wanted to speak very solemnly to them. He promised me they would do nothing bad, but now that the feasting was over, much to my sorrow, he put on his dancing mask and robes. The leading singers stepped out, and soon all were engaged in a spirited chant. They kept excellent time by clapping their hands and beating a drum. . . . The chief, Kadonah, danced with all his might during the singing. He wore a cap which had a mask in front, set with mother of pearl, and trimmed the porcupine quills. The quills enabled him to hold a quantity of white swansdown on the top of his head, which he ejected while dancing by poking his head forward; thus he soon appeared as if in a shower of snow. In the middle of the dance a man approached me with a handful of down and blew it over my head, thus symbolically uniting me in friendship with all the chiefs present, and the tribes they severally represented. After the dancing and singing were over, I felt exceedingly anxious about addressing them, but circumstances seemed so unfavourable on account of the excitement that my heart began to sink. . . . I stood up and requested them to cease talking, and every countenance became fixed attentively on me.

The preacher delivered his message while his Nishga hosts repeated with him the word "Jesus," and he returned to Fort Simpson quite satisfied. He came back to the area at the end of the winter of 1863, accompanied this time by his Anglican bishop. They arrived in the middle of the oolichan season, and as reported by the prelate, about five thousand Natives had gathered at the Nass estuary, including Haida from the Queen Charlotte Islands, Tlingit from Alaska, and people from the interior: "The fish are caught in vast quantities. Some of them are dried in the sun, others are pressed for the sake of the oil or grease, which has a market value as being superior to codliver oil, and which the natives use as butter with their dried salmon." The pair took advantage of the presence of two hundred Metla-katlans on the fishing grounds to say a few prayers and sing some hymns, while the pagans carried on with their own activities. Farther upstream, at the village of "Nikah," the Christians met with some hundred and sixty Indians: "There were chiefs; there were medicine men, with their red rings of bark on the head; there were cannibals and dogeaters, some with faces painted fierce red, other black and red."

On 2 July 1864, a second missionary, Robert Doolan, arrived at Metlakatla. Anxious to make inroads among the Nishga, the founder of the Christian island community decided to send his colleague to the Nass with a native catechist, Samuel Marsden. On July 20, the three of them established the first Christian mission in the area at "Abanshekques," near the present village of Greenville. N.E. Johnson, an Anglican propagandist, has left an enthusiastic account of their arrival:

> "Pity us, great Father in heaven, pity us," said a chief standing before Mr. Duncan. "This chief," he continued, pointing to Mr. Duncan, "has come to tell us about thee. It is good, great Father. We want to hear. Who ever came to tell our forefathers thy will? No, no. But this chief has pitied us and come. He has thy Book. We will hear. We will receive thy word. We will obey."

Duncan then gave a sermon, after which, according to Johnson, another chief said: "We are not to call upon stones and stars now, but Jesus. Jesus will hear. Jesus is our Saviour. Jesus! Jesus! Jesus! Jesus Christ. Good news! Good news! Listen all. Put away your sins. God has sent his Word. Jesus is our Saviour. Take away my sins, Jesus. Make me good, Jesus."

It should be borne in mind that such reports were written for British parishioners in the hope of generating funds for the missionary effort. In his own report to the Church Missionary Society, Doolan showed greater modesty. He was allowed to raise his tent in one of the chiefs' houses and given some salmon to eat. Shortly afterwards, Doolan rented a vacant house for use as a school at the same time.

A worried letter sent to his superiors a year later indicates that events in the village had somewhat overwhelmed him. Asking for a catechist, he described a rather chaotic situation: "We have suffered many hardships to the body from the unsuitableness of our house to withstand the cold; much discouragement at seeing so few anxious about their souls." Evidently he had spent a difficult winter among villagers unprepared to interrupt their traditional festivities for his sake. And the cleric had clearly managed to get on the wrong side of the head-chief:

> A great deal of medicine-work going on, especially at Kinzarda's. I hear he has threatened to take away the breath (as the Indians express it) from some men, for telling us about their medicine-work. Cowdaeg, a boy, is enduring much persecution because he will not join the medicine-work. The poor boy was crying very much to-night. He tells them he is not strong, and does not want to join them. They say they will excuse him the arduous part of

the work, but he will not yield. May God strengthen him! Kin-
zarda speaking very bad of us.

The misunderstanding between missionary and Natives was
total. Doolan made numerous faux pas by ignoring local customs that he saw as valueless. His efforts to stop the winter
ceremonies and the young people's initiation would have been
as hard to explain to the Nishga as an attempt to cancel a Sunday dance or a first communion mass to a group of Italian
villagers. Also shocking to the Nishga was the white man's lack
of respect for their social conventions. With the chiefs the most
influential guardians of tradition, the church aimed its action at
those who had the least interest in preserving the existing order
— poor cousins, and individuals of low rank. Doolan's door was
open to anybody, a principle foreign to hierarchical Nishga
thinking. The missionary was perfectly aware of what was happening: "The chiefs are annoyed that we allow all people to
come into our house. They say they do not like to come in when
so many common people are in. We can scarcely get a man to
work for us, the feeling is so strong, and, as our wood is
exhausted, we have no school."
In Metlakatla, William Duncan realized that the evangelization of the Nishga was facing major difficulties:

One great drawback to its progress (in our way of talking) is, that
the chiefs, as a body, keep aloof. This, no doubt, arises from the
discovery they have made, that in becoming Christians they have
to renounce their pride — forego the revenue accruing from
heathen rites and customs, and have to bestir themselves to a life
of activity and labour in order to support themselves. For this they
are by no means prepared.

Doolan was not the only element upsetting Nishga society. In
the fall of 1865, while the missionary was in Metlakatla for a
short visit, a boat came with a cargo of rum to the mouth of the
river. The smugglers sold alcohol to the Natives during the day
but anchored every night in Alaskan waters, Russian territory,
to escape arrest. One night after he had returned to Abanshekques Doolan witnessed a drunken brawl that turned into an
exchange of fire between two hamlets built on islands in the
river. The incident left two Nishga wounded. On another occasion a man named Moke, under the influence of whisky, threat-

ened his father with a gun. A stray bullet hit a third man, whose friend then fired on Moke with his rifle, leaving the drunkard with a bad stomach wound. As Doolan noted, disconsolately, "The camp is flooded with whisky." He even reported an attempt on his life by a drunken villager; fortunately for him, the man's rifle misfired.

In 1866, two years after his arrival, the situation was basically the same. He had the support of a small group of sympathizers, but for the most part the village was still hostile. In fact, his first attempt to convert a Nishga resulted in a family feud. He won the friendship of a boy named Tacomash from the village of "Lakunkedah" who was suffering from a bad case of bronchitis. No sooner had Tacomash moved in with the missionary at Abanshekques than the father arrived wanting his son back: ". . . he insisted that Tacomash should leave, and that the medicine charmers should rattle over him. . . . Then came the uncle, and spoke about his nephew's leaving, as they wished he should die at his own village."

Yet Tacomash asked to stay. For the next two weeks or so, while the boy was dying, father, mother, uncle, relatives, and friends tried without success to get him back to Lakunkedah. Finally, on 8 May, Tacomash asked to be baptised. He was christened "Samuel Walker." The first Nishga convert died a few hours later. His relatives arrived immediately and, over the missionary's objections, proceeded to give away his belongings as custom required. Doolan was allowed to say a few prayers, but the deceased was taken back to Lakunkedah to be buried according to tradition.

In 1867, the mission reached a new low. Attendance at prayers dwindled to a trickle, something Doolan attributed in part to competition from five smugglers' ships in nearby Russian waters. At Metlakatla, William Duncan decided that it was time to act. The Church Missionary Society had just sent him a young Irishman, Robert Tomlinson, who had studied medicine without completing his degree. Duncan gave him the choice of staying with him or joining Doolan on the Nass; Tomlinson opted for the Nass. Given their signal failure so far with the Nishga, the missionaries decided to modify their strategy: instead of trying to gain ground in a pagan village, they would found a new settlement free of hostile influences, from which they could later radiate throughout the area. It was to be a new Metlakatla experiment.

Tomlinson arrived at Abanshekques in June 1867, impatient to transform the Nishga "from ignorant, bloodthirsty, cruel savages into quiet, useful subjects of our gracious Queen." He soon masterminded the exodus of about fifty Christian sympathizers. Doolan took part in it, though health problems had prompted his resignation and he would be leaving the district that September. The party embarked on rafts and drifted towards the mouth of the river. They had intended to settle on the south shore of the fjord that led to the open sea, near a place known as Nass Harbour, but wind and tide pushed them to the north instead. There they found a promontory to their liking, the delta of a stream where they thought they could farm. So was the mission of Kincolith founded.

Kincolith was conceived on the Metlakatla model, but conditions on the Nass were very different from those at the Tsimshian mission's founding five years earlier. The new Christian village was not the result of voluntary support by a significant faction of the local society; it originated in a decision made by the churchmen in the wake of their failure at Abanshekques. It is not surprising that in 1870, three years later, Kincolith still had only sixty inhabitants. The site did not have Metlakatla's isolation from pagan influences; Kincolith was located near the oolichan grounds, where each year thousands of Natives congregated. And the Nishga village quickly aroused the hostility of the Tsimshian, who were used to camping near by in the fishing season and claimed the area as their own. Tomlinson's strong personality was the only thing that stopped the new community from sinking into the chaos of Doolan's disastrous Abanshekques experiment.

With the Tsimshian viewing the Kincolith Nishga as intruders, it was only a matter of time before some sort of incident occurred. One year after the move, in the spring of 1868, it erupted at Angeeda, one of the hamlets of Abanshekques, during the oolichan season festivities. A Nishga was killed; the villagers retaliated by shooting two Tsimshian chiefs. The retreating Tsimshian met four Kincolith Nishga on their way home from the fishing grounds, unaware of what had happened. Two were shot, a third died while the canoe was sinking, and the man's nephew, a boy, was caught on the shore. He was about to be killed too when a Tsimshian recognized him as a relative from the same clan. The young Nishga was later returned to

Kincolith by a neutral emissary, a man from Tongass in Alaska who had married a Tsimshian woman.

Back at Fort Simpson, the Tsimshian prepared a military expedition and returned to the Nass with a number of canoes. They landed at Kincolith, where only Tomlinson's intervention prevented a bloodbath. The missionary asked the villagers to barricade themselves inside their houses, then met the Tsimshian on the shore, where he requested that they surrender their weapons. Apparently aware of the consequences of involving a white man in their dispute and of possible reprisals by the colonial authorities, the Tsimshian complied, and returned to Simpson.

Hostilities lingered on for twelve months during which Tsimshian and Kincolith Nishga fought a series of skirmishes. The situation was serious enough for the colonial government to intervene. In his official report, Chief Commissioner of Lands and Works Joseph Trutch attributed the conflict to the presence in the area of a smugglers' boat, the *Nanaimo Packer*, and the illegal sale of rum to the Natives. He put the first Nishga casualty down as a case of manslaughter, and ascribed the events that followed to the Native tradition of revenge. Trutch did not take into account the fact that the conflict centred around Kincolith, the village of three of the victims and the target of the Tsimshian reprisal. Although there is no specific record of what triggered the Angeeda incident, the Kincolith controversy could well have been the main reason for the mini-war.

In the spring of 1869, the new governor of the colony of British Columbia, Sir Frederick Seymour, arrived on board the gunboat *Sparrowhawk* to settle the dispute in person. By then, the Nishga and the Tsimshian were eager to put the quarrel to rest, if only because of the disruption that the whole affair was causing to their normal activities on the common fishing grounds. On 2 June, Sir Frederick witnessed an agreement on the *Sparrowhawk;* it was his last official act, as he died of dysentery days later on the return journey.

Summing up the incident, Joseph Trutch gave credit for the settlement to the beneficial influence of the missions. He was also anxious to see some significant changes in official policy. The time had come for white administration to develop a more direct presence in Native societies:

The mode by which these warring tribes were brought to relinquish their feud, and bound over to live in future according to English Law, appears in happy contrast to the manner in which, by bombardment and burning of Indian villages, canoes, &c., the authority of Government has on some former occasions been enforced, with, perhaps, unnecessary infliction of loss of life and impoverishment, and even, in some cases, destruction of entire tribes.

The same events had convinced Reverend Tomlinson of the necessity of official status for the mission; on 14 June 1869, he wrote to Commissioner Trutch asking him to confirm the legality of its presence and applying for "a reserve to be appropriated for the benefit of those Indians who have already, or may hereafter, settle at this Mission Station." The government of British Columbia responded favourably, and in October, Trutch informed Tomlinson: "The reservation you recommend of land around Kincolith for the use of the Indians resident thereon, has been established by notice in the Government Gazette, a copy of which I enclose for your information."

This exchange of correspondence is of great historical significance: it marks the colonial power's first official encroachment on Nishga territory. In writing his letter to Joseph Trutch, Reverend Tomlinson had the privilege of opening a file that to this day has never been closed — the file of the Nishga land claims.

At the same time, Tomlinson took steps to avoid a recurrence of the 1869 trouble. In the winter of 1870, he called a meeting of the Kincolith people and suggested that they allow the Tsimshian to fish for oolichan and build seasonal shore cabins on condition that they agree to respect the Sabbath and the rules of the village. The quarrels were to be abandoned. Though the solution was accepted by all the families but one, it did not prevent incidents from cropping up again. A few years later, the Nishga destroyed some Tsimshian cabins near Kincolith; the Tsimshian retaliated by ransacking the villagers' vegetable gardens. The *Sparrowhawk* agreement had provided for indemnities for the deaths that had taken place, but nothing had been paid by the spring of 1870, and the Tsimshian threatened to start the fighting again. Tomlinson weighed in once more and obtained payment of the settlements. His mediation was made easier by the fact that the previous winter he had given hospitality to a Tsimshian chief stranded on the ice-pack. The chief happened to be the head of the clan responsible for the Angeeda massacre.

These interventions brought radical change to the missionary's status in the district. Tomlinson was the first to recognize his progress:

> The immediate results were, the prevention of bloodshed, a decided change of feeling in the Tsimchean tribes for the better towards us, and lastly, it afforded a proof that we should not measure our actions by the rules of the Nishkah chiefs, who were still heathen, but were a distinct settlement determined to act independently. The secondary results were much more important as concerns ourselves; and the existence of Kincolith as a village. Indeed it may truly be said that our action in this matter burst the last band that had held in control the latent hatred which had been smouldering so long, but hitherto only showing itself in words, and not in actions. So long as the tribes considered that we would stand by them, and be a defence for them, they were loath to do aught that might incense us, but so soon as they perceived that we would act independently, this restraint was removed.

The first years of the mission were difficult ones. In the spring of 1870, Kincolith was struck by famine. An exceptional drop in temperature at the beginning of the oolichan season left hundreds of Natives from various nations stranded without food or proper clothing on the frozen shores of the fjord. The mission had to share its meagre supplies with a hundred refugees, some of whom had had only salmon skins to eat for five days. At the same time, Tomlinson, like Doolan before him, was experiencing fierce hostility from his converts' pagan relatives. That April he reported a new crisis:

> At first efforts were made to induce some of the settlers to leave, and inducements held out to them to do so. These succeeded in one case, but that could not satisfy those whose object was to annihilate the settlement, or at least to so far weaken our hands as to make us willing to fraternize with them at any cost; so that when they had succeeded in drawing one away they made a great rejoicing.

Like Duncan of Metlakatla, Robert Tomlinson linked evangelization with acceptance of a Western mode of life. In his struggle against traditional medicine, "devilry" in his eyes, the missionary did not hesitate to use modern science as a weapon and present it to the pagans as inseparable from Christianity. The strategy was not without its inconveniences, especially when the reverend doctor failed in his therapeutics. In 1870, he operated on an old woman suffering from an undisclosed chronic ailment, and when the patient died twenty days later, Tomlinson found himself in trouble:

> Her brother, who does not belong to us, invited all his relations and friends to his house, and they dressed up a mummy instead of the corpse, which had been buried in our little burying-ground, and denounced me as the murderer, and added many cautions to those around not to have any thing to do with me, lest I should murder them too.

A short time later, he was reporting the deaths of two other surgery patients. This unfortunate turn of events did little to enhance his credibility with the Nishga.

The non-Christians kept trying to lure back their relatives who had settled at Kincolith. One day, a widow who had taken refuge among the Christians was kidnapped by her husband's kinfolk. Worried that this would be seen as a precedent, Tomlinson went to the family's village and obtained the widow's return. In October of 1870 the crisis came to a head:

> Three from our little band of Christians were drawn away into sin, besides several others, and there were signs of unsteadiness and wavering among the others. Day after day only brought fresh tidings of new victories for the enemies of truth, and it almost seemed as if the avowed wish of these would be granted, and that they would draw away the little band until no more of it could be found than is found of the winter's snow when the summer's sun has thawed it. I felt more depressed than I ever remember having been before.

By 1875, Tomlinson thought that the mission was strong enough to attempt a frontal attack on Nishga customs he judged to be incompatible with Christianity, particularly the distribution of property: "Such a custom clearly strikes at the root of any real improvement, and it is needless to say that we have always considered it an essential step for any one who wishes to live at either of the Christian villages of Metlakatla or Kincolith that he should entirely relinquish it." The Fort Simpson Tsimshian had officially renounced the potlatch two years earlier, and Tomlinson now decided to ask the same of the Nishga. Taking advantage of the nation's annual meeting at the mouth of the river for oolichan season, he called a meeting of the chiefs and made a vehement speech against potlatching. He was particularly dismissive of a compromise put forward by the Nishga that would have allowed Natives not resident at Kincolith to keep their customs while relinquishing some of the most blatantly pagan rituals and respecting the day of rest:

> I pointed to the one way through Jesus, and how impossible it was for any one who would walk in His footsteps to continue a custom so directly opposed to His teaching. . . . The majority of the chiefs and principal men and medicine men at once threw off the mask and declared their intention to preserve their old custom intact. They used every effort to prevent any from attending school, and even went so far as to forbid the boys playing at soldiers, for it was, they said, from such beginnings that those at Fort Simpson learned to wish for the ways of the white men.

With Kincolith, the Christian refuge, reeling from crisis to crisis, Tomlinson realized that his mission would never prosper so long as the bulk of Nishga society remained pagan. In 1870 he launched his campaign. The first midsummer reconnaissance up the Nass was marred by an unfortunate blunder:

> On my way down, I inadvertently set fire to a flat land on the river bank, which destroyed an immense number of wild fruit trees, the berries of which are esteemed as a delicacy. A large portion of this land belonged to one of the chiefs, who thereupon fell into a temper with me, before he had even asked me whether I would pay for the mischief.

During a second upriver visit that fall, the incident returned to haunt him as the chief whose trees had gone up in flames used his influence to keep the people from services. Though the cleric was better received in other villages, the Native attitude did not seem to go beyond the norms of curiosity and politeness. He came back with one convert, a man who had accompanied him on his journey. A few years later, in the winter of

1874, he made another attempt, reporting warm receptions in "Kitlachdamix" and "Kitwinshilk," but this trip did not result in the creation of new Christian outposts either.

Trapped in the Kincolith experiment, the Anglicans lacked the manpower to pursue Tomlinson's campaign. It fell to another sect to establish the first permanent Christian community in the Nass Valley. In 1874, the hard-working evangelist Thomas Crosby opened a Methodist mission to the Fort Simpson Tsimshian. In the following year he made his first journey to Nishga territory. His report stated bluntly what the Anglicans had avoided admitting for an entire decade:

> We found the people at the great heathen dance in old Chief Claycut's house. Most of them were covered with paint and feathers and wished to know what I had come for. They didn't want any Missionary troubling them. An old chief said, "God gave you the Bible, but He gave us the dance and the potlatch, and we don't want you here."

Crosby was received with civility nonetheless. He was invited to sit by the fire, and Chief Claycut gave the order to pour something like twenty litres of oolican grease over the flames in his honour. And he persisted, trying in the fall of the same year, at a village called "Kiteeks" twenty kilometres from the river's mouth, to interrupt the performance of a traditional ceremony: "I said, 'Stop!' in a very decided voice. 'I want to preach to you.' I walked up and down in the house, giving them the Law as well as the Gospel."

In March of 1876, however, the Methodist missionary was gratified by developments on the Nass:

> We found the people all at home, and many of the Chiefs spoke, urging that a Missionary be sent at once. One said, "There are fifteen hundred people reaching away up the Naas and on to the headwaters of the Skeena, and this is the door to them all." They urged that we should not fail to send a white Missionary that summer. I left a native with them.

It is hard to know if such a change of heart among the Nishga was genuine or an invention of Crosby's battered optimism. It is possible that they had decided to let the Methodists settle in the valley. The move would be prompted more by practical considerations than by sudden conversion: observing the Metlakatla, Kincolith, and Fort Simpson missions for some years, the Nishga would have seen advantages in accepting white people among them, particularly in terms of medicine, education, and new economic activities. In short, they probably realized that they had to adapt to the changes brought by Europeans, whatever they thought of them.

The hypothesis of a careful welcome is supported by their choice of land for the Methodists. The Nishga did not ask them to settle in an existing village, but assigned them a site — Lakalzap, the location of modern Greenville — that had been abandoned after a dreadful epidemic in which survivors were not left enough time to bury their dead.

Having received the go-ahead from the Nishga, Crosby started the search for a missionary. During a trip to Nanaimo on Vancouver Island, he found as his candidate a young Englishman Alfred Green, in British Columbia since 1874 and teaching at a nearby Methodist school. After a short visit in August, Green and Crosby went to Lakalzap on 10 September 1877. They stopped at Angeeda, the main village two kilometres south of the mission site, where they found with great surprise that the people had organized an impressive ceremony in their honour. A gun was fired, flags were up, they were wearing their best clothes, with some even sporting soldiers' uniforms; the Nishga were clearly showing the importance they attached to the new mission. The missionaries were treated to a speech:

> We, the chiefs and the people of the Naas, welcome you from our hearts on your safe arrival here, to begin in earnest the Mission work you promised us last Spring when you visited us. We have seen the Mission carried on about fifteen miles from us at the mouth of the river for many years, but cannot see much good it has done among our poor people; but as you say you do not come here to trade with us, but only to teach us, we think it will be very different under your instruction.

They asked the clergymen to teach their children how to read and write, and called on the Great Spirit to see that the mission "be like a great rock, not to be moved or washed away." One could hardly believe such a welcome from the people who had seen Doolan make his pitiful attempt thirteen years earlier. But times had changed, and the Methodists had a distinct asset in

their catechist William Pierce, Scottish through his father and
Tsimshian through his mother, who had a good knowledge of
local customs.

The first winter was hard. There were not enough supplies,
and Pierce recorded a Christmas dinner that was particularly
bleak: boiled potatoes and boiled turnips, a boiled porcupine,
and, for "dessert," boiled rice without milk. At the start, four
families moved in with Green and Pierce, and in the course of
the first year a missionary's house and school were built. In spite
of his initial progress, Alfred Green, like Doolan and Tomlinson
before him, soon complained of the strength of tradition: "It is
strange to see how determined these heathen are to get the
Christians back to heathenism. If they cannot get them by persecution they will try them by force, or by kindness work on
their feelings." As at Kincolith, the presence of the mission
divided families. Green reported a conflict between an uncle
and his nephew, a convert who refused to take part in traditional dances. The uncle said:

> My nephew, you are my heir, you see my property; I have been
> saving it up all my life for you, so that when you take my name you
> will be rich and a big Chief. But you are going a different road;
> you are poor; you have no good clothes; you have no boxes filled;
> you won't dance, so the people don't give you presents. It is true
> you have a little house at the Mission; but I cannot see your prop-
> erty. Come to me and I will give you all.

The quarrel was later settled by the conversion of the uncle.

The missionary tactics of the Methodists seem to have been
less totalitarian than those of the nearby Anglicans. The sect did
not try to create a new social organization, concentrating instead
on the spiritual aspect of their mission. The Methodist brand of
Christianity was an "intense" one, with prayer meetings at which
believers bore public witness to their personal experiences. It
was ten years before the mission had enough parishioners and
funds to start building a church, though on an 1881 trip to
England, Green was given sixteen musical instruments and
returned to found a brass band. With a month's intensive coach-
ing, the Nishga made great strides. Green reported joyfully that
their repertoire included " 'The German Hymn,' 'The Fisherman's Prayer,' 'Praise God from Whom all Blessings Flow,' 'God

save the Queen,' 'The Dead March in Saul,' 'Onward Christian Soldiers,' and 'Around the Throne of God in Heaven.' "

In 1889, Alfred Green was transferred to southern British Columbia, and the church found it hard to provide a replacement. Lakalzap, which became Greenville, received successively four ministers, the Reverends D. Jemmings, R.B. Beavis, S.S. Osterhout, and Dr. William Rush, but by 1900 the Methodists were unable to find candidates. Finally, in 1904, after four years without a minister, the parishioners asked the Anglicans to take care of them; since that time, most Greenville Christians have been affiliated with this denomination.

GOSPEL ROAD

As Crosby had been told, Lakalzap was simply the gateway to the real stronghold of paganism in the upper valley. Logically, the Methodists were in a better position than the Anglicans to forge inland, but they lacked the funds and manpower to fuel any sustained missionary effort upstream. During the summer of 1878, however, William Pierce sojourned briefly at "Kit-wun-sikh" near the modern village of Canyon City. In the fall, he moved to Gitlakdamix, the largest of the Nishga villages, eighty kilometres from the sea. Nahoogh, a young chief who offered him hospitality, became his prime target; he was the nephew of Skadeen, head-chief of Gitlakdamix, and heir-apparent to the leadership of the village. During his stay, Pierce obtained Nahoogh's and three other conversions. This encouraging development brought Alfred Green to Gitlakdamix, and he was instantly a witness to the tenacity of Native custom. The villagers were cremating the remains of an old woman; as Green tried vainly to interfere, they removed the heart from the fire and buried it under a tree, wrapped in a dry cedar mat. "Surely, these people need the Gospel," concluded Green.

His church never carried the Word to the people of the upper Nass. It was needful too, and the shortage of funds forced William Pierce out of the area in the spring of 1879. A Native evangelist, George Edgar, was left behind. The Methodists kept a handful of followers at Gitlakdamix and Kit-wun-sikh until the end of the century, but the absence of any permanent mission prevented them from making any great incursions into the upper valley. This distance work fell to the Anglicans.

In 1875, the Kincolith missionary Tomlinson paid a brief visit to Gitlakdamix and was surprised at his welcome: "Why was it that, in a village still sunk in heathenism and tenaciously clinging to their own customs — at a time, too, when they were just about to give away property — we should have had such a reception from one of the chiefs?" He found his explanation. The previous winter, an old Gitlakdamix chief had been stopped by his family from going to Kincolith to get treatment for an inflamed knee. When spring came and the ailment had developed into an ulcer, the chief went to the mission and stayed with a relative. Tomlinson managed to cure him over the summer, and convert him as well: "In an unexpected manner God has opened a door for the entrance of His truth among that tribe."

Tomlinson decided to mount a direct assault on Gitlakdamix. He arrived at the village with several canoeloads of timber for building a school. The Nishga called him to a meeting and let him know that they had not authorized him to settle there. Tomlinson was warned by one of his followers that the head-chief had a dagger under his robe, and that his life was in danger. He was spirited out of the meeting by Tkaganlakhatqu, head of the Wolf clan, who put him in a sympathizer's house. Fourteen years after Doolan, the Anglicans had failed for the second time to establish a Christian settlement in an existing Nishga village. The reason was that, unlike the Methodists of Lakalzap, they had gone uninvited.

The day following this fiasco, Tomlinson modified his plans and reverted to the Metlakatla-Kincolith formula of building a Christian community out of the main stream of Native society. He left with his canoes and landed three kilometres downstream at a deserted spot named Aiyansh — translated by the missionaries as "the place of eternal bloom," but really meaning "early leaves" — where his helpers quickly built a house with the timber they had brought. The party returned to Kincolith leaving the structure unoccupied. Shortly afterwards, Tomlinson ran into doctrinal difficulties with his church and moved to the Skeena region, where he became an independent missionary among the Gitksan. His successor, H. Schutt, did not stay long and was replaced in 1883 by the missionary William Henry Collison, who had spent some time with the Haida of the Queen Charlotte Islands.

Collison would stay with the Nishga for thirty-seven years until his death in 1920.

For a while, Tomlinson's "school" at Aiyansh had birds and squirrels as its only tenants, until a white miner decided to make it his own. Chief Tkaganlakhatqu chased him away and moved in with one of his four wives and some friends. As head of the Wolf clan and leader of the secret society of the Ulala, Tkaganlakhatqu was the second personality in rank in Gitlakdamix. There is no written record of the reasons for his departure from the village, but it is possible that some kind of local rivalry played a role in his move and subsequent rallying to Christianity.

In 1883, the Church Missionary Society appointed James Benjamin McCullagh, a twenty-nine-year-old Irishman, as minister to the upper Nass Valley. McCullagh had not spent his younger years as a church worker; he was stationed in Malta as an officer in the British army when the C.M.S. asked him if he wanted to go to British Columbia. When he arrived at Aiyansh, his first goal was to build a house and start learning the Nishga language. He obtained the final conversion of Tkaganlakhatqu, whom he baptised "Abraham Wright."

From the start, relations were tense between the small Christian mission and the five hundred Gitlakdamix pagans. McCullagh reported that he had been the target of several assassination attempts. The Irishman also had trouble with his own flock: the Aiyansh settlers did not renounce their traditional rituals immediately and the missionary kept stepping in to stop Indian ceremonials around the mission. When one of his old parishioners, a man named Simass, died in midwinter, McCullagh spent a whole night standing in the snow near his grave, convinced that the "Cannibals" were bent on unearthing the corpse and eating it. This presumption of necrophagy on the part of a highly conditioned newcomer was never renewed; with more experience in the field, McCullagh recognized around 1899 in a pamphlet called "Indian Potlatch" that he had never personally witnessed any case of cannibalism, and that if any had occurred, it had been before his time.

Two years after his arrival, McCullagh organized a "company" of Christians led by two chiefs wearing special badges, and put it in charge of evangelization campaigns at the fishing camps. The missionary won a significant victory with the conversion of an heir to the title of Gitlakdamix head-chief, a man named Muguiliksqu. The Indians tried to win him back by organizing banquets in his honour, giving him gifts, and scattering down feathers on his head. Muguiliksqu would not change his mind, but McCullagh had to put up with the usual quiet warfare against the Christians' activities:

> I began my work last winter among them by holding services as usual in one particular house. My congregations were generally very small, and on one occasion I had none. Upon inquiring as to the reason of this, I was told the chiefs had made a "new law" forbidding any person to attend Christian services. I thereupon went from house to house, holding a short service in each, at the conclusion of which I found I had preached that day to a very large congregation, about six times the usual number, so that their new law turned to my purpose.

The small mission grew slowly from year to year, but in 1892, after a holiday in England, McCullagh realized that the situation was basically the same as it had been ten years before: the Nishga still clung to their age-old customs, and Gitlakdamix remained hostile to the Christians.

> Alas! the great attraction among the heathen, during the winter, was the Ulala, or cannibal dance, at which human flesh was rated at one pound, two pounds, and three pounds per bite; many regarding it as a profitable business to offer their flesh (generally their arms) to the dancers. A one-pound biter merely made a deep bruised impression with his teeth; but a two-pound gentleman was allowed to lacerate flesh and imbibe a little blood; while an optimus had the full privilege of tearing a piece away and eating it. Old Gwin-giau reached the summit of his ambition (public notoriety and fame) by being able to take ten bites at three pounds!! Picture to yourselves such scenes, enacted by naked savages, besmeared with ochre and bedecked with feathers, howling and writhing through the fiendish contortions peculiar to this mysterious rite, in the lurid glare of blazing logs, and encircled by an audience drawn from the various Nishga tribes, and you will see then "the heathen at home," perfectly at home in darkness such as this!

During their pastor's absence, the Christian Indians built a three-kilometre "Road of the Gospel" from the mission to Gitlakdamix.

After the advent of the New Year we laid prayerful and determined siege to this citadel of heathenism. Every day, until March
10th, when the tribes left for their spring fishing, a party of forty
or fifty started from Aiyansh, marching along Gospel Road with
banner aloft, singing and praying, straight into the heathen village, where they spent from three to four hours, holding outdoor
and indoor meetings.

In November, having endured eleven months of psychological
warfare and daily commotion in their village, the inhabitants of
Gitlakdamix were losing their patience, especially since the
Christians were now coming with a drum:

> ... the Heathen took a dislike to the drum. Perhaps they thought
> it was too much à la medicine man, or perhaps they may have
> heard that I advised against the use of the drum. Be that as it may,
> they sent a deputation to me, asking me to stop open-air preach-
> ing. If I would engage to stop that, they would give their very best
> attention to the preaching of the Gospel in their own houses.
> However, before I could get a word in, Chief Abraham was on the
> war path against the deputation, belching forth like a volcano
> torrents of burning indignant remonstrance, and, having
> exhausted himself, left the council chamber. I then explained to
> the deputation that I could not, neither had I any desire to stop
> street preaching, nor could Abraham stop it.

On the following Sunday, the Christians came back with their
drum to the centre of the village.

> Here they were met by a determined crowd, which completely
> blocked up their way, while certain of the baser sort made a rush
> with knives to do for the drum. Somehow the drum seemed to be
> charmed, for though T'Gak kept on beating it, they could not get
> their hands on it. The Christians made no reply to the many
> taunting speeches of the Heathen, but getting down on their
> knees began to pray for them. One old medicine man, Hkseije,
> spat four times at George Gozag, as he was praying, but Gozag,
> taking no notice, went on praying. Old Agaud, another medicine
> man, made a rush at the throat of a relative, to give him a good
> shaking, but he was seized with such trembling and weakness,
> when he found himself in the midst of the Christian ranks, that
> when they went down on their knees he flopped down too, which

sight created a panic in the Heathen crowd, who fled precipitately lest some powerful influence should come over them also.

After this epic confrontation, the Christians went home convinced finally of the need for compromise. The people of Aiyansh renounced their drum; in return, the villagers would allow them to preach in their houses every Sunday morning. On 21 December 1893, head-chief Skadeen gave a banquet to put the seal on this agreement. From that day forward, Christians were allowed to move freely in the village. What ten years of sermons had not been able to achieve had been won in under a year of musical terrorism.

Evangelization did not progress, however, by the sole force of the Word. The missionaries had a number of non-religious weapons in their arsenal:

> When the medicine-men found I was really effecting cures, and that the sick were being brought to me rather than to them, they gave out a law that first a sick person should be rattled over, and then he could be brought to me or I to him. Or, if it were not possible to rattle over them before they were attended to by me, they must be rattled over afterwards. How manifestly clever! They would thus be able to take the credit of every recovery, and saddle me with every failure. Then too I made a law, that I would not on any account receive for treatment any person who had been rattled over by a medicine-man.

James McCullagh's edict was not unusual for the time. Doolan and Tomlinson had applied the same policy before him. The miracles of modern science were very useful in winning submission to the Gospel. In his fight against the forces of darkness, the missionary felt able to override the fundamental principle of medicine that the sick are to be treated regardless of their personal beliefs. The end justified the means.

To Natives, McCullagh presented the opposition between medicine and shamanism as absolute, but the missionary knew himself, in a way remarkable for his time and situation, that the line between the two was in may respects arbitrary. He recognized that the reason why medicine cured people was not simply because it treated the body, but because it explained the illness — patients were prepared to put their faith in it. Seen, then, as a system of explanations, medicine was not very different from shamanism and religion. The explanation happened to be "scientific," but it could just as well have been magical or mystical. Like a physician prescribing a pill that contained nothing more than sugar, or a shaman attributing an illness to the presence of an evil spirit, the missionary manipulated the minds of his "patients" without any qualm in order to wrestle with disorders of a clearly mental or psychosomatic nature. Such was the case of the cure of T'Gak.

T'Gak was a man from Gitlakdamix who lived alone and naked in the woods, avoiding human contact. One day he appeared at the door of the Aiyansh church and interrupted the Sunday service with an "idiotic laugh." Members of the congregation tried to catch him, but he jumped into a river and escaped. After three weeks he was finally captured, tied like an animal, and brought to a cabin.

Sitting there before him and looking into his monkey-like eyes, I wondered what I was going to do with him. No matter what I said I failed to kindle a gleam of intelligence in his eyes. At last I tried the line of fear. Pulling out my pocket-knife, I pretended to make a jab at him; he winced, and a flash of apprehension glimmered for an instant in his eye. Putting back my knife, I followed the clue. "You have too much blood, too much blood," I insisted, looking fixedly at him. "I take some blood," I went on, repeating the words many times. It seemed as if the word blood had really penetrated to his brain; and so I made up my mind to try an experiment, rushing in, I suppose, where angels would have feared to tread. I had been delving into Gall and other writers on the brain, and had been much interested, and it occurred to me that if I could reach the brain I might get a result. So, having taken two or three intelligent Indians into my confidence and instructed them in the parts they were to play, we took the patient (I had almost said the victim) and laid him out upon a table and bound him down. His arms were then held out at right angles by two assistants, each of whom had a tin bucket at this feet and a bottle of warm water coloured with red ink in his pocket. In my own hand appeared a little blade of gleaming steel. Again I insisted, "Too much blood, too much blood — I take some blood," looking into his eyes and pressing the forefinger of my right hand on the middle of his brow. Then we blindfolded him, and I noticed a tremor of the lips.

There was a dead silence. With a chip I sharply scratched each arm, my assistants dropping warm water on the places, and this trickling down the forearm fell drop-drop-drop into the buckets. The dropping continued and could be distinctly heard above the deep breathing of my assistants and the ticking of my watch, as I kept my fingers on the pulse.

At a motion of my head, a man cried out: "Awnai gusgaul ile!" ("Oh dear, what a quantity of blood!") Then silence again. Another motion of my head and two others made the same exclamation. The pulse was now distinctly feeble, then it began missing a beat or two; so I thought it was time to stop, and gave the word, "Clear away." There was a bustling sound of washing and wiping and moving buckets; pieces of adhesive plaster were put on each "wound" and the bandage removed from the eyes. Our subject lay as limp as a rag, but in his eye there was a natural look, as he gasped out: "Ukdak nei!" ("I'm hungry!").

We took him to Abraham's shack, put him to bed, and gave him some food, and by and by he fell asleep. Every day I visited him and talked with him, and presently walked about with him, clothed and in his right mind. T'Gak stayed on at Aiyansh, became a candidate for baptism, and was eventually baptised.

The Reverend-Shaman had made a good convert, for T'Gak proved himself as the indefatigable drummer leading the Christian soldiers onward to the final surrender of heathen Gitlakdamix.

After shamanism, the potlatch was the missionary's other obsession. McCullagh recognized that the custom was not, strictly speaking, a religious ceremony, but an essential element of the Nishga political structure.

The Potlatch is political as far as this life and this world concern the Indian, and the event seen by the public is in reality an election. The articles distributed with so much display as free gifts (with the exception of blankets and calico torn up into small strips) are all returnable within a year or two. They are not gifts, as many people imagine, but vote-acknowledgements — a public recognition of the rank or social status of the voter (who records his vote by his presence) by the Potlatcher who is a candidate for some position, favour, or honour in his clan.

The missionary clearly knew that in attacking the potlatch he was condemning a whole social system. His justifications, however, were by no means as clear. They emerge as an uneasy alliance between theology and economics. "Although not an idol itself," he wrote, "the Potlatch puts all the idols of heathendom in the shade, for not only does it swallow up the sustenance of an entire community but the community itself, and only says 'Shimoigit!' (Hail, chief!) in return." He condemned the institution as "glorification of self" and almost in the same breath lined it up with the pernicious egalitarian doctrines of his age: "Jealousy of one another is the characteristic feature of Indian life, and so socialistic are their ideas that no individual dare improve his condition above the general average, while at the same time each clan-section is consumed with a burning desire to make a better show than any other."

Here we are close to the real reason for white opposition to the potlatch: the practice was fundamentally foreign to European economic and social systems and incompatible with capitalist and Protestant ideals of individual accumulation. In McCullagh's words, "It is destructive of individual liberty, and, consequently, of the development of the race; it is inimical to all social progress and education." Wasteful, inequitable, the dreaded potlatch

> consumes five clear months out of every twelve in simply gorging, sleeping and dancing; the most that any of its votaries can earn is all too little for it; the money that ought to be spent upon the necessaries of life is squandered on this idol, which is feted and glutted to its heart's content, while the poor, the aged, the feeble and the sick lie in poverty, filth and rags — dying for want of a little nourishment.

The missionary strove against customs like the potlatch or the practices of secret societies that had obvious links with a mythology foreign to Christianity; he also attacked social behaviour and Native versions of marriage and divorce that did not conform to white standards. For example, a Nishga could divorce his spouse or remarry simply by taking his clan as witness to the new arrangement. The colonial authorities recognized these ceremonies as valid, but McCullagh lobbied legislators to change the situation and entrench the supremacy of British law. He evidently saw himself as much more than a religious leader:

"The pastoral work of a missionary among Indians is widely different to that of the vicar or rector of a parish in England or other civilized country. Here one has to take cognizance of one's parishioners — their domestic life, their dwellings, their sanitary arrangements, their civic life, their laws, government, &c. — as well as their souls."

In accordance with this conception of his role, McCullagh intervened in all aspects of Nishga daily life. In 1885, he founded a "Red Cross Association" for preaching the Gospel to the heathen. Its twelve members, led by "a Captain (Army Church style)," wore a small red Maltese cross and paid monthly dues of fifty cents. By McCullagh's rules, "should any male member of the community fall sick or cease to attend Divine service, he at once comes under the care and ministrations of the Association." The formula was expanded in 1893, when a female version, the "White Cross Association," was created with

fifteen members, distinguished by a small white Maltese cross, all communicants, who form a weekly working party for the purpose of making moccasins, &c., which are sold for the benefit of our church building fund. Last summer we received an order for two pairs of beaded moccasins, one pair of which was intended as a present to the Countess of Aberdeen.

In addition to doing beadwork for the Vicereine, the White Cross stepped in each time a female member of the community stopped going to church.

In 1895, Reverend McCullagh reported that the local school, managed by two native teachers, regularly looked after twenty children and twelve adults, plus, after work, twenty young men from Gitlakdamix who attended night courses. The minister himself wrote several textbooks in Nishga and translated part of the Gospel. In the same year, McCullagh was pleased to note that he had organized a choir and that the Aiyansh church had 125 souls, including 66 communicants, 12 catechumens, two churchwardens, one sexton, and one bell-ringer. Services were conducted in Nishga and English.

Aiyansh was administered politically by a parish council composed of seven chiefs: "The council has considerable power, and their authority is enforced by a force of five constables. Curfew is sounded at 10 p.m.; no one is supposed to be out of doors after that hour except for some reasonable cause." And to short-circuit the traditional network of solidarity in the clan system, the missionary created mutual societies. One of these was a fire-insurance company that, for an annual fee of $2.50, provided indemnification for members up to $170 in case of total loss; a further payment of fifty cents entitled a homeowner to fire-brigade service and repairs to minor damages. Other of McCullagh's innovations included the YMCA and YWCA as well as a "Harmonic Silver Band." On the economic side too, his achievements were impressive — a sawmill, a small printing press, a dispensary, roads, boardwalks, and some single-family cottages. According to visitors, by the end of the century Aiyansh was a rather pretty village.

Like Duncan's Metlakatla before its collapse, the Aiyansh community became a model for travelling Europeans. McCullagh sent numerous letters and pamphlets to church publications in Britain to stimulate giving; but always behind the public image of a prosperous village embracing modern ways was a monolithic community forged by the will of an iron-fisted missionary whose ultimate goal was not merely evangelization, but the complete reconstruction of Native society. For men like McCullagh, Tomlinson, and Duncan, Christianity was a global system that encompassed not only going to church on Sundays and reading the Bible but also washing with soap, working six days out of seven, and eating with one's feet under a table.

The missionaries and the Indians agreed on one point: religion and culture were inseparable. According to McCullagh, the Nishga did not have a separate concept for "religion," but included their spiritual life in an overall practice they called "Am." The potlatch, for instance, was at once the cornerstone of a system of ownership, and thus of production; the reminder of a myth that placed the individual and the clan inside Native history and cosmology; a theatrical performance; a gastronomical, musical, and poetical occasion, and, finally, the way of defining every individual's position in society. The link between the potlatcher and his claim depended on mythology, since he had to know the story, the legend, even the song attached to the place, if he was to prove his title to a certain fishing spot or trapline. The potlatch itself would have collapsed if, to "cleanse" it of paganism, the reference to the underlying myth had been eliminated.

For the missionaries, Christianity too was a part of a whole that could not be dismantled. To their eyes, the sawmill and the bottle of medicine were Christian; evangelization and general progress were inseparable. It is ironical that the system being promoted by the missionaries on the marches of the empire was already being dismissed at the centre, where religion had very little to do with the development of science and technology. Of their laborious legacy very little but a fragmented religious practice now remains. Modern Nishga are generally practising Christians, but Aiyansh and Metlakatla as cities of God exist no longer. Looking back through history, one could say that the role of the missionaries lay less in their stated objective — evangelization — than in a mandate that was given to them by the system as a whole: the destruction of those elements of Indian culture that were inimical to modern capitalism.

Fortunately for the present-day churches, this mission of destruction has had an unforecasted positive consequence: while trying to entrench their Christian utopias, the clergy sheltered the Indians somewhat from direct encroachment by other whites. Helped by a deep sense of morality, they developed the understanding that colonization also meant the theft of land, and they sided with the Natives in the struggle for their rights.

From an instrument of oppression, the Church thus developed into one of defence, acting as a model organization and support group in the fight for the land. In a way, the Nishga "indianized" the new religious institution and adapted it to their own needs. Unto this day, no other major institution in Canada, whether political party, trade union, or government, espouses unflinchingly the cause of Native land claims. The church stands alone, and by some this could be construed as atonement for the errors of its past.

6

THEFT OF THE LAND

. . . in the olden days the white men, commissioner or whatever, he come in and ask the chief. The chief wouldn't speak English. He only thought that man asked, "Whose smokehouse is that?" and he'll say, "Me," by using point of hands, talk by hand. But if he had a broken English like me, he woulda tell that this whole valley is ours. The chiefs of the Nishga, right through the mountains.

Because they call this Nass River "the supper bowl," because they eat out of that one bowl, they call this Nass River "the one bowl," and it's gonna be from the beginning to the end of the world, this river will flow, and nobody's gonna stop it. And all their fish they get it and eat it out of this river. And all the meat, and all the berries, they eat out of the valley. So both the valley and the Nass River, they call it "the supper bowl," because everything they eat out of this it comes naturally all the time, season after season. Nobody stop it. Meant for the Nishga.

Chief Roy Azak, 1981

The Nishga country is large — 14 830 square kilometres. It could cover three quarters of Wales or the State of New Jersey. As far as the Canadian authorities are concerned, however, the Nishga are trespassers on most of their land. The white man's law allows them only 76 square kilometres, equal to a quarter of the County of London, or two fifths of the District of Columbia, only 0.5 per cent of their original territory. And yet the Nishga have neither sold, ceded, nor abandoned their land. It has simply been taken from them without warning, authorization, or compensation.

History was not supposed to have unfolded quite this way. The 1763 royal proclamation that confirmed the style of British rule to the west of the Atlantic colonies was explicit that Natives were not to be "molested or disturbed in the Possession of such Parts of Our Dominion and Territories as, not having been ceded to, or purchased by Us, are reserved to them, or any of them, as their Hunting Grounds." When the British government decided in 1849 to transform Vancouver Island into a colony of the Crown and rescind the monopoly held by the Hudson's Bay Company, James Douglas, first governor and the Bay company's chief factor, tried to respect the principles laid down in the proclamation. His stated policy was "to purchase the native rights in the land, in every case, prior to the settlement of any district." From 1850 to 1854, he signed fourteen treaties with a number of Vancouver Island groups so that white colonists would settle only on lands Natives had either ceded or sold to the Crown. The governor's prices were ridiculously low. He bought the real estate on which the provincial capital was built for thirty shillings per family, and the adjacent area of the Saanich Peninsula for three blankets per square mile.

In 1858, the mainland followed the example set by Vancouver Island and was granted colonial status under the name "British Columbia." Douglas, by now governor of both colonies (they were united in 1866), tried to apply the same Native policy, but conditions had changed. The first gold rush had attracted to the lower Fraser Valley and the southern interior thousands of adventurers who were putting irresistible pressure on Native lands, and to compound the problem Douglas could no longer count on the Imperial treasury. London refused to allocate the funds necessary for the purchase of lands coveted by incoming white settlers, and when in 1861 the Colonial Office finally rejected a request for three thousand pounds, the governor was forced to abandon his policy.

He did try, however, to soften the impact of white encroachment, ordering his administration to establish "reserves" which were supposed to include all lands that the Natives claimed. In Douglas's mind, the reserves were properties that could not be alienated because they belonged to the Crown, and their creation was a humanitarian measure which would shelter the indigenous population. The reality was quite different: suddenly, the Natives were denied ownership of their ancestral territories and parked, without their consent and with no compensation, on some very small parcels of land.

The fact is that the governor's rules were not respected in the field. Each time conflict arose between Native rights and settlers' appetites, the civil servants plumped for the latter. As soon as Douglas retired in 1864, his policy was shelved. His successors consigned Native questions to a single civil servant, Commissioner of Lands and Works Joseph William Trutch. From 1864 to 1871, the date of union between British Columbia and the Canadian federation, Trutch sided systematically with the colonists' interests. He stated the new policy clearly in 1870, when two churchmen, William Green and George Hills, complained to London about the treatment to which the Natives were being subjected: "The title of the Indians in fee of the public lands, or any portion thereof, has never been acknowledged by Government, but, on the contrary, is distinctly denied." In 1865, the British Columbia government had opened the gates to white settlement with a "Land Ordinance" that provided free grants for colonists — 160 acres per family with the possibility of purchasing a further 480 acres from the Crown. At the same time, Trutch gave his subordinates a yardstick of ten acres per family for establishing reserves.

The land question was reopened by the 1871 union of British Columbia with Canada. According to the British North America Act that created the Canadian federation, Native affairs were a federal responsibility, while the provinces had jurisdiction over lands. Clause 13 of the Terms of Union between British Columbia and Canada tried to deal with potential conflict by stipulating: "The charge of the Indians, and the trusteeship and management of the lands reserved for their use and benefit, shall be assumed by the Dominion Government, and a policy as liberal as that hitherto pursued by the British Columbia Government shall be continued by the Dominion Government after the Union." This "liberal" policy meant that at the request of the federal government, the province would designate lands for Native use; in case of disagreement the conflict would be referred to the Secretary of State for the colonies in London.

The Ottawa government realized very quickly that the policy of the province was not "liberal" at all. In the rest of the Dominion, the practice at that time was to carve out reserves on the basis of 80 acres per family: on the Prairies, the first treaties signed between 1871 and 1873 made provision for tracts of land ranging from 160 to 640 acres. Meanwhile, British Columbia was still insisting on ten. The conflict became obvious when, in the spring of 1873, the new federal Superintendent of Indian Affairs for British Columbia, Dr. Israel Wood Powell, received a copy of a Dominion order-in-council suggesting that "each family be assigned a location of eighty acres of land of average quality."

The crisis broke in 1874 when the Victoria legislature passed its first Land Act, a law implying in its definition of "Crown land" that the public domain had been acquired from a previous owner. It made no provision for the creation of reserves. The Dominion government used its consitutional prerogative of disallowance and quashed the provincial law in March 1875.

The Canadian justice minister, Télésphore Fournier, was in total contradiction with Victoria's announced policy in holding that "there is not a shadow of a doubt, that from the earliest times, England has always felt it imperative to meet the Indians in council, and to obtain surrender of tracts of Canada, as from time to time were required for the purpose of settlement." The quarrel was thus not simply over average areas for reserves, but over the obligation to negotiate with the Indians prior to white settlement. The doctrine Fournier expressed might have lent itself to a direct challenge to the very legitimacy of European settlement, but the Canadian government chose to avoid the issue. By the terms of an 1875 compromise between Ottawa and Victoria, the allotment of reserve lands in British Columbia would not be carried out on the basis of specific acreages, but decided according to local conditions. In 1876, the federal government retreated even further, agreeing not even to raise the question of "aboriginal title" before establishing reserves. A joint Reserves Allotment Commission was set up with representatives of both governments. Its chairman, chosen by both parties, was Gilbert Sproat, an admirer of the Native policy of former Governor James Douglas.

Sproat spent the next three years crisscrossing the southern part of the province and listening to the numerous complaints of Natives who, from the mouth of the Fraser up to Shuswap Lake, were losing their lands at an alarming rate. The commissioner soon became a target of violent criticism by colonists who accused him of "prodigality" towards the Natives. The whites easily won the support of the Victoria government, which undermined Sproat's work by systematically refusing to print his rulings in the provincial Gazette. Another provincial tactic was to distribute the best land in an area before the commission had arrived and had a chance to identify reserves. And in certain cases, Victoria disregarded Sproat's decisions completely, granting white settlers properties already included in reserves. These boycotting manoeuvres culminated in an 1879 amendment to the Land Act by which any reserve allotment would be declared invalid that had not been registered under a new set of regulations. After three years of work in the field, not one of the commission's conclusions was inscribed in the provincial Land Registry. Sproat was left with no choice but to resign, and he did so in 1880.

He was replaced by a friend of the colonists, Peter O'Reilly, who happened to be brother-in-law to Lands and Works Commissioner Joseph Trutch, the architect of the province's anti-Native policy. Holding the post of reserve commissioner for eighteen years, O'Reilly was responsible for establishing the size and location of most of British Columbia's modern reserves. Unlike Sproat, he spent little time in the field. Decisions were made in Victoria among bureaucrats and politicians; there was virtually no consultation with Native groups.

O'Reilly's appointment coincided with the beginning of a radical change in the numerical weight of the province's Native population. In 1881, there were 25 661 Indians in a total of 49 459 inhabitants of British Columbia; ten years later, after the completion of the transcontinental railroad, they represented only one third of a provincial population of 98 173, and by the beginning of the twentieth century, in 1901, they had dwindled to minority of 25 488 in a total 178 657 inhabitants.

As the O'Reilly years began, the north coast of British Columbia had not yet been visited by the commission, but the Nishga were suffering from white encroachment nonetheless. Some settlers had already "staked their claims" to Native land; one such was John Mathieson, an old Scottish convert of William Pierce, who in April 1879 registered a pre-emption of 380 acres on properties of the people of Gitlakdamix. For the most part, however, white men coming to the Nass had to acknowledge Nishga ownership of the country before their presence was tolerated. This situation was memorably expressed by the missionary Alfred Green in an 1888 letter to the federal authorities:

I came to the Naas River first in the spring of 1877, and was advised to look out and pre-empt a piece of land to erect mission buildings on, and to use for a boys' industrial school. But I found the idea of ownership so strong among the Indians, that I had to give that project up. I soon found that this feeling was general. Every mountain, every valley, every stream was named, and every piece belonged to some particular family. This claim was recognized by all the white men, viz., Harvey Snow, James Grey, J.J. Robinson, who rented small sites from the Indians for fishing purposes, and paid the Indians regular rent for the same. When the two last named men applied and received Crown grants from the Provincial Government, and the Indians were made to give up their gardens and to remove their houses off the land that had been granted to these white men, so strong was the feeling against these white men taking this land, that Grey only got his surveyed by promising a sawmill should be built on it. The ten acres at Fishery Bay was not, and never has been, surveyed.

The Methodist clergyman reported a more serious incident that had been caused by white interference in the salmon fishery, the main occupation of the Nishga people.

In 1880, Mr. H.E. Croasdaile had a foreman named Mr. Nice, and he erected a large trap to catch salmon in the Naas River. The day that it was towed and placed in position the Indians became very excited, and stopped the work. Mr. Nice wrote, asking me to go down, as he was afraid the Indians would shoot him. I went; and the Indians, to the number of 700, met together. I heard them and urged them to leave the matter with Dr. Powell.

Green wrote a letter on the Natives' behalf, and Powell had acknowledged its receipt, but "I know the Indians did not hear from him again, and the trap was allowed to remain in the place the Indians complained of, till carried off by the ice."

By that time Ottawa had already capitulated to the colonists in power at Victoria, and it is thus not surprising that Superintendent Powell gave no real answer to the Nishga letter. The federal bureaucrat was blatantly impolite when a delegation of Nass River people led by one of their highest-ranking leaders, Chief Mountain, travelled all the way to Victoria to lodge their complaint with the Canadian government. One of those delegates, Charles Russ, later testified to the superintendent's arrogance:

I know that Dr. Powell does not care for us, for I was sent by the Indians, with Chief Mountain, to Victoria, to go and talk to him about our troubles. I paid my way on the steamer, and Mountain and I went, with Mr. Crosby and Mr. Green, to talk to Dr. Powell. He told us another day he would see us and answer us, but he did not hear our other words; and, after a long time, we returned home without any answer; and so we know that he did not want to assist us.

Powell was certainly not the only official to treat the Nass people in such cavalier fashion. On 7 October 1881, Peter O'Reilly arrived at Kincolith to impose the reserve system on the Nishga. He spent only thirteen days touring the valley, interviewing the people, and reaching a decision over a territory larger than the State of Connecticut. His recommendations were drafted by 20 October and approved by the provincial government on 8 May 1882. O'Reilly's visit has come down as part of Nishga oral tradition, and their collective testimony reflects its lightning speed. The reserve commissioner arrived in the middle of the fishing season when the villages were half-deserted and asked innocuous questions about the ownership of certain buildings. At no time, claim the Nisgha, did he try to explain his real purpose, which was the seizure of most of the land and the establishment of reserves. Yet the present locations of the Nishga reserves are the direct result of that whistle-stop tour of a century ago.

The commissioner did recognize, in his May 1882 official report, that "the reserves above referred do not include the whole of the lands it may be necessary to assign to these Indians as owing to the lateness of the season I was unable to visit all the places claimed by them for fishing and other purposes." And speaking with the province's premier five years later, he further admitted that he had paid no attention at all to what the Nishga had to say: "Every inlet is claimed by someone, and were I to include all these, it would virtually declare the whole country a reserve." His method had been simply to identify the locations of dwellings and add to these a few fishing spots along the main watercourses. This work done, he had evaluated the Nishga population at 867, though it was probably greater, and assigned them 9 954 acres of unsurveyed land, or about 11 acres per person.

In November 1888, Chief Tat-ca-kaks of Lakalzap lodged an affidavit concerning the commissioner's action.

I wish to say that every mountain and every stream has its name in our language, and every piece of the country here is known by the name our forefathers gave them. And we are not satisfied with Mr. O'Reilly coming and measuring off our land. We do not understand how he comes to get this power to cut up our land without our being willing. When Mr. O'Reilly came we told him how much land we wanted, but he would not do what we asked. God gave this land to our fathers a long time ago, and they made gardens and made homes, and when they died they gave them to us. And strange Indians of other tribes who came here, wanting to fish the "oolachans," always asked our fathers for the privilege to come and fish here and always paid something for it. So this shows that all recognize that this belonged to us, and we have never been willing that our land should be surveyed.

O'Reilly had laid out the reserves without a survey of the land. This was started in the summer of 1886 by a party under Capt. William Jemmett, surveyor for the Indian Reserve Commission. When Jemmett tried to define their boundaries more precisely, the people of the upper Nass refused to let him carry out his work. Two decades later, Archdeacon Collison of Kincolith recollected in testimony before the McKenna-McBride Royal Commission on Indian Reserves that "an allotment of land was made which was accepted by the Christian Indians, although not favourable by the heathen chiefs — they took up the stakes and threw them in the river, denying the rights of outsiders to come and measure up the land." Chief Skadeen of Gitlakdamix gave his own version of the events in a signed affidavit:

My heart is very sick because the white man want to take our land away from us, and do not make a strong promise to us on paper. We want a treaty, and want the government to give us something for our land. God gave us the land, and we picked our berries, got our furs, made our houses, and made our canoes; all our living came off of this land, and out of this water, and now our hearts are made sick by the white chiefs taking nearly all our land from us. We do not want a reserve if we do not have a treaty, for the reserve is not large enough for us to live on. Our berries and hunting grounds are not in the reserves. Mr. O'Reilly did not do right; when he was here he said he would take away my power and give it to another man. Mr. O'Reilly did not make me chief of Gitlakdamix; my power came from my forefathers, and all in the

village acknowledge that I am their chief, but because I did not
want our land surveyed he said he would take my power away and
give it to some one else. God gave us a good survey when he gave
us the land, and we do not want Mr. O'Reilly to survey the land
unless the government make a treaty with us, and give us a present for our land.

The story of the establishment of the reserves was handed
down from generation to generation. In 1983 Chief Frank
Calder, founder of the present Nishga Tribal Council, was able
to give the following account:

You'll have to take their word for it, and you'll have to take my
word for it. It's by word of mouth. One of the last line of chiefs
passed it by word of mouth. It was on a beautiful day at the old
Gitlakdamix, the very old, original one. . . . So, this particular day,
a beautiful day, somebody reported to the chiefs that there's five
people across, over Gitlakdamix. And they're looking through
some strange instrument. So the chiefs said, since this was later in
the day, but nevertheless they were so interested, they all looked
across there. Big population in those days, you know. By God, yes,
it's a tent, there is smoke coming out beside the tent, and they
counted five people. So one of the chiefs sent a young brave
across. 'Cause they don't have oars, you know, in those days either,
you paddle, but it's a fast river, so you have to go on pole . . .
He beached the canoe. The guy never argued. He was told not
to argue. Find out what they're doing. The young fellow goes up
there. He says what are you doing? Ah, you haven't heard. Well, I
tell you, not in exact words. But the Queen wants to survey a line
down the river, you know. So far down that way it's gonna cross
the river and then it's gonna come back up, and it's gonna go a
ways behind your village, and it's gonna cross the river again and
come down here. That's what we're doing. Well, I don't know if
the boy said thank you, I don't know if there is any words to say
thank you, you know. But he came back. He told the chiefs how, at
Gitlakdamix late at night. Eight o'clock, the Indians were timing it,
'cause as soon as they saw that smoke they figured those people
are going to have their breakfast. Eight o'clock every canoe
beached started headin' across. Every Nishga has a Hudson Bay
musket. They marched up. Never argued to ask them what they
were doing. They just said, "Get off my land." The guys left. Who
wouldn't leave with all these guys with their muskets?

And in my studies, there were two impacts of that order. The old man told me — old Chief Nagoums Calder, one of the top chiefs in the river, who raised me — don't you ever forget, my son, the impacts. He's talking Indian, he doesn't know English, he's talking Indian, Nishga. In all your studies, as you grow up, don't ever forget what the order meant. "Get off my land." "Saayeen! Saayeen!" "Get off." The refusal of the Nishgas of the Indians to be confined in what is now known as reservation system. It was a complete refusal for that system to be established. And number two, the birth of the land question.

The Nishga were not the only ones to protest being parked on small reserves. The same land question, linked to a religious controversy, was taking on dramatic proportions at this time among the Metlakatla Tsimshian.

The matter started as an ecclesiastical squabble. Contrary to instructions of the Church Missionary Society, William Duncan refused to apply the Anglican doctrine in its entirety to his Native flock. In his view, the Tsimshian were not ready to practise all the rites of the church, and he refused to celebrate communion among them. He also rejected the idea of ordination for himself or any of the missionaries sent to help them. In 1879, the Anglican Church decided to carve a new diocese in the region, the diocese of New Caledonia, and when the new bishop, William Ridley, arrived at Metlakatla, a bitter dogmatic and personal conflict developed with the mission's founder. In 1881, matters came to a head and Bishop Ridley expelled William Duncan from the church.

Up to this point Duncan had been a model missionary, consulted regularly by the authorities for his expertise in Native affairs. Within a few years, however, he was to become a pariah seen by officialdom as a dangerous agitator. The radical change in his behaviour began when his religious differences with Ridley erupted into a fundamental dispute over the Natives' ancestral rights to their land.

As far back as 1864, Duncan had secured a reserve within a radius of one mile around the Metlakatla mission from his friend and admirer, Governor Douglas, in order to forestall a challenge to the Christian presence by the pagan Tsimshian. As well, two acres in the village itself had been granted to the Church Missionary Society for its buildings. In the wake of the 1881 schism, Bishop Ridley laid claim to these acres, known as

Mission Point, but the Metlakatlan majority, faithful to Duncan, carried off several of the buildings from the Missionary Society's lot. The prelate was left with only a school, and was even prevented from settling in the village at all following some bitter confrontations with the islanders.

The authorities tried to ease the tension by appointing an official commission of inquiry under Superintendent Powell. In September 1884, however, Bishop Ridley renewed hostilities by trying to set foot in Metlakatla and sending a surveyor, E.E. Shearburne, to measure the society's land. The islanders resisted, forcing Shearburne to leave the village. A second commission of inquiry then brought to light the proportions the conflict had assumed.

Duncan, it appeared, was now challenging the very principle of the reserve system. In 1880, he had accepted the idea of reserves along the coast mainly to stop further incursions on Indian fishing grounds by the white people already operating in the area. By 1884, the missionary was reproaching O'Reilly for having set up reserves at all in the absence of any formal consultation with the Tsimshian or explanation of the official land policy. He advised the commission to reopen the file on Native lands not included in existing reserves.

The commissioners, however, fell back on the province's official stand:

> The question of Indian lands is constitutionally settled by the British North America Act (an Imperial statute) and the Terms of Union between British Columbia and Canada. The commissioners consider that at Metlakatla and the North-West Coast every effort has been made to locate large and sufficient reserves in accordance with the provision of the laws above mentioned, and that particularly as regards the Tsimpseans, the reserve made by Mr. O'Reilly is more than ample for Indian purposes.

The seizing of Mission Point by the Metlakatlans was not seen by the commissioners as simply a religious commotion; it had been an open challenge to government power on a property that was considered to fall within provincial jurisdiction. The Tsimshian had asserted sovereignty over land outside their reserves and were furthermore refusing to accept a new white civil servant, the Indian Agent appointed to them under the provisions of Canada's new Indian Act. The commission recommended that a gunboat be sent to Metlakatla to protect the surveyors of Mission Point.

In the spring of 1885, when Duncan was in England, the provincial government sent out a new surveyor, C.P. Tuck. The Tsimshian protested but allowed him to do his work. However when he came back to the island in September 1886 to complete the survey, the villagers pulled up his spikes every morning and effectively prevented him from measuring anything at all. Eventually, a month later, they confiscated his instruments and expelled him altogether. Victoria reacted by sending the gunboat *Cormorant* with police on board. They arrested eight islanders and forced completion of the survey. Utterly demoralized, the main body of Metlakatlans resolved to abandon their village. During the summer of 1887, six or seven hundred of them left Canada for ever and, with William Duncan, founded a new Christian community on Annette Island in the Alaskan archipelago, which was given to them by the American government.

The expulsions of surveyors at Gitlakdamix and Metlakatla were remarkable instances of the depth of Native resistance to the reserve system. The tragic conclusion of the Metlakatla experiment came as proof of the fundamentally violent nature of white power and the impossibility of physical opposition to the organized theft of the land. Yet the traumatic changes imposed on the Nishga did not leave them bowed in submission. They simply picked themselves up for a new battle on the political front, and waited for the next government manoeuvre.

The Canadian parliamentary system of government is supposed to function in a democratic and equitable manner. By its very nature, however, it will do things that are offensive to minorities and, indeed, things to which minorities would never agree if they were given the chance of exercising power themselves. There come times in the process when whole segments of the governed population cease to believe that they can influence in any way the behaviour of the state. When this happens — when governments have protected for too long the same powerful vested interests, when their actions seem to breed only disbelief and disrespect, or, less dramatically, when they want to avoid blame for unpopular decisions or damaging issues — they have at their disposal a political instrument that can extricate them from these tricky situations. This instrument is known as the Royal Commission of Inquiry.

The system of public inquiry by panels of respected and sup-
posedly neutral citizens has the advantage of defusing poten-
tially explosive issues by transferring conflict from the ground
of action to the safer sidelines of palaver. Hearings also help to
reintegrate protesters within the system by drawing them into
often aimless dialogue and giving them the impression that they
have a voice in the decision-making process. Yet more often
than not, royal commissioners have been dictated to as well as
approved of by the political power, and their public investiga-
tion becomes a caricature of direct democracy.

British Columbia's Northwest coast in 1887 was a perfect theatre for the introduction of this subterfuge. The reserve system
challenged, survey teams thrown out, religious schism, the Metlakatlan exodus to Alaska — the situation was threatening to
explode into a wholesale rejection of white authority in the
region. The Royal Commission of Inquiry into the North-West
Coast Indians came to the scene well and truly briefed. In
unmistakable terms, the Honourable Alexander Edmund Bas-
ton Davie, Premier and Attorney-General of British Columbia,
instructed his nominee J.B. Planta as to what type of "impartial-
ity" he expected from the commission: "You will please be careful — while assuring the Indians that all they say will be
reported to the proper authorities — not to give undertakings
or make promises, and in particular you will be careful to dis-
countenance, should it arise, any claim of Indian land title to
Provincial lands."

On 17 October of that year the commissioners, Clement
Cornwall for the Dominion of Canada and Planta for British
Columbia, arrived at Kincolith, where they heard, among oth-
ers, the Native schoolteacher Frederick Allen:

Ever since Mr. O'Reilly was here the chiefs of Kincolith have been
troubled and dissatisfied about their land. Mr. O'Reilly did not
consult with them or have a talk with them about it, and he did not
give them a choice about their land. After he said he had given us
our land he left, and then we knew nothing until Capt. Jemmett
surveyed it and showed us the boundary; then we saw it was too
small. There was no wood upon it and no way of hunting. . . . We
want the whole of Observatory Inlet and surrounding country
with the streams entering it. We catch salmon in them and hunt
over it all, and we get wood and berries there. And on Portland
Canal there are several streams we want secured. Each chief has

always had certain places where he and his tribe always hunted and caught salmon. We do not want the whole of that Inlet (Canal), only some places. We have good reasons for wanting these places secured to us. Sometimes the salmon is scarce in one stream, then we go to another. All the Naas Indians when the salmon is scarce up the river go to these inlets.

The next day, at Nass Harbour, the commissioners received a similar message from the Greenville Nishga. Unlike the people of Gitlakdamix, the lower-valley villagers had not expelled the surveyors, but they did feel that they had been duped by O'Reilly. The most important chief in the village, Victoria Long-arm, could not, by Nishga protocol, appear in person. Her husband, Chief John Calder, spoke on her behalf:

I am not going to speak to you of myself at all: I am going to speak to you the words of the chiefess of the Naas River, Victoria Long-arm. There are many chiefs. At Greenville, where Victoria lives, there are Mountain, myself, and Nease Youse, and half a mile from us at another village there are Tat-qua-gaas, Kledach, Nee-ish-les-yarn, Laik, Kitchon, Waalsh, Nish Chan. These are chiefs, but my wife is acknowledged to be chief over all on the river. My wife has one word, and that word she has sent me to bring to you is that "our land is too small." It is not large. It is not as much as we can use. We can't live on it. It is not what we asked for; not so large as we expected. When Mr. O'Reilly came up, my wife and the other chiefs told him what we wanted. Mr. O'Reilly did not give it. When the surveyor came up last year, we asked him to a meeting. He came. We pointed out what land we wanted, but he didn't give it. He gave just what Mr. O'Reilly did; and that is where the trouble began, and it has been growing in our hearts ever since.

Another speaker was Charles Russ, a Greenville sub-chief:

We have no word in our language for "reserve." We have the word "land," "our land," "our property." Your name for our land is "reserve," but every mountain, every stream, and all we see, we call our forefathers' land and streams. It is just lately the white people are changing the name. Now it is called the Indian reserve, instead of the Naas people's land. If you ask the Hydahs, Alaskas, Stick-eens, Bella Bellas, and Fort Ruperts, they will tell you that all this country is the Naas people's land, and we don't know when any change was made, or when it was taken from us. But now it is called "reserve" we want the word "treaty" with it. The change that was made from "our land" to "reserve" was made by the white people, and "treaty" is to come from them too . . .

My father was a chief of Metlakatlah, and my mother a Naas woman; that is why I am on the Naas. My father did not want his land and his father's land called a reserve; that is why he got up and left the country for Alaska; and we don't like the word "reserve" any more than he did; but now, if we have a treaty, we will be willing to live on a reserve.

Mr. Planta — By the word "treaty" you mean a paper making the reserve sure to you, do you not?

C. Russ — You see we only ask a little land for ourselves, and outside there is a great deal of land; we give that to you. Come, now [*extending his hands*] what are you going to give us, if it is only a little, with a strong promise, and then it will be finished?

The commissioners then explained the official policy:

Mr. Planta — The whole question of the Indian lands in British Columbia was settled long ago by law, and the Government cannot go beyond the law. Once the Provincial Government had the sole charge of the Indians, but about twenty years ago the Imperial Parliament passed a statute called the "British North America Act," and under its powers the Queen made an Order in Council, which admitted British Columbia into the Dominion upon certain conditions. . . . Under this law [*reading from "Terms of Union"*], "the charge of the Indians, and the trusteeship and management of the lands reserved for their use and benefit," belongs entirely to the Dominion Government, and all the Provincial Government has to do in the matter is to reserve enough lands for the Indians' use.

Mr. Cornwall — It is as well for you to understand that there is no probability of your views as to the land being entertained.

C. Russ — We hear your words and you have heard the words of our chiefs, but the words you have read to us we never heard before in our lives. When they made the laws that you speak about they had never been to see us; they did not know what we used or what we wanted. I would like to ask, sirs, if there was one chief of the Naas present when that law was made, and whether they asked him to speak for the Naas people? Or did they write a letter asking them about it? Why, they never even sent us a letter to tell us it was done. You see these chiefs present laugh. We cannot believe the words we have heard, that the land was not acknowledged to be ours. We took the Queen's flag and laws to honour them. We never thought when we did that that she was taking the land away from us.

Mr. Planta — The Provincial Government will always perform the duty cast upon them by clause 13 of the Terms of Union, by setting apart and handing over to the Dominion Government such tracts of land as may be deemed reasonably sufficient for all the purposes of the Indians, but cannot go further than that.

C. Russ — Set it apart; how did the Queen get the land from our forefathers to set it apart for us? It is ours to give to the Queen, and we don't understand how she could have it to give to us.

[*Here an old blind Indian named Neis Puck jumps up and demands a hearing.*]

Neis Puck — I am the oldest man here and I can't sit any longer and hear that it is not our fathers' land. Who is the chief that gave this land to the Queen? Give us his name, we have never heard it.

The next day, 19 October, the commissioners were once again confronted with the stubborn reality of the Native land claims issue. Planta made a vain attempt to reassure those present:

You may rest assured that you are as secure in the possession of any land set aside for a reserve as anyone can possibly be. It is impossible to touch it without your consent, and if it is taken with your consent, its full value will have to be paid for it. A large sum has been paid by the Railway Company for the piece of land taken at Victoria. Indians listen with open ears to all sorts of tales told them, but it is surprising you can believe such a tale as that. If we had come for nothing else it would have been well for us to come and explain this. The sole object of the Government is to protect the Indians in their persons and property.

David MacKay, another Greenville chief, replied:

> What we don't like about the Government is their saying this: "We
> will give you this much land." How can they give it when it is our
> own? We cannot understand it. They have never bought it from us
> or our forefathers. They have never fought and conquered our
> people and taken the land in that way, and yet they say now that
> they will give us so much land — our own land. These chiefs do
> not talk foolishly, they know the land is their own; our forefathers
> for generations and generations past had their land here all
> around us; chiefs have had their own hunting grounds, their
> salmon streams, and places where they got their berries; it has
> always been so. It is not only during the last four or five years that
> we have seen the land; we have always seen and owned it; it is no
> new thing, it has been ours for generations. If we had only seen it
> for twenty years and claimed it as our own, it would have been
> foolish, but it has been ours for thousands of years.

He was followed by Am-Clamman, sub-chief of Kit-wil-luk-
shilts:

> You saw us laughing yesterday when Neis Puck got up and spoke,
> because you opened the book and told us the land was the Queen's
> and not the Indians'. That is what we laughed at. No one ever does
> that, claiming property that belongs to other people. We nearly
> fainted when we heard that this land was claimed by the Queen.
> The land is like the money in our pockets, no one has a right to
> claim it.

Back in Victoria, Cornwall and Planta drafted their conclusions. Faithful to their orders, they simply recommended an
unspecified increase of reserve area as well as the appointment
of an Indian agent, even though the Nishga had specifically
rejected this last idea. And when the moment came to deal with
the central question, the seizing of traditional Native lands, the
commissioners proved that they could fudge with the best of
their superiors.

> The basis of the claims advanced was the assertion of the "Indian
> title" to the whole country. The commissioners had to combat and
> deny this by stating the law on the subject, as required by their
> instructions, and it was done temperately but explained. . . . The

Greenville and Upper Naas people demand that a treaty be made with them with reference to the land in their neighbourhood, outside of the reserves, which they desire to appropriate; they mean that they require either a sum laid down or annual subsidies, or, in lieu of payment, they propose that they should be allowed to pick out land, outside of the reserves, to the extent of 160 acres for each individual.

Cornwall and Planta lashed out with special venom at the upper-Nass Nishga who had dared challenge the wisdom of the white man: "The Indians . . . probably imagine that they know a great deal and are thoroughly able to say what is good for themselves, so in a way that would not call for particular attention were it not seriously intended, they hold themselves as above and beyond the existing laws which affect them as Indians; such ideas ought to be firmly but kindly dealt with and changed."

If firmness and kindness formed the general thrust of the public report, frankness was reserved for official eyes only. In a confidential document sent to both governments, Commissioner Cornwall explained that certain things could not be stated openly; one of these was the charge that the Methodist church and the ex-Anglican minister Tomlinson were behind the Native unrest. So as not to fuel further incidents, the report advised against giving the chiefs a clear answer on their general claim. In confidence, however, Cornwall was prepared to be realistic about the ownership issue: if the Native claims had any basis, he pointed out to his masters, the property grants made by the province to settlers were not legal. Since this eventuality was unthinkable, there was only one possible conclusion: the Native title had to be invalid, regardless of law and precedent.

But to return to the question of the Indian title to lands. It has long been determined that Government can not in any way allow this. There is no ground for the assertion that the fee of the lands ever rested in the natives although in many parts of the old Provinces of Canada the Indian title was, as it is called, extinguished by the force of purchasing the same for infinitesimally small sums, and a like course has been pursued in the North West Territories, yet it has not by any means been done all over those provinces, and where it has been done it was only, I conceive, because it was deemed politic and expedient to do so. No doubt it would have been politic and expedient to do so in this Province years ago, but it was not done, and now, one would say, it is impossible to do it. The mere idea of the necessity of such a course invalidates at once every title and real property in the country, although those titles have been granted by the Crown. Which is absurd.

The Indian in his wild state has no idea of property in or title to land. . . . The beasts of the field have as much ownership in the land as he has.

Even in this "wild state" the Native could see that the government had no intention of dealing seriously with his claim. After the "kind" words of the 1887 royal commissioners came the "firm" reality of the Indian Act. Dialogue ended abruptly at the beginning of 1888 with the appointment of Indian Agent Charles Todd to introduce white law into the area. This new imposition called up a flurry of petitions along the Nass. On 2 March 1888, the following letter appeared in the Victoria *Weekly Colonist*:

Will you, in your paper, let the people know that we do not want an Indian agent, and that we will not have anything to do with one. We gave our words to the commissioners that came here last October, and they told us to wait for an answer. Now we do not take an agent to be an answer, and we want to see the answer before we see an Indian agent, for we can go to the American side and get what we want in peace if we cannot have it here. It was a "Boston" ship that first came to Naas River and found us.

(*signed*) Claigtuck, Scotein, Sabasha, Yat-Ca-Geiks, Chiefs.

At the same time, Superintendent of Indian Affairs Powell received a similar petition "from all the people of Kislakdanox, Kiswanselth and Kiskaludeen," and signed by three of their chiefs. And lest the message be lost, Indian Agent Todd was also petitioned in the same vein. On 7 January, chiefs Skadeen and "Mimasth" of Gitlakdamix said flatly, "We don't want an agent, that's all we got to say." On the following day, Chief "Sabasa" of "Quickmowah" wrote to the agent telling him, "You did not hear our words we had been sent to the Commissioners that we dont want the Agent unles the Government give how large we want to our land. All the people of the River their are never wants the Agent because we don't like you to take care our own land. . . . We want to get answer from Commission before see you, all people one word do not see you now."

The movement even reached the Anglican village of Kincolith, where only the Reverend Collison's action stopped the signing of yet another petition. At least, this is the version we have from a Methodist Nishga, David Mackay: "I know the people at Kincolith want a treaty too. I heard them ask Mr. Collison to write a letter to Dr. Powell, telling him they wanted a treaty. Mr. Collison replied, 'He would not; that if he wrote it he would be hanged,' and so he frightened the people; but they want a treaty." A letter to Agent Todd by Clayduk, Gatcakayas, Victoria, Mountain, and Ness Jash summed up the general feeling: "We do not want to see your face."

The unrest stirred up by the creation of the reserves was accelerating a new process: some missionaries sided with the Natives and helped them organize as a political lobby. The Methodists were particularly active. Thomas Crosby and Alfred Green had accompanied Chief Mountain and Charles Russ to Victoria, where they were refused an audience by Superintendent Powell. When Green complained about a grant of ten acres of land to a white man at Fishery Bay, Powell called the Methodist missionaries dangerous agitators. In a May 1886 letter to his Ottawa superiors, the federal civil servant advanced the ridiculous proposition that without the activities of Green and Crosby, the Indians would be perfectly satisfied with their lot.

> ... The evidence before the Metlakahtla commission of enquiry and statements to myself go to shew that their greatest exertions have been made to create antipathy against the proper authorities, and thus breed disloyalty and ill feeling. In any other portion of the Province there is not the slightest trouble with the Indians, nor to my knowledge have any vexatious questions arisen in their minds as to their aboriginal rights to the whole country, except where they have in the first instance been fomented and agitated by these teachings.

Green conveyed the sense of basic distrust between officials and missionaries in a report to his church:

> The past year has been a most trying one. The unrest of all the Indians over the "Indian Land Question" and the exodus of the people of Metlakhatla to Alaska, have kept the Indians in a constant state of excitement, and have greatly hindered the spread of the Gospel.

A government commission was here ten days ago, and the Indians had the opportunity to present their troubles, and to make
known their desires. The Indians are not unreasonable. They wish
for larger reserves, and a treaty with the Government, with payment for the land surrendered; or instead of payment, 160 acres
of land for each Indian outside of the reserved village sites, to be
their private property. Last January, the Indians insisted on Bro.
Crosby and me going with a deputation of Indians to Victoria, to
ask the Governments to send a commission, with a view of ending
the ever-increasing danger. Over ice and snow, and then a rough
canoe passage into Alaska, where we caught the American steamer
for Victoria. But after our trouble, expense, and danger, the
Dominion officials refused to see us with the Provincial Government, though the latter were willing. Had those officials conde-
scended to see the poor, despised Methodist missionaries, and had
they listened to facts, and sent a commission early in the spring,
and dealt justly and liberally with the Indians, the Metlakhatla
community of a thousand Christian Indians might have been
saved to our country. Many other Indians have been seriously
thinking of leaving their new villages and the graves of their
fathers, and abandoning the whole work of the last eleven years,
and begin life anew in the Alaska forest, rather than submit to
have their lands taken from them without a treaty, and only small
reserves to live on granted them. Not only the Christian Indians
feel strongly on this question, but the Heathens also; and they, not
controlled by the Gospel of peace, are ever wanting to draw the
Christian Indians to some extreme measure. It has been very
difficult to manage them. . . . They [the officials] call us "mislead-
ers," because we possess the confidence of the Indians.

The Native deputation mentioned by Green trekked to Victoria in January 1887. The authorities refused to see the Lakalzap
missionary and his Port Simpson colleague Thomas Crosby, but
the joint Nishga-Tsimshian delegation was granted a meeting
with Premier Smithe, Superintendent Powell, Indian Reserve
Commissioner O'Reilly, and various other officials. The Natives
were heard on 3 February, and the transcript of the encounter
is revealing.

Hon. Mr. Smithe — . . . When they [the Indians] shall be able to
read and write and understand the same as white men, then there
will be no need for any special protection for Indians, who will

exercise the franchise as part and parcel of the general community, exercising all the rights and privileges of Her Majesty's other subjects. But you have to grow from infancy to childhood, and from childhood to manhood. ... You mentioned the word "treaty." Now will you ask some one to explain, in connection with the land, exactly what it is that you want?

Burton (speaking for John Wesley, of Naas) — My fathers have sent me from Naas to speak before you. When Judge O'Reilly was there some years ago the chiefs of the Naas were away from home; the only one there being my father [Mountain] who told Judge O'Reilly that he was not satisfied with the size of the land he had given them. It was not for Mountain (my father) alone that he asked for the land; it was for all the Indians on the Naas and for those outside who came on the Naas in the spring of every year for the oolachans. Our reserve is very little; and we have not got any timber land; neither have we got our hunting grounds. These are what we want, and what we came for. We want you to cut out a bigger reserve for us, and what we want after that is a treaty.

Hon. Mr. Smithe — What do you mean by a treaty?

Wesley — I have mentioned after a certain amount of land is cut out for the Indians, outside of that we want such a law as the law of England and the Dominion Government which made a treaty with the Indians.

Hon. Mr. Smithe — Where did you hear that?

Wesley — It is in the law books.

Hon. Mr. Smithe — Who told you so?

Wesley — There are a good many Indians that can read and write, and they are the ones who say this themselves.

Hon. Mr. Smithe — And they told you this, did they?

Wesley — Yes.

Hon. Mr. Smithe — Well, I should like them to produce the book that they read this in. I have never seen that book.

Wesley — We could not tell you the book just now; but we can probably find it for you if you really want to see it.

Hon. Mr. Smithe — There is no such law either English or Dominion that I know of; and the Indians, or their friends, have been misled on that point. Now, you seemed a little while ago to desire to be placed as nearly as possible on the same footing as white men. You say that you ought to be as good as white men, and I quite agree with this; and all we wish is, and all we wait for is, for you to get a little advanced beyond where you are now; when you will be able to read and write, think and understand as (and thus be just as good as) white men. All men are of the same flesh and blood, and there is no difference between them, except that the white man knows and has been taught more. Now you are going entirely out of that position, and want to be placed in a better position. White men, you know, hunt as well as Indians. I, myself, am very fond of hunting, and am free to go upon the hills with my rifle and kill game; but I have no more right to go there than you have. You, also, have a perfect right to go there, as every other Indian. The land belongs to Queen Victoria, who permits us to go on that wild land — on land that has not been cultivated — that has not been paid for by some white man; and we are glad to make laws to regulate it, and have the privilege of hunting there. But you wish to have the "exclusive" right of hunting over these lands, which is more than any white man claims or desires . . .

Now, why do you want those hunting grounds? It seemed to me to be the desire of everybody — both the Indians and their teachers — to raise the Indians out of the position which they have held in the past, when they were little better than wild animals that rove over the hills, when they required a large extent of land to gather berries from, or for hunting over. This being their only means of subsistence, one could understand that it was necesary for them to have this greater extent of country. But now the Indians have been taught other and better ways, and are leaving and giving up their old habits, and they do not require to go picking berries over the hills as their forefathers did. This wish is absolutely nothing but mere sentiment, and it seems to me far better to be contented to accept the same position as a white man in that regard; to be the same in the eyes of the law; to ask no more and to take no less . . .

The Indians, indeed, are specially favoured. When a white man comes into the country no land is given to him, no reserve is made for him, and he does not own a single inch until he has paid for it. The land all belongs to the Queen. The laws provide that if a white man requires a piece of land he must go to the Land Office and pay for it, and it is his. The Indian is placed in a better position: a reserve is given to each tribe, and they are not required to pay for it. It is the Queen's land just the same, but the Queen gives it to her Indian children because they do not know so well how to make their own living, the same as a white man, and special indulgence is extended to them and special care shown. Thus, instead of being treated as a white man, the Indian is treated better. . . . Do you understand what I say?

Burton — I understand. [*Translates to Wesley*] As I said before, we have come for nothing but to see about the land which we know is ours, and we come before you, as he says, for you to settle it. All the villages of the Naas River have counselled together that they do not want to cause you any trouble, all they want being peace. By hunting grounds he [Wesley] means that by the laws among the Indians every chief has a hunting ground, and fishing ground, and goes there to dry salmon all the winter; and that they do not want to be interfered with on that account, but they never refuse anyone to go on that ground to hunt. These chiefs keep these hunting grounds free, not to themselves, and quarrels have never been known upon them yet; but there is a chief on every inlet, and he calls it his own where he hunts. And right on this very hunting ground there is a little timber, which they wish you to give them the right to cut, as they always thought it was theirs. It is not only a hunting ground but a fishing ground, and there is timber there.

Hon. Mr. Smithe — Do you understand that, Mr. O'Reilly?

Mr. O'Reilly — Perfectly. It is easily explained. They each have a little spot which they are in the habit of calling their own. Every inlet is claimed by some one, and were I to include all these, it would virtually declare the whole country a reserve; this arrangement I could not justify. To lay out all the inlets pointed out and claimed by them, would be impossible. They were given the right to all streams which run through their reserves, and every fishing ground pointed out by them, of every sort or kind, was reserved for them. There was no difficulty in doing this, as the fish of special value to the Indians the white men do not care for, therefore their interests do not clash. But to declare every inlet, nook, and stream an Indian reserve would virtually be to declare the whole country a reserve . . .

Dr. Powell (Superintendent of Indian Affairs) — I think the grievance they have is, that they want a treaty.

Hon. Mr. Davie — That is what they want.

Hon. Mr. Smithe — They are simply misguided.

Dr. Powell — There is no doubt of it.

The only tangible result of this protest was a second blitz through the Nass Valley by Indian Reserve Commissioner Peter O'Reilly. The minutes of his eleven-day visit reveal an important split among the Nishga. Those under the direct influence of the Anglican missionaries — the Kincolith people and the followers of Chief Abraham in Aiyansh — had resigned themselves to the Indian Act. Their strategy was simply to lobby O'Reilly for better reserves. This prompted the leaders of the Greenville area to issue a public letter of reprimand to their neighbours:

To the people of Kincolith,
We the people of the Upper Naas, desire to know why you are letting the land be surveyed without speaking to us, and the people of Fort Simpson, and Skeena first. If you try to get land reserved for yourselves without letting us know, it will make trouble amongst us . . .

(*sgd*) Tat-ger-gat; (*sgd*) Victoria.

O'Reilly met the protesters the next day at Stoney Point.

Job Calder — I am speaking for Victoria [the chieftaness]. She is my wife, she does not want the people to speak much, but she wants you to do what they wish. Victoria, and all the chiefs from this part of the Naas, wish our reserve to extend from Canaan, on both sides of the river, to Hal i colth [about 19 miles], from mountain to mountain. We want to be paid for the land outside the reserve, and we want a treaty. We want a title. If you cannot do this now, we dont wish you to do anything. We dont want you to measure our land.

Commissioner — I must now tell you again that you will never get such a title as you claim, and that you will not be paid for your land.

Kle dach, 1st Chief — I did not see you when you came up. People generally knock before they come into a house and get permission to come in. The surveyor came in the same way almost secretly. We did not know about it till he had finished it. We did not send for you, but now we have a good chance to speak our mind. It troubled us things being done secretly. We have never coveted anyone's good land elsewhere. When one wants to borrow property, they should go to the owners. The Government would not like us to take anything from them. If the river is taken away from the chiefs, they will go out of their minds. The chiefs of the river never requested that anyone should be sent to measure their land. If you cannot promise a title, and you cannot pay us for the land, dont measure any more.

At Aiyansh on 3 September, Captain Jemmett was exposed as having lied to the Indians in order to complete his survey. Chief Skadeen testified that "we asked the surveyor what was to become of the land outside the reserves. I said this because he surveyed only along the river, and I had asked back to the mountains. Captain Jemmett said the timber outside the reserve was mine." O'Reilly was quick to deny the chief's interpretation of Jemmett's promise, and he reiterated that there was no Native claim on lands outside the reserves. He added another lie of his own when he insisted that the surveying procedure had nothing to do with plans for white settlement: "You say white men want to take your land; name one."

Chief Skadeen, unaware that Jemmett had already built up enough data to draft maps of the reserves, proceeded to anathematize the holding of further surveys.

My forefathers owned the whole of the land, and God put them on it. Would the Queen like us to go, and survey her land? If we did, they would put us in prison. When I went to Victoria, I wanted a place to pitch my tent, and they wanted me to pay for the little place, and said they did not want me there. All the land around is ours, the hunting places on the mountains are ours. All the chiefs on the Naas own the river, and the land around it. It is not to be doubted that God gave the land to myself, and all the chiefs; we get our living from it, so I, and all the other chiefs say the land is not be be surveyed. I have said NO once, and I am not going to change my mind.

O'Reilly responded with a threat: "I tell you as a friend that if you advise your people to break the law the Government will soon put another chief in your place."

It would have been hard to find an ear deafer to Native anguish. Back in Victoria, O'Reilly wrote:

Like the Indians ,at Fort Simpson these people [the Greenville Nishga] declined to have any reserves unless their title was recognized, and they were paid for all the land outside the reserves. In that event they would claim as their reserve, from a place named "Canaan," five miles below Greenville, to a point known as "Hal-i-colth" fourteen miles above, including the entire valley from mountain to mountain . . .

On the 3rd September I arrived at "Kit wil luc shilt," the middle village on the Nass river, where I attended a meeting of the Indians, the chief Sebassah being the principal speaker. He stated that the chiefs of the different villages had agreed that unless the whole valley of the Nass river was given to them, they would not have any reserves. They also objected to the Indian Agent coming among them and to the enforcement of the Indian Act. I remained here several hours and explained fully the mistake they were making . . .

On the following day I met the Indians of "Kit lac da max" (the upper Nass village), and those of Iyennis at the village of the latter. Here the Indians were divided in opinion. The Kit-lac-da-max people with their chief Scotteen adhered to the theory prepounded at Fort Simpson, Greenville, and "Kit wil luc shilt," viz that the country belonged to them, and that they would not be satisfied until they had received payment for all the land outside the reserves, which were to include the entire valley of the Nass river, extending from mountain to mountain. On the other hand the representatives of "Iyennis" stated through their chief, Abraham, that the Indians on the Nass had no grievance whatever, that he was satisfied with the treatment they were receiving at the hands of the Government and thankful that an Indian Agent had been appointed, that were it not for disturbing rumours which were circulated among them, by the chiefs and others at the lower villages, the Indians would be quite content . . .

I can now confidently state for your information, that the Indians of the Tsimpsean, and Nass tribes have been liberally dealt with, and that the reserves which have been laid out for them are amply sufficient for all their requirements. All their fisheries, and cultivated gardens that were made known to me, or of which I could gather information, have now been reserved, and were it not for the fact, that an idea has been instilled into the minds of these Indians that the country is theirs, and that they should be paid for it, the constant irritation you hear so much of in regard to their land would soon die out.

7

THEFT OF THE RESOURCES

For the Nishga, the legal loss of the land had no immediate implications. As long as no one tried to move into the area, their villages and houses remained where they had always been, and the rivers and the forests were used as if nothing untoward had happened. Nor, in this area, was there any compelling reason for establishing the reserve system. In faraway southern British Columbia, immigrants were carving farms and ranches out of Native territory, but in the north, there was no direct pressure from eager colonists to inspire a government to seize 99.5 per cent of the humid and rugged country of the Nass. The only "reasons" were the general application of the principle of white supremacy coupled with the denial of Native title in any form.

The loss of the land would not remain an abstraction for long, however. Settlers began pre-emptions, and for many Nishga families the idea of the reserve took on concrete meaning as they discovered that the white man's law had turned them into squatters on their own home ground. One case, that of a hamlet named Grease Harbour, is particularly well documented. On 15 October 1915, the McKenna-McBride Commission heard testimony from two Nishga, Michael Inspring and Daniel Guno.

Mr. Commissioner Macdowall — We are here today to take the statements of Michael Inspring, Guno, and Derrick. We shall take these statements to Victoria and will lay them before the full Commission when this matter together with all the matters relating to the Naas Valley will receive full consideration.

Michael Inspring — I will first put a question to you Commissioners. I want to know what mission you have come on here whether of peace or trouble?

Mr. Commissioner Macdowall — We have come here in the interests of the Government and to all good men whether they be white men or Indians it is a matter of importance to have good government.

Michael Inspring — What else can I say besides what has been told you already by the Chiefs of the village of Aiyansh and Gitlakdamix. As you see we have been using these grounds from the earliest days until now. In our statement we told you that we want this land for our own use, but there is one grievance that I want to speak about in regard to this one piece of ground. Ever since the time that I and my brother started here; he started here about five years ahead of me and I came in after him, but ever since we started here we have had trouble at times. I have been threatened by some of the pre-emptors just because I talk to them they have threatened to shoot me. They would not permit us to go ahead with our work here; that is why you see the amount of work we have put in on our gardens; and they are going further and the pre-emptors are collecting here and they are threatening us that if we don't leave this place they will put us in jail. And gentlemen we require as you have come in the mission of peace we would like you to aid us in getting rid of these men because this land belongs to us. We haven't taken this land for the simple reason because we know that the government has put a reserve on it but we know and we are certain that we have lived here from time immemorial. And we know that this land belongs to us and they have put up houses and the houses have rotted away. Some of our people have even died at this place and have graves here and if you want to see the graves we can point them out to you. This is another reason why we know that this land belonged to the Indians from time immemorial. That is all . . .

Mr. Commissioner Carmichael — Have you your house on here?

Answer — This is my house in which you are now and I have started to build another one.

Question — How long has this house been built?

Answer — I cannot answer any further. I built this house before the pre-emptors came.

Question — Do you know whether that was before it was made into a Provincial Reserve?

Answer — Long before that. It is only three years since this has been set aside as a Provincial Reserve.

Question — Have you a garden here?

Answer — I have a garden starting here and running along behind the house and I have also cleared quite a large piece of land. I have done all the clearing that you see around here. I cleared all this land around here; I cut the trees away myself and then Mr. Taylor came along and built his cache and agreed that he would only use it for one year after which it would be mine . . .

Question — You have been here for a number of years before any of the pre-emptors came before it was made into a Provincial Reserve, you built this house in which we are now some years ago but you cannot say how many, that you have cultivated gardens and made clearings on this section of what is now known as a Provincial Reserve?

Answer — That is correct.

Question — Had you made those gardens and made the clearing that you speak of before this part of the country or the land was made into a Provincial Reserve?

Answer — Yes, sir.

Question — And your claim is that you thought it was part of an Indian land when you put your house here?

Answer — Yes . . .

Commissioner Macdowall — How wide a frontage on the river here do you claim?

Answer — I claim the whole frontage. It was used by the Indians before me . . .

Question — You made rather serious statement about some white settlers threatening to shoot you. Would you give me the names of those white settlers who threatened to shoot you?

Answer — A man by the name of Juggins had his gun in his hand just at the top of the hill and in the other hand he held a pocket knife and he said, "Get out of here or I will shoot you."

Question — When was that?

Answer — Two years ago.

Question — Was anyone present at the time?

Answer — I had two boys with me.

Question — How old were the boys?

Answer — One was twelve and the other was younger.

Question — Whose boys were they?

Answer — One belonged to my sister Eliza. The father of the boy is dead.

Mr. Commissioner Macdowall [*to Mr. C.L. Cullin*] — Are there any other questions you would like to ask?

Answer — No, I think that is all.

[*Daniel Guno is called and sworn and makes the following statement.*]

It is now 9 years and 6 months since we first came to live here. I lived here for five years without hearing a word from anybody. After the five years a surveyor came along. When the surveyor came I asked him, "what is your business here?" and he said,

"Nothing. I have not come to disturb you at all; I simply came because the Government wants to know how many acres of land there is in this country." Three years ago Surveyor Taylor came along and it was he that surveyed the pre-emptions. I asked him and he told me that the Provincial Government had made a law that none of the pre-emptions would come within half a mile of the Indian settlement, and when I heard this I wasn't troubled, but now they grieve me and as it were make fun of me.

They come and cut my fences and go into my gardens, and lately Michael's mother and his children and my children went up to cut the bark of a tree which we use for medicine and Olson threatened me and from that time my heart began to tremble. There was another man by the name of James Smythe went up there to cut small trees as was our usual custom to make into poles for poling our boats and the same man came to him and threatened him also. That is all I have to say about that man. There is another man that came here by the name of Arthur Priestly and he has also threatened me and also as it were made fun of me. This man came along here. He had no business to come here as he has his own house farther down the river and he was not hard up. He came along and started building and that is why I say he is making fun of me, and he stated if the Royal Commission came here and said he had to go he would go but in the meantime he would pay me rent up to the end of December and a week ago I went to collect the rent and he said, "Get out, you have no title here."

Another man by the name of Studdy came along, broke down my fence and went into my garden and erected a tent house — partly tent and partly wood — and said he was working for the Government and he said the Government has never helped me with a potato or anything and this man has put his tent in my garden and spoilt part of my crops. From this I know that if the Government takes us away from here my children will die. I have had ten children — two are dead and eight are still alive. I don't want gentlemen to go outside of anything that you have heard from the Chiefs. My request is the same as theirs and I am no stranger here. This is my own country and the place where I have always lived. That is why, gentlemen, the reserves are detestable to the Indians. If they in the first place had agreed to the reserves being set apart the reserves would not be as small as they are now. They would have covered all the territory we have asked for.

Mr. Commissioner Carmichael — Is your house on the portion of land known as the Indian Reserve?

Answer — I have a house on the reserve at Aiyansh and I also have a house here just across this little creek . . .

Question — The 9 years and 6 months that you speak of — have you been here all of that time on what is known as the Provincial Reserve?

Answer — The early spring I come here and live here until the time is due that I go working in the canneries. I then move down to here until the very cold weather sets in and then I move down to Aiyansh about Christmas time . . .

Question — When did you start making your gardens here?

Answer — There were gardens here before me and as soon as I came here and built my house I used the same gardens.

Question — Do you know who made the gardens that were here when you came?

Answer — A man by the name of Kakque and another man by the name of Philip Ward.

Question — Were they white men?

Answer — Timothy Derrick's uncle was Kakque and my father's uncle is Philip Ward.

Question — So they were both Indians?

Answer — Yes.

Question — And they were in occupation here before you came here?

Answer — Yes.

Question — What vegetables do you grow in your garden?

Answer — I grow potatoes, turnips, and grass seed.

Question — Have you any vegetable gardens or means of livelihood anywhere else?

Answer — No.

Question — If you had to remove from this Provincial Reserve and start in to live on any of the Indian Reserves would you have to start again making gardens and building your home?

Answer — It is impossible for me to leave.

Question — That is not an answer to my question.

Answer — I am not free as far as the application of this place goes, the same as asked for by all the Chiefs of the other villages.

Question — Have you got anything in the way of poultry on your place down here on this land?

Answer — Yes.

Question — Any cattle?

Answer — No, but I have an awful lot of children and they are my cattle. Before I get old I expect to make ten more.

Mr. Commissioner Shaw — I understand where Studdy built his home was not actually in your vegetable garden but on a grass plot that you had sowed?

Answer — Yes, on the grass that I had sown, but his wood pile he put on top of my turnip patch.

Mr. Commissioner Carmichael — To what extent did it injure your patch?

Answer — It may not have hurt my turnip patch but it hurt my heart more.

Question — Did any of your neighbours or friends remonstrate with this man when he went to this piece of land which you call your own?

Answer — I came to an agreement with Mr. Gordon and also with Mr. Philipson and Charlie Morgan is my witness that if anyone should come to disturb my holdings that they would prevent it. I asked Gordon why he allowed this and Gordon said, "I don't know." Many of my things have been disturbed even my stove pipe in my house and I have spoken to Gordon about it.

Question — Do you pretend to think that Studdy stole your stovepipe and other things?

Answer — I don't blame anyone but I know the Indian law is that anyone occupying the land in the absence of the real owner they always say he is the culprit.

Question — Does Priestly own that very nice log house in which he is now living?

Answer — The house belongs to a man by the name of Jasper and Priestly is renting it.

Question — What did Priestly agree to pay you rent for?

Answer — Because he built his store in a part of the ground which was a part of my garden.

Question — When you said a few minutes ago that the house belonged to Mr. Jasper Derrick, did he pay Mr. Derrick rent for that house?

Answer — I don't know whether he had paid him yet.

Question — Is Jasper Derrick an Indian?

Answer — Yes . . .

Mr. Commissioner Macdowall — How many graves are there in this graveyard up on the hill?

Answer — There is one man buried over here at the foot of the hill a relative of William Gogag. There is another buried up where you can see all fences around the graves, and just above where

Olson lives there is a place where he used to cremate. In the old days we used to cremate our dead.

After their return to Victoria, the commissioners reviewed the question and decided that the Nishga had to be expelled from their traditional land. The Indian agent responsible for the Nass Valley, Charles Perry, contributed to the discussion.

Question — Now 34 and 35 are the Grease Harbour Lots. And this point is known as Grease Harbour. Is that correct?

Agent Perry — Yes.

Question — What improvements have the Indians at this point?

Answer — They have a root house, two residences, outbuildings and fencing, and I would say in all about two acres of cultivated land, some in hay, truck gardens, and some in a turnip patch.

Question — And in addition to the houses there are one or two houses partially constructed?

Answer — Yes . . .

Question — What were the names of the two men who occupied this piece of land?

Answer — Michael Inspring and Daniel Guno.

Question — Are they bona fide members of the Aiyansh Band?

Answer — Yes.

Question — Do you know how long it is since they started making improvements on this land?

Answer — They say about nine years ago.

Question — You have no personal knowledge of it?

Answer — No, not being a Reserve I had no occasion to go there.

Question — Do you know whether this piece of land was at any time pre-empted by anyone?

Answer — I understand it was pre-empted by a man named Clay and in a Provincial map, I think it was dated 1912, this pre-emption is shown there, but since that time an issue has arisen between the Province and Mr. Clay which may become a matter of litigation.

Question — Do you know the status of this piece of land at the present moment?

Answer — Yes, it is a Provincial Reserve.

Question — Reserve for what purpose?

Answer — I could not say.

Question — This is the outlet to the river from a white settlement lying north of the point. Is it north?

Answer — Lying all around it as a matter of fact.

Question — As a matter of fact are there not a number of settlers in and around this particular point?

Answer — I understand there are about fifty.

Question — And in order to get out this is their landing place and a wagon road leads from this point to the settlement at the back?

Answer — Yes, if the Government build a bridge there.

Question — Would you consider it will be to the advantage of these settlers and to the Government if this were a Government Reserve?

Answer — Yes, most decidedly.

Question — And would you consider if it became an Indian Reserve that it would be inimical to white interests?

Answer — Yes.

Question — As conditions exist today, would you recommend that this be constituted an Indian Reserve leaving out of consideration Indian occupation?

Answer — No.

Question — And if it is constituted a reserve what suggestion would you make as to the improvements that the Indians have there?

Answer — I would say that it is advisable that these Indians be compensated for any improvements they have on it, that is provided they were going to be removed from the place . . .

Question — What would you consider the value of the improvements that they have at Grease Harbour?

Answer — Personally, I think that if the Indians were paid a thousand dollars that they should be prepared to clear from this place if they are required to do so.

The commissioners asked Perry what would amount to a fair settlement. The agent proposed one thousand dollars in compensation for improvements on the land and another thousand for relocation elsewhere. Since the creation of a reserve would have been "inimical to white interests," the McKenna-McBride Commission excluded Grease Harbour from its final list.

In spite of several attempts like the Grease Harbour settlement, European farmers were never successful in the area. Agriculture in the Nass is marginal — the landscape mountainous, the climate harsh in winter and very wet all year round, and communication with the outside world consistently difficult. The establishment of missions brought in a few merchants, and a handful of settlers ended up around Aiyansh after the Klondike gold rush. In 1915, C.L. Cullin, provincial inspector of pre-emptions, was enthusiastic about the great potential of the Nass:

There are upwards of eighty settlers in this district. The means of transportation are as yet poor, it being necessary to take a gasoline-launch at the mouth of the Nass and proceed fifty miles up river before the valley opens up. This is a land of promise and will some day be a greater producer of all farm offerings. As yet, the settlers grow just sufficient for local consumption, and most of them are busily engaged preparing for the future and the advent of roads and railways. The summer climate leaves little to be desired, and although the snowfall may run as much as 3 feet, the early coming of spring clears most of it away by the end of March or middle of April. The soil is of the richest river-silt, and the benches of the river are high and sloping, giving the best natural drainage. The timber is of medium growth. There are many open spots of some acres in extent. As the valley widens out, going up the river, the area of meadow land increases. This section will be one of the finest in the country for stock-raising.

These prophecies came to naught. Most of the settlers left during the First World War, and fewer came back — fifteen families, according to a 1923 report. The Great Depression dealt a fatal blow to white hopes in the valley; by the end of the Second World War, only one family remained from the original Aiyansh colony; more recently, a small group of young white people, going back to the land, have taken up residence there. Nishga country, then, has never been a colony of settlement. It has remained, like most of Canada, a colony of exploitation, a "white reserve" of natural resources set aside for private interests — nowadays forest and metal-mining corporations.

In the later nineteenth century, the big private interests were those of the fishing companies. In fact, the creation of the reserves in the 1880s coincided with the appearance of the first salmon canneries in the area. From being a food source for the Natives, salmon suddenly became an export earner precious to white entrepreneurs. This development worried the Nishga, and in August 1881 several chiefs of the Upper Nass sent a warning to Indian Affairs Superintendent Powell.

The chiefs complain that this year up to the present the supply of salmon visiting the up stream, has been very small, and that consequently their stock of winter food will be much reduced. The chiefs attribute the present scarcity of salmon to the fact of the fishing operations of Messrs. Croasdaile & Green, Wellwood & Co. intercepting the runs. The chiefs learn, without at present knowing the truth of the report, that it is intended to commence canning operations by the Nass Harbor Co. next year, and that if so, a greater number of boats will be employed than have been in use this year, and consequently the run of salmon up river will be still further reduced. The chiefs have no wish to interfere with the legitimate employment of their white friends, but they naturally ask that the white men should not be allowed to take all the salmon.

> (*signed*) Sebasha, head chief of Kitwinshilk, Queekmow,
> Gliushood, Abraham, Ooyaa, Andaiman.

The opening of the canneries called for expropriation of the Native fishing grounds. The Ottawa government achieved this by bringing in a system of fishing permits. The Nishga did not easily accept this new erosion of their rights, as is apparent in an 1888 report by Fishery Guardian John McNab:

I visited the Naas River again on the 24th of July, when I issued a few more licences. There was a good run of salmon, but a scarcity of fishermen. When at Naas Harbor I received a letter from the chief of the Indian village at Kincolith, near the entrance of the Naas River, requesting me to call at his village as he has something of importance to communicate. I landed there on my way back, and found the chief and a number of the principal men of the village assembled in the chief's house. They asked many questions about the law in regard to catching salmon on the Naas River; wanted to know exactly how much money I had collected this year, and what I had done with it. After being satisfied on these points, the chief very gravely informed me that I had done very wrong in collecting money for fishing on the Nass, without having asked permission from him, that the river belonged to him and to his people, that it was right that white men should buy licences, but that he and his people should receive the money, that they were entitled to it all; but that as I had been sent to collect it, they were willing that I should retain half for my trouble. After a consultation amongst themselves, I was told that they had intended to demand half the money collected this year, but would let it pass until next year, and charge me to inform the Government to that effect, which I respectfully take this method of doing.

As with the land question, the denial of substantial Native rights in the fisheries was a significant departure from the principles that had prevailed at the start of colonization. Treaties signed by Governor Douglas between 1850 and 1854 had always concluded with the explicit understanding that Native groups were "at liberty to hunt over the unoccupied lands, and to carry on our fisheries as formerly." And in an 1879 letter to his superiors, Alexander Anderson, the federal fishery inspector for British Columbia acknowledged that the freedom used by the Native was having no adverse effect on stocks: "I would willingly quiet the alarm of those zealous agitators (few, possibly, in number) who contend that the untrammelled exercise of the aboriginal must necessarily cause the ruin of the fisheries. These objectors are oblivious of the fact that, up at least to the advent of the white man, the fisheries throughout the Province were admittedly unimpaired."

Nevertheless, the Canadian government in 1878 decided to interfere with Native fishing rights by introducing an initial restriction — a ban on the use of nets in the fresh waters of British Columbia. This regulation, badly designed for local conditions, was poorly enforced, but it was the first in a series of bureaucratic attacks on the Natives' economic independence. In the same year, the federal fisheries department made a new distinction between food and commercial fishing which allowed Anderson in 1881 to prohibit cannery sales of salmon the Fraser River Natives caught using their traditional methods. The ruling completely ignored the fact that Native people had always bartered fish and from the beginning of the nineteenth century had supplied white settlers with smoked and fresh salmon.

The distinction between native and commercial fisheries was made official in an 1888 federal regulation:

> Fishing by means of nets or other apparatus without leases or licences from the Minister of Marine and Fisheries is prohibited in all waters of the Province of British Columbia. Provided always that Indians shall, at all times, have liberty to fish for the purpose of providing food for themselves, but not for sale, barter, or traffic, by any means other than with drift nets, or spearing.

This bureaucratic cavil was highly questionable from the start. The principle was inscribed in no legislation; it was merely a reading from law by some federal officials, and derived its dubious validity from vague powers of regulation conferred on the minister under the Fisheries Act. And it was shaky for a more fundamental reason: the implicit assumption that the department was acting in a legal vacuum, that the traditional fishing rights recognized in the 1763 proclamation and Douglas's treaties were annulled by some undocumented loss of ownership by the Indians. Fisheries minister Charles Tupper was most explicit when he requested in 1891 that the reserve commissioner and the various Indian agents

> be instructed that they must use all their influence to make Indians under their supervision understand that in extending to them the valuable privilege they now enjoy of taking fish for their own use, whenever and howsoever they choose, such permission is not to be considered as a right, but as an act of grace, which may be withdrawn at any time, should it be found that it is abused, or used for other purposes than those for which it is granted, or in such a manner as to embarrass the action of this Department and interfere with its officers, in the performance of their duties.

A serious challenge to this policy was delivered in 1906. To control upstream salmon catches and accommodate the canneries, the department banned the use of traditional fishing weirs on the Babine River, a main tributary of the Skeena, and arrested nine transgressors to show that it meant business. The resultant uproar in the region forced Ottawa to sign a special "Barricade Agreement" which was in contradiction with official doctrine on two important counts. By promising the Babine people compensation in the form of free nets and the use of added lands in return for giving up their weirs, the agreement implicitly recognized the existence of Native fishing rights. Also, by acknowledging the Natives' right to sell their excess catch, it abandoned the odious official distinction between food and commercial fisheries.

The champions of white colonization often argue that the lands and resources taken were "underdeveloped," and cite as proof the marginal economic state which is the lot of many Natives. The Nishga case proves on the contrary that the Native population was able to adapt as well as the white men were to the changes that came with commercial fishing. Simply, they were shut out of the main stream of the new industry by repressive government regulation. On 4 October 1914, the Kincolith Nishga explained to the McKenna-McBride Royal Commission of Inquiry on Indian Reserves how their partial eviction was engineered: although they had purchased twenty motor boats, federal regulations did not allow them to compete with white fishermen. Their complaints were later substantiated by local Indian Agent Charles Perry. Perry testified to the commission that Ottawa had imposed two kinds of fishing licences — "independent" and "attached." An "independent" licence enabled the fisherman to sell his fish to any buyer, while "attached" licences were granted only to canneries, which meant that the fisherman was forced to sell his catch to a single outlet.

Question — Can you give any reason why the Independent Licences are not issued to any of the Indians of your Agency?

Answer — Yes, because the cannerymen say that if independent licences were granted to the Indians, the Japs would want them. The Japs being naturalized British subjects are entitled to them, and of course the cannerymen contend that if these licences were issued to the Indians they would have to issue them likewise to the Japanese.

Question — In your opinion would the white men approve or disapprove of the Indians having these licences?

Answer — I believe they would disapprove.

Question — For what reasons?

Answer — When the government allowed an unlimited number of licences to be granted, so many were issued that quite a number of the fishermen said it was impossible for them to make a living. Last season there were 425 white men fishing over and above the 175 that had fished before under the independent licences.

Question — Who took out those 175?

Answer — White men.

Question — Did the Indians apply for any of these?

Answer — No, because they were for white men, and the Indians knew they could not get them if they did apply.

Question — Is it by regulations of the Fisheries Department or by the will of the cannerymen that independent licences are not issued to Indians?

Answer — Under the regulations of the Department Indians are not allowed to have independent licences.

The commissioners asked Agent Perry if he thought that Natives were suffering any hardship as a result of the discriminatory policy of the Department of Fisheries.

Yes. I certainly do, and on this account I asked Ottawa if they would issue twenty as an experiment. Mr. Scott, the Deputy Superintendent General took up the matter with the Fisheries Board and they declined, and his recommendations were turned down on the ground that the Indians could get all the employment they wanted at the canneries. The Indians are well able to provide their own boats and gear, and in my opinion if they were granted independent licences they would get a better price for their catch.

Would the Indians, once granted "independent" licences, give as much satisfaction to the canneries as white or Japanese fishermen?

Yes, because it would be to their advantage to fish more steadily than what they are doing at present, because they would be able to get 25¢ a fish while fishing under an independent licence, whereas they only get 12½¢ a fish while fishing under the attached licences. In fact I have seen where they could have got 30¢ a fish if the Indians had been in a position to have sold them.

In their final report, the commissioners recognized the Native complaints as valid: they were "unanimously of opinion that the Indians of Northern British Columbia are — but should not be — discriminated against in the issuance and use of these 'independent' fishing licences; and that there is no authority conferred by the law, or intent therein expressed or suggested, for such a class or racial discrimination."

In the beginning of the salmon canning business in the North and for years thereafter only attached licences were issued. Then independent licences were introduced, and the policy was adopted of diminishing year by year the "attached" and increasing the number of "independent" until the attached licences would cease and the canneries of the North, as those of the Fraser River, be made to depend upon the catch of independent fishermen for their supply of salmon. The Indians being debarred in the meantime from independent licences will in a few years be completely cut off in the North from the salmon fishing industry.

Even though the discriminatory measures were later repealed, they had managed to prevent the Natives from gaining control over the commercial fishing industry in its formative years. The banks also played a major role by refusing needed funds for modernization to Native fishermen who, under the Indian Act, were not considered as full adults and not allowed to borrow money or mortgage property freely. In 1979, British Columbia Natives owned only 8.8 per cent of the province's fishing fleet.

The unresolved question of traditional rights still clouds the future of fisheries on Canada's Pacific coast. According to an internal research paper prepared for the fisheries department by V.H.B. Giraud in 1975, "There has been a great deal of unrest in the Indian population in the last 2–3 years brought on, no doubt, by the delays in both federal and provincial government action in making decisions regarding land claims. This unrest has overflowed to the food fishery and claims of native food fishing rights." Giraud kept the faith by arguing that the department had been right in consistently rejecting the Native claims:

The regulations of 1878 did not provide for an Indian food fishery. It was the Department of Fisheries, starting with Inspector Alexander C. Anderson in that year, which established these fishing rights as they are today. The commissions that studied food fish regulations have all agreed that the Federal Department of Fisheries had the right to regulate the fisheries in British Columbia and that the Indians fishing for food were bound by these regulations. Court decisions and Appeal Court decisions have upheld the British Columbia Fishery Regulations. As the regulations exist today an Indian fishing for food without a permit, fishing during closed times, etc., is guilty of an offence against these regulations.

The classic logic of bureaucracies, with regulations defending fellow regulations, has never impressed the Nishga or other Native peoples. In the spirit of their forefathers of 1888 who requested the white men to pay them a fishing fee, the Greenville and Gitlakdamix Nishga in 1932 refused credibility to the federal fishing licences. Fishery Inspector J. Boyd complained of their intransigence in a 15 September report:

> I would refer to my letter of the 9th instant advising that Indian permits issued in favour of the Chief Councillors of Gitlakdamix and Greenville had been refused and that a further attempt was being made to have them accepted. Inspector McIver has now been advised by Constable Newnham that the Chief Councillor of Greenville has again refused to accept the permit. Constable Newnham has not yet had an opportunity of interviewing the Chief Councillor of Gitlakdamix.

The fundamental position of the Nishga people has remained constant through a century of white encroachment on their fishing resources. In a July 1981 statement to the Royal Commission of Inquiry on Pacific Fisheries Policy, the Nishga Tribal Council stood firm:

> In Nishga-claimed fishing areas, the Nishga strongly oppose being subject to any tax, since they do not believe they should have to pay for access to their own resource. Access to non-Nishga areas is another matter. In principle the Nishga are not opposed to paying for access to other fishing areas, provided, of course, the Nishga land claims are settled. The Nishga would then be willing to pay for access into non-Nishga areas just as they would charge a fee for others to have access to the Nishga resource.

And on the fundamental question of fishing rights, the Tribal Council stated that "since the Nishga have never surrendered aboriginal title to the Land Claim Area or its resources, their position, understandably, is that they still own, control and have management authority over this territory and all resources within it, including fisheries."

ASSAULT ON CULTURE

W ill you be good enough to acquaint the Indians of your local-
ity that a Law was passed last year by the Dominion Parliament which came into force the 1st January, this year,
enacting among other things, that any person who engages
directly or indirectly in celebrating the Indian Festival known as
"Potlatch" or the Indian Dance, known as "Tamanawas" is guilty
of misdemeanor, and shall be liable to be imprisoned therefor, for
a term of six months.

Missionaries had been waging bitter war on the potlatch for a
number of years when this April 1885 circular from Indian
Affairs Superintendent Powell announced that the federal government had finally followed their advice and criminalized their
enemy. There was an initial problem: the Potlatch Law had
been badly drafted, and Powell was afraid that its immediate
enforcement would mean the sudden cancellation of all debts
among Natives. He instructed his staff not to prevent exchanges
of goods for the time being, and to allow Natives to assemble for
the purpose of returning property.

In the Nass Valley, one of the hotbeds of the potlatch, missionaries were incensed by the "weakness" of the authorities.
Rev. Alfred Green protested to Ottawa in April 1886 about this
toleration of the customary distribution of goods.

This is really the vital point of the potlatch, for, as at each time they meet, they give presents, this potlatching must go on forever. I hold Dr. Powell responsible for this terrible state of affairs existing in that region during the last year, for had he not sent that circular, the whole thing would have died out. As it is the Indians state openly in their feasts that they have the authority of Dr. Powell for their actions, and furthermore, when complaints are made to Judge Elliott, he will not take action in the matter (shielding himself with Dr. Powell's circular). It is thus the law of the land is openly violated and ignored, and respect for the government greatly lessened in the hearts of the Indians.

The Potlatch Law was tested a few years later with the arrest of a Kwawkgeulth Indian named Hemasak in August 1889. Justice B. Begbie promptly released him on a writ of habeas corpus, ruling in essence that the law did not provide a proper definition of the word "potlatch" and was therefore too vague to be enforced. The church lobby obtained a modification of the act, and a July 1895 amendment led to a second wave of arrests. This time, the missionaries took the matter into their own hands. McCullagh sent his constables to arrest and jail two Nishga potlatchers and serve summonses on twelve others. Some Nishga reacted by petitioning Ottawa for a halt to missionary interference with their customs. They defended the potlatch as a "method that we have of showing our good will toward one another, and we believe that it is our right just as much as it is the right of our white brethren to make presents to each other."

The Nishga continued to ignore the Potlatch Law, and church and state continued to harass them. The controversy reached the press when in February 1896 three Nass River Indians, Amos Gosnell, William Jeffrey, and Billy Williams, sent a remarkable petition to the New Westminster *Daily Columbian* and the Victoria *Daily Colonist:*

In an interview with Mr. Powell, Indian commissioner, we were informed by an explanation of how that any person giving a potlatch would be imprisoned for six months. It is the desire of the Indian department to civilize us, which meets with our approbation; but we were born Indians, educated according to the laws of our ancestry, and, as nature dictates to us, we enjoy their vested rights as an inheritance. We came to Victoria to obtain our natural rights.

We see in this a contradictory state of affairs adorning your civilization. Churches are numerous; theatres are located in the various sections of the town; and saloons multiply in numbers; all of which are in conformity with your laws, consequently we wish to know whether the ministers of the gospel have annihilated the rights of white men in these pleasures leading to heaven and hell exactly in different directions. They have kindly forced us out, as we are "not in it" . . .

You have your Christmases, Fourths of July, and 24ths of May, all of which you celebrate without interference sine qua non. Money is spent in squandrous profusion with no benefit to the poor of your race. We go to the entertainments of your theatres and you charge us money for the privilege. We give our dances at which our guests are welcomed by the testimonial of donations, according to our custom — the inheritance of our fathers. If we wish to perform an act moral in its nature, with no injury or damage, and pay for it, no law in equity can divest us of such right.

We see the Salvation Army parade the streets of your city with music and drum, enchanting the town; leading wanderers, and helping the poor — by making him pay for all he gets. We are puzzled to know whether in the estimation of civilization we are human or fish on the tributaries of the Naas river, that the felicities of our ancestors should be denied us.

Our lands and our fishing grounds are converted to other hands; licences are imposed for fishing the waters of the White Crest mountains, which we pay with pleasure, for such is your law, and we only ask in connection that our potlatches may meet with your approbation.

We see in your graveyards the white marble and granite monuments which cost you money in testimony of your grief for the dead. When our people die we erect a large pole, call our people together, distribute our personal property with them in payment for their sympathy and condolence; comfort to us in the sad hours of our affliction. This is what is called a potlatch — the privilege denied us.

It is a chimera that under the British flag slavery does not exist.

        (*signed*) Wise-as-you, Simh-Sam, Naas-Quah-So.

Reverend McCullagh reacted with a letter to the Indian Commissioner of British Columbia in which he recognized that he was unable to prevent even the Christian Nishga from potlatching.

> It is generally supposed that this question of the potlatch is one of Christian against heathen and vice versa. This is not the case. The ringleaders of the potlatch are Christians. The delegation which went to Victoria last Summer was composed partly of Christians, viz.: Amos Gosling, William Jeffry, and Moses Gagwilen; ... Quksho, alias Mathew Nass, who assaulted Nish-yek, is Christian; Stephen Laklaub, who incited the Indians to disobey the summons, is a Christian; of the seven potlatch cases dealt with by me this winter four are Christians ...
>
> Thus it is that in enforcing Sec. 114 of the Indian Act the Government will not be taking the part of Christians against heathens. Left to themselves the heathen Chiefs would give no trouble; it is when two or more evil-disposed Christians, who profess to know everything, gain an influence over them that they go astray. Of course the Chiefs are not without blame, for they leave no stone unturned to surround themselves with such characters.

The controversy was dividing the Natives themselves, and in March 1898 a group of McCullagh's Aiyansh followers petitioned Ottawa in favour of the Potlatch Law. They wanted to keep up "in civilization and progress" with the Native groups that had already given up the custom: "We have got several good cases of Potlatching now ready for trial where much property was destroyed. We have witnesses ready and are prepared to pay a lawyer. Mr. Todd has taken down some of the facts. Let the law be put in force." It was also in 1898 that the Anglicans finally broke down the resistance of their main opponent Skadeen, head-chief of Gitlakdamix. According to the Reverend Collision, Skadeen left his friends performing a potlatch ceremony at Angeeda to follow a Church Army group which had come to preach the Gospel. The chief explained his decision in vivid imagery: "Do you see that mountain? If a landslide took place and was rushing down its breasts, could any of you arrest its progress or turn it back again? Well, it is even so with me." He moved to Kincolith and two days later announced his conversion to Christianity. The old chief was baptised publicly at Fishery Bay, and by Collison's account remained faithful to his new religion. According to McCullagh, however, Skadeen "returned to his heathen surroundings after a few years, and died virtually a heathen in 1904."

One year after the death of Chief Skadeen, McCullagh issued a cry of victory in a report delayed "by events so glorious and victorious that I am glad and thankful to be able, by God's blessing, to conclude ... with news undreamed-of when I began: there is not a heathen left on the Naas at this date!" At long last, the missionaries were able to accomplish what they had wanted to do for decades — "clean" the valley of all traces of heathenism, ridding it of all the artifacts of the old Native ways. The lucrative traffic in "curios" was attracting dealers but also collectors, whose main interest was to preserve whatever they could from destruction.

In 1901, the province's archivist, Arthur Newcombe, had bought eight ritual objects for $160 from the white Nass Harbour merchant George Palmer. In November of 1905, he made a trip to Nishga country and took delivery of 132 items that had been gathered, according to his notes, by J.B. McCullagh. Some of these articles were shipped by Collison of Kincolith. The list included chiefs' head-dresses, shaman charms, sets of gambling sticks, stone adzes, wooden chests, rattles, daggers, carved spoons, whistles, baskets, dishes, a chilkat blanket of mountain-goat wool, a bow, some arrows. ... A whole culture was leaving the valley in bits and pieces. Newcombe's notebook contains drawings of some of these items, exquisite pieces that must have been a delight to the eyes and the hearts of the ancient Nishga. One senses the despair of those who had to part with familiar objects of such beauty; in another context, they would have been Aunt Hilda's silver, Cousin Elizabeth's engagement ring, or Grandfather's favourite armchair.

But McCullagh had claimed victory too soon. In the fall of 1910, his converts were holding their old festivities once again.

The months of October, November and December, 1910, I shall never forget! The recent loss of the mission buildings and all our worldly goods [by fire], together with the straitened circumstances in which we found ourselves, were but a featherweight on my heart compared with the distress occasioned by the dishonour done to the ineffable Name by those who bore it, whose brows I had once solemnly signed with the sign of the Cross, in token that thereafter they should not be ashamed to confess the faith of Christ crucified. And now, behold, their greatest ambition was to make a glory of death! Day in and day out, feasts for the dead, offerings for the dead, honour for totems, honour for crests, gravestones erected with processional and musical honours! Eight beasts were slain during those three dark months to provide feasts for the dead. It was history repeating itself, "They joined themselves unto Baal-Peor, and ate the offerings of the dead" (Ps. cvi. 28).

According to the missionary, the head-chief of Gitlakdamix made a speech advocating a return to paganism, but a few days later, "The work of grace began to be renewed in their hearts. From Gitlakdamix and Aiyansh penitents came to me seeking to make their peace with God, one of the first being the chief."

McCullagh gave no explanation for this turnaround, but the incident was seemingly the last expression of open revolt against Christianity in the Nass Valley. The sale of traditional artifacts started up again with even Indian Agent Charles Perry taking part. C.F. Newcombe, the son of the provincial archivist, made a trip to the Nass in 1912 guided by Max Collison, son of the Kincolith missionary. In a single week he acquired an impressive inventory of items that had clearly been assembled for his arrival. His list of purchases contains fewer "curios" such as spoons and baskets, and more ritual objects that would multiply in value many times over in the future: at Kincolith, 3 masks — $7, 2 masks — $7; at Greenville, a potlatch outfit — $24.50, 4 masks — $18, a mask, gambling sticks, etc. — $19.75, a chief's chest — $20, 4 masks, a charm, and a war club — $19.25, a dog eater and cannibal's crown and other small items — $18.50, ladles, spoons, etc. — $11; and back again at Kincolith, a button blanket with a man-wolf design — $20. In 1916, a major symbol of resistance fell when the Gitlakdamix chief bearing the hereditary title of "Skadeen" contacted the younger Newcombe to offer a number of objects, including a chief's hat: "It cost $65.00 and put it down to $37.00 to you." Somebody wrote on the letter, "Offered $15.00."

Finally, the missionaries turned their wrath on the last prominent landmarks of Nishga culture, the totem poles. According to both the anthropologists Marius Barbeau and C.F.

Newcombe, most of the Gitlakdamix poles were cut down in 1918 and used as firewood in a campaign of vandalism that modern Nishga attribute to the churches. Admirers of Native art, anthropologists, and curators tried to save what they could by placing some of these poles in museums around the world, but in a 1930 report to the Museum of the American Indian in New York, C.F. Newcombe was forced to admit that the situation was appalling: "The village of Angeeda has been abandoned since 1880 — fifty years. Most of the other poles formerly standing there have disappeared either through decay or removal. Only a few old Indians know where they stood or can give their description. This deserted village is in an out of the way place and is practically never visited by the present generation of Indians." And concerning the general situation in the Pacific Northwest, Newcombe concluded sadly that "the needs of most of the museums seem to have been satisfied. Yet a few more poles could still be placed and conserved in museums. The possibilities are being canvassed. The poles that are still left standing in the forests — there are many of them — are practically lost. They will soon disappear."

Chief Roy Azak of Canyon City recalled in 1981 "when they really forbid the totem poles. My dad got a really good totem pole. It belonged to the old people and he cut one down here and he had to cut it in half. It was so long. It's called 'The Shadow.' Well, big totem pole. He sold it and if you go to New York you'll find that totem pole. I think it's outside in a park somewhere in New York." In 1929, the Museum of the American Indian in New York purchased a fifty-foot totem pole, the pole of "Gwaneks and Weerlarhae," known as "Henry Adzek's father's pole" and carved by Qaderh of the Gitlakdamix Wolf clan. According to Marius Barbeau this pole was erected in a courtyard of the museum's annex in the Bronx, the token, in Chief Azak's words, of a tragic misunderstanding:

The white man made a mistake, felt that the Indians worshipped this. Nobody kneeled down before the totem pole, I never heard, I asked my grandfather, that anybody kneeled down in front of the totem pole and worshipped the totem pole. It's just to show the tradition, what tribe you're in, and how many locals you got around, that belongs to your family. That was all written down on that. It's just like a history writing. It's all written on a pole. . . .

Whatever happens ... they put it on the totem pole. And the wolf saved somebody in our family, or if the chief want that wolf-prince to be his crest, he didn't just go out and shoot that in ten minutes or half an hour. He had to follow that wolf, he had to suffer, he had to follow that wolf for maybe weeks, months, before he catch up with him.

Also in 1981, Chief James Gosnell expressed the tenacity of Nishga beliefs so consistently misconstrued by the representatives of church and state.

> The early missionaries really, they too, tried to stamp out the Indian way of life, you know, the culture, the potlatch and those kinds of things. Up until about, oh I would say, twenty years ago, I think, when they changed. You see, the church people, or the religious people, they had the idea that we had no belief, that we were just human beings. Period. But yet that was not the case. Our people always worshipped the Supreme Being, up there they say, you know, up in the sky. ... They always believed that there was someone that had more power and authority than us, ourselves, and that we had to hope of the era after. You see, the white men were not aware of all these things. Our people's belief is that God gave us the land upon which we're living and all the natural resources that's there for our use of survival. All our songs, our dances, all, everything, our way of life, is given to us by God. This is the basic belief.
>
> The Church was of the opinion that the settlement of the dead that we were trying to, or attempting to communicate with that dead person, such is not the case. The settlement of our dead, we need the promotion of our chieftainship title from the dead person to whoever is next in line of succession. That's all it's all about, very sacred, you know, to us. We honour that and all that is done through our clan system ...
>
> There were many people, not necessarily Nishga people, but Indian people throughout B.C. were imprisoned because of the practice of our own culture, the potlatch, as they call it in other parts. But it is not all of it, it's only part of it. ... Our people never did even abide by those, they call them Potlatch Laws. You know, our people carried out their own tradition all the time. That's how we were able to maintain some if it, or most of it, until right now. They never did abide by those laws. In those days, they had these

so-called "Indian agents" going in there and telling the people that it is unlawful, so people just ignored it. And now during that period of time, and until 1958, we were totally isolated, there's no road, or anyway, the only transporation was the river. And I don't think any white men would like to travel that river. We were totally isolated. So on the basis of isolation, we were able to just carry on our tradition, our way of life in respect to potlatch and that sort of things.

THE NISHGA GO TO LONDON

The Indian seemed to be regarded as a negligible quantity in this race, for his hunting and fishing grounds are now all mapped off as the property of others, without so much as "by your leave" to him. Consequently he feels distressed in his mind, sore, hurt, aggrieved. He thinks that his ancient rights should have been respected, and that his long record of loyalty to the "Great Queen" better rewarded. Of his own native wit he understands that some sort of settlement should have been made with him by the Government for the alienation of his lands. He misses something to which he cannot quite give a name. I think it is Justice.

The Indian loves his country with a deep, passionate, understanding love, even as I myself have grown to love its wild haunts. The rippling streams, the verdant slopes, the pine-studded parks, the glorious blueberry patches and strawberry dells, the dense bush, the beaver meadows and muskegs, the heavily-timbered forest with its mossy carpet and winding ways, the silent lake, the river with its everlasting supply of fish, the hunting and the trapping, and the labours and the joys of home — all this he sees coolly appropriated by strangers, whose only conception of him is that he is "a jolly nuisance." It must be hard on him when he takes his family off as of yore to the spring hunt, and they once more gather round the old camp-tree to make their temporary home, to find the old tree blazed and a

notice inscribed thereon — DON'T HUNT HERE ANY MORE, I HAVE
STAKED THIS LAND (*signed*) WHITE MAN.

He reads this and the warm blood runs cold to his heart. Then his
cheeks begin to feel hot and burning; there is a choking sensation in
his throat; his teeth are set and his eyes blaze. Look at him, as he
stands alone by his rights against the magnitude and weight of the
whole British Empire! He does not cringe, he does not lose his head
— he burns, and cries, "Oh, I feel as if my heart would burst."

When it came to their feeling for the immemorial land, missionaries like James McCullagh found themselves on the Native
side. The reasons for this were by no means simple. One may
certainly have been to keep a "closed shop," isolate their flocks
from infections carried by secular whites into the Utopias they
were attempting to create. Yet it is also obvious from their writings that they felt a genuine sympathy for the Natives' plight.
The Methodists were the first to take a militant attitude towards
government. The Anglicans evolved more slowly and more
ambiguously, and hesitated between two basic positions: should
the Natives be integrated as fast as possible into white society,
thus achieving "equality" status through their disappearance as
a group, or should they retain their identity and control of their
traditional territories, which meant the settlement of their
grievances and a halt on white encroachment? McCullagh of
Aiyansh moved gradually towards the second position, while his
colleague Collison from Kincolith favoured the first, as shown in
his 1915 testimony to the McKenna-McBride Commission:
"Kincolith was one of the first villages to take up not only the
reserve system, it was also the seat of the first appointed Indian
agent, and in other ways led in the adoption of present method
being always on the right side. . . . Church and state should work
hand in hand to effect reformation and civilization among the
Native people of the northern coast."

The process favoured by Collison was termed "enfranchisement" in the Indian Act; a single Native or aboriginal band
could renounce their "Indian status" voluntarily and be integrated with white society. This solution, however, whatever its
intrinsic merit, was not possible in British Columbia. The Terms
of Union had provided for the province to set aside lands for
Native use, but Victoria took the position that these reserves
must revert to the Crown as soon as Natives became "enfran-
chised" and thus no longer officially "Indians." In this legal

legerdemain the Native people, by renouncing their status, would lose the little land that had been left to them.

Most missionaries opted, therefore, for a more direct defence of the Indians' traditional rights, and helped organize a political lobby in favour of the land claims. The Methodist missionary Alfred Green was probably instrumental in the formation of the first Nishga Land Committee in 1890. Led by a Lakalzap chief, Arthur Calder, it was made up of elected representatives from three local chapters — Kincolith, Lakalzap, and Canyon City–Aiyansh. When the Methodists retreated from the Nass valley because of a shortage of ministers, the Anglicans became involved in its activities. At the McKenna-McBride Commission hearings in December 1915, Indian Agent Charles Perry publicly accused McCullagh of fuelling Native protest through his English-Nishga newspaper, the *Hagaga.*

> I have a copy of his paper — it has a direct tendency to influence the Indians against the Government, and more than that he printed a notice of the Indians which was stuck up on the trees asking white men to keep off their lands until their claims were settled. This notice reads as follows:

INDIAN PROTEST

Against white settlers coming into the Aiyansh Valley, Naas River, B.C.

Whereas we, the Indian people of the above mentioned valley, being lawful and original inhabitants and possessors of all the lands contained there from time immemorial: and being assured in our possession of the same by the proclamation of His Majesty, King George III, under date of 7th October, 1763, which proclamation we hold as our Charter of Rights under the British Crown;

And whereas, it is provided in the said proclamation that no private person do presume to make any purchase from us of any lands; so reserved to us until we shall have ceded from the same to the representatives of the Crown in public meeting between us and them;

And whereas, up to the present time, our lands have not been ceded by us to the Crown, nor in any form alienated from us by any agreement or settlement between the representatives of the Crown and ourselves;

And whereas, our case is now before the Privy Council in England, and we are expecting a settlement of the difficulty at present existing between ourselves and the Government of this Province at an early date;

We do therefore, standing well within our constitutional rights, forbid you to stake off land in this valley, and do hereby protest against your proceeding further into our country with that end in view — until such time as a satisfactory settlement be made between the representatives of the Crown and ourselves.

Issued by the members of the Indian Land Committee, elected by the Indians of the Upper Naas.

signed: J.K. Flyaway, J.R. Badweather, Git-lak-damiks. S.A. Zeedawit, A.M. Nahneigh, J. Nakmauz, Aiyansh. Amos G. Neesgwaksaw, Samuel Weeshakes, Johnnie O-yea, Gwinhoa. Dated at Aiyansh, B.C., this 17th day of May, 1910.

Although it received precious help from the missionaries, the Nishga Land Committee was not a mere appendix of the church. The pagan village of Gitlakdamix had been one of the strongest centres of protest against the imposition of the reserve system in the 1880s, and the committee was simply continuing in more modern guise the traditional Nishga resistance to the legal theft of their lands. The Native objective was not only to obtain larger reserves but also to reach a settlement for all the territory seized by the province in 1881. And the Nishga were now not the only ones to raise their voices; the land agitation was spreading to all parts of British Columbia. In 1906, Joe Capilano, a chief from the region of the city of Vancouver, went to London and presented a petition on Native grievances to King Edward VII. Chief Capilano was received politely, but the Imperial authorities refrained from giving him any answer.

At the same time, the land question was the cause of growing tension between the two levels of government in Canada. The 1876 compromise and the creation of the Reserve Allotment Commission had not solved all the problems; Ottawa and Victoria remained in conflict over three fundamental points. First, it was becoming more and more evident that the province was in bad faith on its commitment to continued "liberality" in the assignment of reserve lands. In 1901, Victoria even had the audacity to ask for a reduction in size of already existing reserves to make more room for white colonists. The second area of contention was the issue of Native title that Ottawa had passed over in 1876; the federal government, stung by the province's inflexibility, was now showing signs of returning to its

traditional position of "extinguishment" of title by negotiation
and treaty. Finally, Ottawa and Victoria were in disagreement
over "reversionary interest," the provincial claim to ownership
of reserve land "abandoned" by its occupants through either
demographic evolution or "enfranchisement."

This last issue came to a head in 1906 when the Grand Trunk
Pacific Railway tried to get part of the Tsimshian reserve for a
new ocean terminal. The federal government asked Victoria to
waive its "reversionary interest" in the matter, but Premier Richard McBride took the view that any land removed from a
reserve must immediately revert to the province. Two years
later, British Columbia strengthened its land Act, giving itself
the power to regain control over lands that at any time ceased to
be used by the Natives. The 1876 federal-provincial accord was
defunct. Victoria disbanded the Reserve Allotment Commission, and as a symbolic gesture sold some 161 acres of repos-
sessed Native reserves to individuals.

Although the British North America Act made "the Indians
and their lands" a federal responsibility, the 1876 agreement
had allowed the province to assert its presence in the field. By
1908, however, not only had this duality become untenable, but
the Natives of British Columbia were living under the most
insecure system of land tenure anywhere in Canada. At Victoria
they organized a lobby group, the "Conference of Friends of the
Indians of British Columbia," while in Ottawa A.E. O'Meara, a
Toronto lawyer who was also a minister, led the fight with an
organization known as the "Moral and Social Reform Council of
Canada." These two groups repeatedly asked both governments
to submit the question of the validity of Native title for a ruling
by the Judicial Committee of the Privy Council in London.

In May 1910, legal experts of the provincial and federal governments agreed on a list of ten questions to be referred to the
Imperial authorities. The first three had to do with the legitimacy of Native title and the other seven with the size of the
reserves. O'Meara approved the list on the Natives' behalf, but
Premier McBride rejected the document because of the three
questions on aboriginal title. From his point of view, the
reserves were provincial properties like the off-reserve territories, and the Natives could have no possible claim to them.

On 3 March 1911, a delegation from the Nishga nation went
to Victoria to protest McBride's attitude and notify the provincial government of its intention to push for recognition of its

land claims. In Ottawa meanwhile, the Liberal Prime Minister of Canada, Sir Wilfrid Laurier, confided to a Native delegation that they had very little hope of a settlement without taking the province to court:

> The British Columbia Government contends that the Indians have no claim. If the case could be referred to the Supreme Court and the Privy Council it would bring the matter to an issue at once. Unfortunately, Mr. McBride would not agree to that submission. He only agreed to leave out of the question the very thing we want to have a decision upon. We do not know if we can force a Government into court. If we can find a way I may say we shall surely do so, because everybody will agree it is a matter of good government to have no one resting under a grievance.

Ottawa never pressed the issue. Shortly after Laurier made these remarks, the Liberals lost an election and the victorious Conservatives led by Prime Minister Robert Borden opted for a new compromise with the province. In 1912, the federal government appointed a special commissioner, Dr. J.A.J. McKenna, with the mission of repairing the rift with Victoria. McKenna wooed Premier McBride in a memorandum of 29 July:

> I understand that you will not deviate from the position which you have so clearly taken and frequently defined, i.e., that the province's title to its lands is unburdened by any Indian title, and that your government will not be a party, directly or indirectly, to a reference to the Courts of the claim set up. . . . As stated at our conversations, I agree with you as to the seriousness of now raising the question, and, as far as the present negotiations go, it is dropped.

Having thus once again evaded the issue of Native title, McKenna proposed that the size of the reserves be the subject of a commission of inquiry. The lands cut off from existing reserves would be sold by the province, and both governments would share in the profit. The reserves of extinct tribes would revert to the provincial Crown, while Victoria would transfer jurisdiction of the remaining reserves to Ottawa. The compromise was accepted by both governments and, on 23 April 1913, a joint royal commission was appointed that became known as

the McKenna-McBride Commission. After two years of hearings, it basically confirmed the locations of the reserves set up by
O'Reilly and assigned the Natives of British Columbia the
reduced territories to which they are still confined today.

This wave of anti-Native policies prompted the Nishga to
change their strategy. Since O'Meara and his friends had failed
in their efforts to present a collective defence in the name of all
the indigenous peoples of British Columbia, the Nishga decided
to carry on the fight under their own banner. At a 22 January
1913 meeting in Kincolith, they adopted a "Statement of the
Nishga Nation or Tribe of Indians" that reaffirmed tribal ownership of their traditional territory with all its natural resources,
including fisheries. Though they cited George III's proclamation and other documents in favour of their claim, the Nishga
based their position on a principle that went beyond political
authority, the principle of fundamental human rights. The
statement defined the broad lines of an eventual settlement:

> While we claim the right to be compensated for those portions of
> our territory which we may agree to surrender, we claim as even
> more important the right to reserve other portions permanently
> for our own use and benefit, and beyond doubt the portions which
> we would desire so to reserve would include much of the land
> which has been sold by the Province. We are not opposed to the
> coming of the white people into our territory, provided this be
> carried out justly and in accordance with the British principles
> embodied in the Royal Proclamation. If therefore as we expect the
> aboriginal rights which we claim should be established by the deci-
> sion of His Majesty's Privy Council, we would be prepared to take
> a moderate and reasonable position.

The Nishga strategy was to ignore Ottawa and Victoria, who
were obviously accomplices on the Indian question, and go
directly to the Imperial government. The move made perfect
sense: Canada was still at that time technically a colony of Great
Britain, subject to the same British monarchy in whose name the
first white authorities had taken possession of Native land; from
the Nishga point of view, it was up to the British to assume the
consequences and decide the matter in the highest court of the
empire. The Nishga were also convinced that Westminster,
given its remoteness from the settlers' influence, would be more
likely to hear the case on its merits. The Nishga hired the

London law firm of Fox and Preece, and on 21 May 1913, a petition was brought in their name before the Privy Council.

The 1913 "Nishga Petition" is a remarkable document, considering the cultural gap that existed at the time between the ideas animating Native society and the legalistic nit-picking of the white bureaucrats. Here were beings far from the crude savages depicted by all the racists, a people that had surveyed their new circumstances adroitly and managed to translate their fundamental position into an alien language for the forum of debate. The petition began by describing with precision the exact borders of traditional Nishga territory. It went on to contend that "when sovereignty over the territory included within the aforesaid limits was assumed by Great Britain such sovereignty was accepted by the said Nation or Tribe, and the right of the said Nation or Tribe to possess, occupy, and use the said territory was recognized by Great Britain." The petition asserted further that "no part of the said territory has been ceded to or purchased by the Crown, and no part thereof has been purchased from the said Nation or Tribe by the Crown or any person acting on behalf of the Crown, at a public meeting or assembly or otherwise, or by any other person whomsoever." Reproducing large extracts from the Royal Proclamation of 1763, it challenged all the land legislation enacted by British Columbia. The privy councillors were asked to confirm the Nishga's territorial rights and declare the provincial Land Act invalid.

Publication of the document caused a stir and turned the Nishga into the flag-bearers of Native resistance in Canada. However, the Imperial authorities refused to deal with the issue, and trapped the Nishga in a bureaucratic vicious circle: to be received in London, the petition had to be sponsored by the Canadian government, but Ottawa did not want to refer the question to the British unless it was amended to a point where the answer would have had no practical consequences.

The federal response came in a July 1914 document drafted by Duncan Scott, Deputy Minister of Indian Affairs. Scott's analysis preserved all the ambiguities of Ottawa's historical position on Native land claims. Like his predecessors, the deputy minister recognized that the question of aboriginal rights had never been settled, but he was not prepared to accept the Nishga definition of these rights: "The Privy Council, to which the Nishga Nation desire to appeal, has already pronounced

upon the nature of the Indian title, describing it as 'a personal
and usufructuary right dependent upon the good-will of the
Sovereign.' It follows that the Indian title, when acknowledged
by the Crown, cannot be separated from what the Crown elects
to grant." Even if Native land title were to be clearly defined it
would not automatically follow, in the deputy minister's view,
that the government would have to enter into treaties: "It is
optional, when, if at all, the Crown may proceed to extinguish
the Indian title, and, therefore, if it is decided that the Indians
of British Columbia have a title of this nature there can be no
claim for deferred benefit from the Crown."

In February 1915, a new organization was formed in southern British Columbia to support the Nishga claim and, with it,
settlement of the land question generally in the province. Under
the leadership of Andrew Paull, a young Squamish chief, and
Peter Kelly, a Haida Methodist minister, the "Allied Tribes of
British Columbia" launched an extensive campaign to publicize
the issue on every reserve in the province. Meanwhile, the
Nishga, who had not formally joined the organization, sent
delegations to Ottawa in 1915 and again in 1916 to ask the
Dominion government to refer their case to the Privy Council.

They met a wall of official silence. Ottawa and Victoria hoped
agitation would subside once the McKenna-McBride Commission had defined the new boundaries of the reserves. The hearings of the official inquiry became a convenient alibi for the
governments' inaction. When its recommendations were finally
adopted in 1924, British Columbia's Native population was left
with 2965 square kilometres of reserve land, or fourteen hectares a head, in a province with a total area of 948 596 square
kilometres. The Nishga "received" 7590 hectares, half of one
per cent of their former territory.

> They tried to talk to these people. If they want the land, sure, we'll
> negotiate it with them. And at that point in time, they said what we
> are saying today, that we are prepared to share the wealth of the
> land. Our people, don't forget, were aware that the valley was
> loaded with natural resources, you know, at that point in time.
> They said that we are prepared to share this not only with you,
> we've been sharing it with our neighbouring tribes, you know,
> throughout time. No, all that fell on deaf ears, you know. They
> wouldn't hear that. Time and time went on, this was going on way
> before I was born, I'm fifty-seven years old this year. They

attempted settlement. The governments of those days just wouldn't listen to them. Instead, in 1927 I believe, the federal and provincial governments created a hoax, saying that any Indian or bands of Indians that will meet and discuss about the land shall be arrested and prosecuted. Mind you, they even respected that baloney, too, you know, until the 1940s or the 1950s.

Chief James Gosnell, 1981

The McKenna-McBride Commission had dealt with reserves as part of the federal-provincial squabble over Crown lands; it never addressed the issue of Native claims. All through the war years, the Canadian government kept trying to defuse the issue and neutralize the Nishga petition. The federal strategem was classic hypocrisy: Ottawa was ready to send the question of Native title to arbitration, but there would be a small condition.

The Indians of British Columbia shall, by their Chiefs or representatives, in a binding way, agree, if the Court, or, on appeal, the Privy Council, decides that they have a title to lands of the Province, to surrender such title, receiving from the Dominion benefits to be granted for extinguishment of title in accordance with past usage of the Crown in satisfying the Indian land claim to surrendered territories, and to accept the finding of the Royal Commission on Indian Affairs in British Columbia, as approved by the Governments of the Dominion and the Province as a full allotment of Reserve lands to be administered for their benefit as part of compensation.

In short, the Nishga must surrender their rights regardless of the verdict, and in the case of a favourable ruling it would be up to Ottawa and Victoria to decide unilaterally what the amount of compensation should be. The Canadian government did not expect the Nishga to fall into such an obvious trap, but used their refusal as a reason for blocking the referral.

By 1918, the Nishga knew officially that the Privy Council would not hear their case without Canada's consent. In the following year, the Allied Tribes of British Columbia tried to break the deadlock with a concrete proposal for settlement in a twenty-point submission to the province. They asked for bigger reserves based on 160 acres per person, plus compensation for all territories lost; the main part of this compensation would have taken the form of modern medical and school systems. In

1923, the Nishga made a similar proposal, requesting $2.5 million as compensation for the loss of non-reserve land. Both plans included recognition of fishing, hunting, and trapping rights.

Though these submissions were precise enough to open up the possibility of a negotiated settlement, the Canadian government acted as if the Native demands were incomprehensible. In a 1925 parliamentary debate, Charles Stewart, the federal interior minister, claimed that he had been unable to get clarification of the Native position.

> Do they lay claim to all lands in British Columbia in view of the fact that in ninety per cent of the cases no treaty had been signed between the tribes and representatives of the Crown? After a great deal of discussion I found that they did not want to lay claim to the land in its entirety, but they do say that before an adjustment can take place they should have certain specified and unspecified provisions made for them by the government of Canada. This is all so vague and difficult of understanding that it is very hard to arrive at any concrete definition of what their claims are.

This persistent inability to understand their position failed to discourage the Native campaigners, and in July of the same year the Allied Tribes once again petitioned Ottawa for either a settlement or a referral to London. Although the Indian question had by then been canvassed virtually to extinction, the government put the case before a joint committee of the Senate and the House of Commons. After five days of hearings in the spring of 1927, the parliamentarians had only this to say:

> The Committee note with regret the existence of agitation, not only in British Columbia, but with Indians in other parts of the Dominion, which agitation may be called mischievous, by which the Indians are deceived and led to expect benefits from claims more or less fictitious. Such agitation, often carried on by designing white men, is to be deplored, and should be discountenanced, as the Government of the country is at all times ready to protect the interests of the Indians and to redress real grievances where such are shown to exist.

The committee flatly rejected the Natives' claims and closed the door to any future negotiation:

It is the unanimous opinion of the members thereof that the petitioners have not established any claim to the lands of British Columbia based on aboriginal or other title, and that the position taken by the Government in 1914 . . . afforded the Indians full opportunity to put their claim to rest. As they have declined to do so, it is the further opinion of your Committee that the matter should now be regarded as finally closed.

When the committee's recommendations were adopted, Parliament included an annual grant of $100,000 to be added to the budget of the Department of Indian Affairs to match the yearly payments made to Natives in other provinces who had signed treaties with the whites, and to be used for improving education, health, and living conditions on the reserves. The members of Parliament viewed the payment, thereafter known as the "B.C. Special," as a settlement, but since the Natives themselves had not consented to it, the measure was no more than a sham. This money is still being paid today and amounts to two dollars for each registered Native in the province. For the white man, the "B.C. Special" is undeniably a good deal: where else could one rent so much land for so little, and, furthermore, without the consent of the original owners?

Since from its point of view the question had not been settled, the Canadian Parliament decided to put a stop to the land controversy by making it illegal to press Native land claims. Such basic rights as freedom of speech and opinion were denied to an important minority by a system that could not restrain its repressive tendencies. By challenging the legitimacy of the British Columbia land grab, Native people had attacked the very nature of white power, and for this they had to be chastised. Section 141 of the Indian Act, passed in 1927, defined a new and unusual offence:

Every person who, without the consent of the Superintendent General expressed in writing, receives, obtains, solicits or requests from any Indian any payment or contribution for the purpose of raising a fund or providing money for the prosecution of any claim which the tribe or band of Indians to which such Indian belongs, or of which he is a member, has or is represented to have for the recovery of any claim or money for the benefit of the said tribe or band, shall be guilty of an offence and liable upon summary conviction for each such offence to a penalty not exceeding two hundred dollars and not less than fifty dollars or to imprisonment for a term not exceeding two months.

Nor did the anti-Native zeal of the 1927 Parliament stop at the prohibition of land claims. With another piece of legislation, the Dominion's lawgivers mounted a new attack, more precise and more refined this time, against the potlatch and thus the Native culture.

Every Indian or other person who engages in or assists in celebrating or encourages either directly or indirectly another to celebrate any Indian festival, dance or other ceremony of which the giving away or paying or giving back of gift or money, goods, articles takes place before, at or after the celebration of the same, or who encourages or assists in any celebration or dance of which the wounding or mutilation of the dead or living body of any human being or animal forms a part or is a feature, is guilty of an offence and is liable on summary conviction for a term not exceeding six months and not less than two months.

NISHGA LAND IS NOT FOR SALE

For a time, the trauma of 1927, with the effective anathemas against potlatching and land claims, seemed to have brought Native resistance to a halt. The Allied Tribes of British Columbia collapsed. The Nishga Land Committee subsided into a lengthy hibernation. Since cultural and political action had to remain for the most part under ground, Native energies were focussed on the day-to-day defence of immediate interests. In 1931, Tsimshian and Haida leaders founded the Native Brotherhood of British Columbia to work at improving economic and social conditions in the coastal fishing nations. The Kwawkgeulth and Squamish soon joined in, and by 1942 the association had Nishga branches in Kincolith and Greenville. The brotherhood dealt chiefly with problems related to the fishery, often in the guise of a union, but it was also active in the fields of education and health. After the Second World War, a similar organization, the North American Indian Brotherhood, was created in the interior of the province under the leadership of Andrew Paull, a veteran of the Allied Tribes and the Native Brotherhood.

The land question remained taboo, but the policies of postwar governments began to evolve in more liberal directions. A worldwide decolonization movement was emerging from the ruins of shattered empires. It was borne home to the elites of Canada that the country's Native people could not be kept in the half-light for ever. A slow process of readjustment was begun in mid-1946 with the appointment of a special joint committee of the Senate and House of Commons to study the Indian Act. It sat for two years. Amending legislation was brought down in June 1950 and withdrawn shortly afterwards to allow for further consultation. On 28 February and the first three days of March 1951, the federal government held meetings with Native leaders from across the country to canvass their opinions. Among them were four from British Columbia: William Scow and Peter Kelly for the Native Brotherhood, Daniel Manuel for the Upper Nicola band, and Andrew Paull for the North American Indian Brotherhood.

The new Indian Act of June 1951 brought some fresh air into the statute book, but the legislation's main components, "Indian" status and the reserve system, remained unaltered. The most significant change was a partial redistribution of administrative duties in favour of local government at the band level, although this was still subject to the "supervisory role" of the minister and his right of veto over band decisions. The prohibition against the sale and possession of intoxicants was dropped, as well as the potlatch and land-claims provisions in the old law. As for the right to vote federally, the Native people of Canada had to wait until the next round of reform in 1960 to receive that privilege.

Not surprisingly, the Nishga were among the first Native groups to take advantage of the changes. It was a Nishga, Frank Calder, who in 1949 became the first Native elected to a Canadian parliamentary institution. The new member for the riding of Atlin was then aged thirty-four. He entered the British Columbia Legislative Assembly under the banner of the Cooperative Commonwealth Federation, forerunner of the present New Democratic Party. The entry of a Frank Calder into the white political reserve was the outcome of a deliberate decision taken by the Nishga people at the turn of the century: if Native society was to survive, its young elite had to be armed with the weapons of the outside world.

Frank Calder's life started at the edge of myth. In 1915, the former leader of the Nishga Land Committee, Chief Long-Arm — Arthur Calder — had lost his infant son while travelling on the Nass River. Shortly afterwards, an elderly woman had a vision and announced that Mrs. Calder's younger sister was pregnant with the reincarnated boy. The male child born on

3 August 1915 was handed over by his natural parents and adopted by the chief under the name Frank Calder.

In 1919, I was four years old. Arthur Calder took me to Kincolith into Walter Haldane's house, where all the leading chiefs were gonna talk land claims. There weren't claims in those days, the land question, that's the name. . . . Jeffrey Benson, who died not too long ago, got married the same year, 1919. And he and his wife were secretaries. He was there, he was the young man who was doing the secretarial work in that meeting. And the story that is well known in Kincolith, because that's where it happened, is Arthur Calder picked me up and stood me on the table and said to the gathering: and this is the boy I am going to send to a white area, and I'm gonna make him speak like a white man, I'm gonna make him walk like a white man, I'm gonna make him eat like a white man. Everything that that guy does, this little boy is gonna do. We don't need no interpreters. By the time he is ready, he is the boy that's gonna be using our language, his language, and he is the one that's going to bring this case to the highest court in the land.

As early as age nine, young Calder was invited to take part in the activities of the land committee — "the books were placed in my hands on this." To give him a white man's education, his parents sent him to an Indian residential school in Chilliwack near Vancouver, where he spent thirteen years. He went on to the University of British Columbia as the first status Indian ever admitted to that institution and he graduated from the Anglican Theological College with a licentiate in 1946. His student days gave him splendid opportunities to learn from the experience of Native leaders and particularly Andrew Paull, whom he calls his "tutor." Deciding against ordination, Calder plunged into the world of politics and spent his next few years in the provincial legislature as a champion of Native equality in areas as diverse as pensions, citizenship, trapping, fishing, and medical and social services. His moral status among the Nishga soared when, in 1958, he became one of their most important hereditary chiefs, assuming the title of Chief Long-Arm from his natural father Henry Clark: succeeding Arthur Calder, Clark died without the traditional nephew to come after him.

Calder had also resurrected the old land committee and registered a new Nishga tribal council as a non-profit association.

The council held its founding convention in October 1955 and quickly regrouped the whole Nishga nation. Primordial among its objectives was the settlement of the land question. The Nishga were about to join battle and become once again the focus of Native land claims in Canada.

In 1959, the tribal council brought the Privy Council petition of 1913 up to date with a new position paper. The emphasis this time was on resources — fish, timber, minerals — as well as the land itself.

> We claim to be the aboriginal inhabitants of the territory defined, and that under the terminology of the proclamation, we are the tribal owners of said territory, and that no part of it be taken from the Nishga nation or tribe of Indians, or the land and natural resources, such as timber resources, be sold and disposed of until the same has been purchased by the Crown.
>
> We claim that our aboriginal rights have been guaranteed by the proclamation of King George the Third and recognized by acts of parliament of Great Britain, and by our aboriginal rights, we claim tribal ownership of all fisheries, minerals, timber, and other natural resources within the realm of the territory outlined.

The council tried to get its position endorsed by other aboriginal groups. The Native Brotherhood, however, at its Kamloops convention, refused to sponsor a proposal to revive the land claims. The idea seemed too dangerous, since the Nishga were by now convinced that their case would have to be tested in the courts. Other Native leaders feared that such a challenge, if it failed, would forever jeopardize Native land claims in the country. The Nishga drew up their own brief and took it to a joint Senate–House of Commons committee on Indian Affairs to petition the federal authorities once again.

On 26 May 1960, this committee heard two representatives of the tribal council, Calder and Rod Robinson. Robinson stressed the urgency of a settlement. Development was rapidly eroding traditional Nishga rights:

> I wish to elaborate on the subject of traplines. There are 60 registered traplines in existence in the Nass valley, and there are 160 persons trapping on those 60 traplines. You will no doubt wonder why, out of the total population, only a very few persons pursue this traditional occupation of our people. Over the past years fur

markets have been on a steady decline, and during the years when fur prices were still good, the average take-home pay realized at the time was between $800 to $1000. Today some of these traplines have already been destroyed by the logging operations, as mentioned in our brief; and, as industry moves further into our territory, more traplines will be destroyed. As stated in our brief, we go on record as welcoming industrial expansion; but the fact remains that we must be compensated for our damaged properties.

What did the Nishga want — land, money, or both? The MPs and senators wanted to know. Frank Calder explained that Native views on the land question remained as they had always been:

We contend the Nishga have never been conquered and, therefore, no treaties, acts, or regulations have come into being to govern the B.C. Indian, as far as we are concerned, in that particular area.

It appears to us that we are in a separate category. When B.C., in 1871, joined Confederation, the Indians automatically came under a treaty which was already in existence in 1869 in Canada. In other words, the Indians in B.C. took no part, nor were they ever consulted into what entered into the Indian Act. As far as we are concerned, there has been no major connection, no treaties, and we contend that our aboriginal rights must be considered in the discussions and deliberations in regard to land in British Columbia. We contend that we definitely are entitled to all lands that we formerly held.

Parliamentarians were puzzled:

Mr. McQuillan, MP — Mr. Chairman, this is only one of a number of such claims, I believe. Any Indian tribe could base a claim on the same basis that this claim has been based. I just wonder what it is hoped to achieve. I think the Indians must be realistic enough to realize that they cannot get this back. They say they were never conquered; but I am sure they would soon be conquered if they tried to do that in every place in British Columbia. I just wondered what their aim is in putting forward this claim.

Mr. Calder — We are not claiming the land back, in the manner that when we do get it back we are the rulers: that is definitely not our claim. We want recognition that we do have rights within the

territory defined — and perhaps our brothers on the outside have
the same feeling.

We know that we have rights, and we want them recognized by
the governments. The governments in the past have refused us
these rights. We can argue until we are blue in the face: the government says this; we say this: and we say that when there is
disagreement, it should be settled in court.

The answer to my friend's question is, as I stated, that we are
not after the taking back of the land and then being rulers over it.
We know we will never get it back. It is well settled now. We only
want our title recognized and compensation paid.

Ownership of the untouched section of the territory and compensation for lands alienated to outside interests: such were the
basic principles of any acceptable settlement. But as Frank
Calder pointed out, the Nishga did not want to argue until they
were "blue in the face." For the tribal council, a court challenge
had become unavoidable.

The Nass River Indians and, I imagine, their brothers in the B.C.
interior and elsewhere, are prepared now to face realities and,
particularly, to face this subject in court because, as long as this
case rests as it is now, there will definitely be unrest in the minds
and thoughts of the Indians in British Columbia. There will be no
rest in the minds until this subject has been given a proper hearing
and judgement placed upon it by the courts — which we hope, this
committee will find for us.

We definitely are looking for a way, and we are here to ask your
assistance to find a way for us to meet the B.C. government, and
yourselves, perhaps, in court because, after all analyses have been
looked over, we are prepared to meet the B.C. government. We
do not know what the future holds in regard to the present government. However, we do know this: the British Columbia government have avoided this issue. They have refused to give reference by which we could face them in court. We do hope, when you
have given your final report, that you will be good enough to put
in all your efforts to find a way by which we can face one another
in court or, if not in court, in a round-table discussion, from which
we can arrive at a solution.

In 1963, a benign incident reopened the whole file on Native
title. Two Nanaimo Natives named White and Bob were

arrested for killing six deer on Crown land. Their lawyer, Thomas Berger, obtained an acquittal. The core of his case was an 1854 document signed by Gov. James Douglas which recognized the Natives' ancestral hunting rights. Judge Swencisky of the County Court ruled that this document was indeed a treaty, and that "the aboriginal right of the Nanaimo Indian tribes to hunt on unoccupied land, which was confirmed to them by the royal proclamation of 1763, has never been abrogated or extinguished and is still in full force and effect." This ruling was later upheld by the Appeal Court of British Columbia. *Regina v. White and Bob* had ramifications far beyond the demise of a half-dozen Vancouver Island deer. The judgement acknowledged not only that the Nanaimo Natives were allowed by treaty to hunt on Crown land but also, and more importantly, that the treaty confirmed a previous right that had never been impaired. It could thus be interpreted as recognition of the fact that in areas where the Natives had never signed treaties, there still existed aboriginal rights which had not been abolished by any subsequent legislation. When the case reached the Supreme Court of Canada on appeal in 1965, the federal panel confirmed the hunters' acquittal. Their ruling was made on the sole basis of the treaty's validity and without regard to the aboriginal rights issue. Nonetheless, *Regina v. White and Bob* opened up the possibility of a new wave of land claims.

In the Nishga Tribal Council, these developments reinforced the belief that the time had come to go to court. As in 1960, however, British Columbia Natives were divided on the issue. The Native Brotherhood, which had contributed financially to the defence of White and Bob, refused once again to become involved. The Nishga went it alone. They wanted their case heard in 1967 in time for the commemoration of the hundredth anniversary of the Canadian federation, but the actual trial did not start until 1969. Their lawyer was the Thomas Berger of the White and Bob case, who as a judge some years later led a commission of inquiry into the proposed Mackenzie Valley pipeline, a project which threatened the environment and livelihood of Native groups in the Northwest Territories. The Berger Commission recommended a moratorium on development before the settlement of land claims — a controversial and enlightened recommendation that has been largely circumvented.

The first decision to be taken by Berger and the tribal council was where to attack. Should they sue Victoria, or Ottawa, or both? The Nishga decided on British Columbia, since the land and all resources except for fisheries were within provincial jurisdiction. Another complication was a century-old dispute with the Kitwancool people who claimed some land in the upper Nass Valley. To avoid bringing third parties into the case, the Nishga decided to forget their own claim to that area for the duration of the trail.

Would the Canadian government side with the Nishga people against British Columbia? It had done so in 1875 when justice minister Fournier fought provincial land laws, and again in 1911 when Prime Minister Laurier weighed the possibility of taking Victoria to court. Yet when Berger asked Ottawa to join the Nishga in their lawsuit, the Canadian government declined. The true colours of the federal authorities emerged in an August 1969 statement by Prime Minister Pierre Trudeau:

> But aboriginal rights, this really means saying, "We were here before you. You came and you took the land from us and perhaps you cheated us by giving us some worthless things in return for vast expanses of land and we want to reopen this question. We want you to preserve our aboriginal rights and to restore them to us." And our answer . . . our answer is "No." If we think of restoring aboriginal rights to the Indians, well what about the French who were defeated at the Plains of Abraham? Shouldn't we restore rights to them? And what about the Acadians who were deported — shouldn't we compensate for this? And what about the other Canadians, the immigrants? What about the Japanese Canadians who were so badly treated at the end or during the last war? What can we do to redeem the past? I can only say as President Kennedy said when he was asked about what he would do to compensate for the injustices that the Negroes had received in American society. We will be just in our time. This is all we can do. We must be just today.

The Nishga action was begun on 27 September 1967. In their statement of claim, they asked the Supreme Court of British Columbia to issue "a declaration that the aboriginal title (also known as Indian title) of the Plaintiffs to their ancient tribal territory has never been lawfully extinguished." The Nishga claimed that they had kept the right to possess, use, and occupy their tribal territory by virtue of the 1763 royal proclamation or, if not, by Imperial legislation, since "no part of the said territory was ever ceded to or purchased by Great Britain or the United Kingdom and no part of the said territory was ever ceded to or purchased by the Colony of British Columbia." The action was brought against the province of British Columbia, whose land legislation, the Nishga argued, was invalid: "The Plaintiffs say that the Land Act and other statutes of the province of British Columbia do not apply to the lands comprising the tribal territory of the Nishga tribe so as to confer any title or interest in the said lands unencumbered by the aboriginal title of the Nishga tribe." The provincial government followed with its statement of defence on 23 January 1968. Not surprisingly, it revolved around the traditional position that "the Indian title of the Plaintiff (if any) has long since been extinguished by original discovery and/or by valid legislation of the Colony of British Columbia and the Province of British Columbia."

The "Calder case" went to trial in April 1969. Frank Calder as president of the Nishga Tribal Council and some of the other plaintiffs, a number of Nishga chiefs representing all four bands of the Nass Valley, were the first witnesses heard. Calder's testimony was very similar to statements made by the other leaders. Berger first asked his client to confirm that he was a member of the Nishga of Nass Bay, the area where his forefathers had also lived.

Q — Can you tell his lordship, Mr. Calder, whether all of the Indians who live in the four communities on the Naas River are members of the Nishga tribe?

A — Yes, they are members of the Nishga Tribe . . .

Q — What language do the members of the Nishga tribe speak?

A — They speak Nishga, known as Nishga today.

Q — Is that language related to any other languages that are spoken on the north Pacific coast?

A — It is not the exact . . . our neighbouring two tribes, we more or less understand each other, but Nishga itself is in the Naas River, and there is no other neighbouring tribe that has that language.

Q — What are the names of the two neighbouring tribes who have a limited understanding of your language?

A — Gitksan and Tsimshian.

Q — Do you regard yourself as a member of the Nishga tribe?

A — Yes, I do.

Q — Do you know if the Indian people who are members of the four Indian bands on the Naas River regard themselves as members of the Nishga tribe?

A — Yes, they do.

Q — Apart from their language, do they share anything else in common?

A — Besides the language, they share our whole way of life . . .

Q — Now, Mr. Calder, I am showing you exhibit 2, which is a map Mr. Brown [the province's lawyer] and I have agreed upon. Does the territory outlined in the map constitute the ancient territory of the Nishga people?

A — Yes, it does . . .

Q — Have the Nishga people ever signed any document or treaty surrendering their aboriginal title to the territory outlined in the map, exhibit 2?

A — The Nishgas have not signed any treaty or any document that would indicate extinguishment of the title.

Q — Can you tell his lordship whether the Nishgas today make use of the lands and waters outlined in the map, exhibit 2?

A — Put it this way, in answer to your question, from time immemorial the Nishgas have used the Naas River and all its tributaries within the boundaries so submitted, the lands in Observatory Inlet, the lands in Portland Canal, and part of Portland Inlet. We still hunt within those lands and fish in the waters, streams, and rivers, we still do, as in time past, have our campsites in these areas and we go there periodically, seasonally, according to the game and the fishing season, and we still maintain these sites and as far as we know, they have been there as far back as we can remember.

We still roam these territories, we still pitch our homes there whenever it is required according to our livelihood, and we use the land as in time past, we bury our dead within the territory so defined and we still exercise the privilege of free men within the territory so defined.

The main non-Nishga witnesses were two experts: William Ireland, archivist of the province of British Columbia, and Professor Wilson Duff, one of the foremost authorities on Native history. Ireland produced an impressive list of documents, maps, censuses, and studies proving that the Nishga had been the occupants of the area for as long as records had existed. The defence chose not to challenge this point. However, Ireland's testimony turned out to strengthen the government case on another issue — the date of British sovereignty over the area and hence the applicability of the famous royal proclamation to the Nass Valley. The records revealed great uncertainty as to the actual date when the region ceased to be "terra incognita," unknown territory.

Duff gave the court a brilliant exposition on the Nishga relation to the land.

Berger — Who has, since time immemorial, inhabited the area delineated on the map?

Duff — The Nishga Indians.

Q — Can you tell the court what position the Indians in the areas adjacent to that delineated on the map took regarding the occupancy of the Nishga tribe of that area?

A — All of the surrounding tribes knew the Nishga as the homogeneous group of Indians occupying the area delineated on the map. They knew of them collectively under the term Nishga. They knew that they spoke their own dialect, that they occupied and were owners of that territory and they respected these tribal boundaries of the territory.

The anthropologist was shown a map of the reserves as delineated by the McKenna-McBride Commission.

Q — Now, are you able to tell the court whether the Nishga tribe
made use of the land and the waters delineated on the map
beyond the limits of the reserve that appear on this map in the
McKenna-McBride report?

A — Yes.

Q — Is there any significance to the location of the reserves on
the Portland Canal and Observatory Inlet and the Nass River?

A — Yes, I think I can say that in many cases these small
reserves were located, for example, on the Portland Canal at the
mouth of the tributary stream, at the mouth of a valley. The
reserve is a small piece of land at the mouth of the stream which,
to a degree, protects the Indian fishing rights to the stream.

Q — Now, prior to the establishment of these reserves, what use
would the Indian people have made of the areas which flow into
the mouths of the streams and rivers?

A — The general pattern in these cases would be that the ownership of the mouth of the stream and the seasonal villages, or
habitations that were built there, signify the ownership and use of
the entire valley. It would be used as a fishing site itself and a
fishing site on the river, but in addition to that, the people who
made use of this area would have the right to go up the valley for
berry picking up on the slopes, for hunting and trapping in the
valley and up the forest slopes, usually for the hunting of mountain goats. In other words, they made use, more or less intensive
use of the entire valley rather than just the point at the mouth of
the stream . . .

Q — Can you tell his lordship the extent of the use to which the
Nishgas have put the lands and waters in the area delineated on
exhibit 2 [the claim area] and how intensive that use was?

A — This could be quite a long statement.

Q — Well, I think we can live with it.

A — And much of it has already been said. However, the territories in general were recognized by the people themselves and by other tribes as the territory of the Nishga tribe. Certain of these territories were used in common for certain purposes, for example, obtaining of logs and timber for houses, and canoes, totem poles, and the other parts of the culture that were made of wood, like the dishes and the boxes and masks, and a great variety of other things, and the obtainment of bark, which was made into forms of cloth and mats and ceremonial gear. These would tend to be used in common.

Other areas weren't tribal territories, would be allotted or owned by family groups of the tribe and these would be used, different parts, with different degrees of intensity. For example, the beaches where the shellfish were gathered would be intensively used. The salmon streams would be most intensively used, sometimes at different times of the year, because different kinds of salmon can run at different times of the year.

The lower parts of the valley where hunting and trapping were done would be intensively used, not just for food and the hides and skins and bone and horn material that was used by the Indian culture, but for furs of different kinds of large and small animals which were either used by the Indians or traded by them.

These people were great traders and they exploited their territories to a great degree for materials to trade to other Indians and later to the white man.

The farther slopes up the valleys, many of them would be good mountain-goat hunting areas. This was an important animal for hunting. Other slopes would be good places for trapping of marmots, the marmot being equally important, and there are a great number of lesser resources, things like minerals of certain kinds for tools and lichen and mosses of certain kinds that were made into dyes. It becomes a very long list.

Q — Go ahead.

A — Now, in addition to this, the waterways were used for the hunting of sea animals as well as fishing of different kinds. They were used also as highways, routes of travel for trade amongst themselves and for their annual migration from winter to summer villages, and a great variety of minor resources from water, like shellfish of different kinds, fish eggs, herring eggs. . . . There is a great list of such minor resources in addition.

Q — To what extent would the use and exploitation of the resources of the Nishga territory have extended in terms of that territory? Would it have extended only through a limited part of the territory or through the whole territory?

A — To a greater or lesser degree of intensity it would extend through the whole territory except for the most barren and inaccessible parts, which were not used or wanted by anyone. But the ownership of an entire drainage basin marked out by the mountain peaks would be recognized as resting within one or other groups of Nishga Indians and these boundaries, this ownership would be respected by others.

Q — Now, can you make any comparison between the area that is represented by the Indian Reserves in the map, in the third volume of the McKenna-McBride Report; can you make any comparison between that area represented by those reserves and the area of the whole Nishga territory that was used and exploited by the Nishgas before their confinement to reserves?

Q — Well, I think the comparison is simply here, and these are several tiny plots of land, whereas on the map the entire tract was used for some purpose or other with some greater or lesser degree of intensity.

Under cross-examination by the province's lawyer, Duff explained that, contrary to an assumption common among white people, the coastal tribes and the Nishga had always had a very precise notion of property. Ownership was documented in their own very different way, through kinship groups and their chiefs, but it was nonetheless a concept widely recognized and understood.

It took the Supreme Court of British Columbia a month to reject the Nishga claim. Mr. Justice Gould ruled that the Nass Valley had been at the time of the royal proclamation "terra incognita," but he added that this fact did not dispose of the Native claim. Did the Nishga have aboriginal rights at the time of contact, and what was the exact meaning of the phrase "aborignal title"? The judge decided to break no new legal ground on the question, since he agreed with the main point put forward by the defence: whatever rights the Nishga might have enjoyed in the past had been superseded by the white man's law.

I am of the view that between November 19, 1866, and May 16, 1871, during which time there can be no doubt that the sole sovereignty over the area of British Columbia as we now know it flowed from the Crown Imperial, such rights, if any, as the Nishgas may have had, were firmly and totally extinguished by overt acts of the Crown Imperial by way of proclamation, ordinance, and proclaimed statute. This entails the examination of a series of legislative events spanning in time from December 2, 1858, to June 1, 1870, thirteen in all . . .

All thirteen reveal a unity of intention to exercise, and the legislative exercising, of absolute sovereignty over all the lands of British Columbia, a sovereignty inconsistent with any conflicting interest, including one as to "aboriginal title, otherwise known as the Indian title," to quote the statement of claim.

The Nishga quickly filed an appeal, but in a unanimous decision of May 1970 the appeal court of British Columbia upheld the Gould ruling. The B.C. court had rejected the Nishga claim on the sole strength of the stated supremacy of colonial and provincial laws over Indian rights. The Court of Appeal went further and offered an opinion on Native title at the time of contact. Chief Justice H.W. Davey ruled that the early Nishga were a "primitive people" lacking the political and social sophistication that, in his eyes, were necessary to justify official recognition by the Crown.

In spite of the commendation by Mr. Duff, a well-known anthropologist, of the native culture of the Indians on the mainland of British Columbia, they were undoubtedly at the time of settlement a very primitive people with few of the institutions of civilized society, and none at all of our notions of private property. I am not overlooking Mr. Duff's evidence that the boundaries of the Nishga territory were well known to the tribes and to their neighbours, and respected by all. These were territorial, not proprietary, boundaries, and had no connection with notions of ownership of particular parcels of land. Also Mr. Duff said that on occasion a chief would earmark a particular piece of property for the exclusive use of a particular family, but I see no evidence that this practice was general; even if it was, it would only support claims of the particular occupant, and not claims to the communal use by the whole tribe over all its tribal territory.

Following general practice in judicial rulings, the appeal court did not concern itself with the moral validity of Native grievances. Its role was to interpret the law, not to decide whether the law was just. For J.A. Tysoe, another member of the appeal panel, it was up to the politicians, not the justice system, to settle the Native title issue:

> It is my opinion that the matter of the possession of Indian title by the Nishga Indians and of any rights thereunder and the claim of the appellants in this action is for government, and not for the courts of British Columbia. I think it is clear from the cases I have set out supra that whatever rights the Nishga Indians may think they have under Indian title are not enforceable in the courts as they have not been recognized and incorporated in the municipal law. I think it necessarily follows from those cases that this court is without authority to pass upon the question whether these appellants possess Indian title.

In the interval, the Nishga case had attracted some considerable interest from Native leaders thinking of promoting their own claims. In the spring of 1969, the federal government had agreed, after a meeting with Indian representatives from all corners of the country, to create a national committee responsible for reviewing the question of treaties and land claims. This was also the time of a proposal from Prime Minister Trudeau for repeal of the Indian Act. This solution, which would have abolished separate legal status for Native people, was applauded by all the political parties, but rejected almost unanimously by spokesmen for the Natives themselves. Frank Calder was one of the few Native figures to endorse Trudeau's suggestion, but in fact his overall position differed greatly from the federal plan. His approval of repeal was conditional on acceptance of the same land claims the prime minister had specifically rejected. Frank Calder diverged from the rest of the Native movement on a matter of strategy, but not on the final goal. He too was fighting against assimilation — the idea behind abolishing the Indian Act — and for recognition of his nation's territorial rights.

The Nishga failure on appeal led to further dissension. The National Indian Brotherhood, an organization created in 1969, called for a pause in Frank Calder's action while Native leaders held talks with the federal government. Its fear was that a Nishga defeat in the Supreme Court of Canada would close the door definitively on all Native land claims in the country. The Nishga, however, refused to halt their proceedings, and laid their case before the federal judges in November 1971. In the fourteen months it took them to reach a verdict, the Native lands issue received wide publicity in Canada.

In Quebec, six thousand James Bay Cree, who were threatened by massive flooding of their homeland by a $14-billion hydro-electric project, sued the provincial government in the fall of 1972. In the Yukon and the Northwest Territories, another megaproject, a pipeline to run from the Mackenzie Delta to southern Canadian centres, also endangered traditional Native ways of life and generated more controversy.

It was in this climate of mounting Native unrest and public awareness that the Supreme Court of Canada rendered its verdict on the Nishga case. The January 1973 ruling turned out to contain a major surprise: the federal judges had not been able to agree among themselves. Three judges had ruled in favour of the claim, three had rejected it, and the seventh had refused to rule on a technicality. According to this seventh judge, Mr. Justice Pigeon, the Nishga could not sue the province without a "fiat," an authorization from Victoria itself: "I would point out that in the United States, claims in respect of the taking of lands outside of reserves and not covered by any treaty were not held justiciable until legislative provisions had removed the obstacle created by the doctrine of immunity. In Canada, immunity from suit has been removed by legislation at the federal level and in most provinces. However, this has not yet been done in British Columbia." One Nishga among many, Chief Rod Robinson, has found this logic more than a little strange: "One judge ruled on a technicality that we had not obtained a fiat from the provincial government. Put it in simple language: if someone stole your property, you had to get that person's permission, the robber that stole your property, to even go to court and sue him. That is exactly what it means."

Technically, as Thomas Berger has commented, the Nishga had lost four to three. Yet for the first time, the highest court in the land had recognized, through the opinion of six judges, that the concept of aboriginal title was not a mere chimera; that it had existed at least up to the time of contact. The six judges split over the present state of Native rights to the land, not their existence. Mr. Justice Judson, with two of his colleagues, sided with Judge Gould of the British Columbia court in asserting that colonial land legislation had erased any previous Indian rights: "The sovereign authority elected to exercise complete dominion over the lands in question, adverse to any right of occupancy which the Nishga might have had, when, by legislation, it opened up such lands for settlement, subject to the reserves of land set aside for Indian occupation." Even in rejecting the Nishga claim, however, Judson acknowledged the existence of an aboriginal title common to all Native peoples prior to colonization: "The fact is that when the settlers came the Indians were there, organized in societies and occupying the land as their forefathers had done for centuries. This is what Indian title means."

And an equal number of judges held that this Native title had not been extinguished in the Nishga's case. In expressing the minority opinion of his colleagues, Mr. Justice Hall pointed to a major flaw in the reasoning of those who denied the existence of such rights: "In enumerating the indicia of ownership, the trial judge overlooked that possession is of itself proof of ownership. Prima facie, therefore, the Nishgas are the owners of the lands that have been in their possession from time immemorial and, therefore the burden of establishing that their right has been extinguished rests squarely on the respondent." Furthermore,

Surely the Canadian treaties, made with much solemnity on behalf of the Crown, were intended to extinguish the Indian title. What other purpose did they serve? If they were not intended to extinguish the Indian right, they were a gross fraud and that is not to be assumed . . . If there was no Indian title extant in B.C. in 1899, why was the treaty (n.8, in the northeast of the province) negotiated and ratified?

Hall had harsh words for his junior colleague in the British Columbia appeal court:

Chief Justice Davey in the judgement under appeal, with all the historical research and material available since 1823 and notwithstanding the evidence in the record which Gould J. found was given "with total integrity" said of the Indians of the mainland of British Columbia: ". . . they were undoubtedly at the time of settlement a very primitive people with few of the institutions of civilized society, and none at all of our notions of private property."

In so saying this in 1970, he was assessing the Indian culture of

1858 by the same standards that the Europeans applied to the Indians of North America two or more centuries before.

The impasse seemed to be total. The court of last resort in the Canadian system had failed to produce a clear opinion on the vital question of Nishga rights to the land. What this meant, in effect, was that the judges had thrown the ball back to the politicians. And curiously enough, the Liberal government did not duck this time. Prime Minister Trudeau met with Frank Calder, and on 8 August 1973, Indian affairs minister Jean Chrétien announced a complete about-face on the land claims issue. Negotiations would be opened with all groups which had never signed treaties and were still using their traditional territories. The minister was careful, however, not to promise any land concessions, settling for a vague formula that stated his willingness "to deal with claims related to the loss of traditional use and occupancy of lands where Native title has never been extinguished by treaty or superseded by law."

What was the reason for this abrupt change in federal policy? In refusing to rule on aboriginal rights, the Supreme Court of Canada had imposed no obligation on the Trudeau government to deal with the issue. Ottawa could have reverted to its traditional attitude of simply ignoring the problem. What prompted the federal change of heart at this point was the fact that, quite apart from the deadlock between the Nishga and British Columbia, the land-claim question was mushrooming into a major political problem right across Canada. The Inuit of the Arctic, the Dene of the Northwest Territories, the Yukon Indians, and the Cree of Quebec were all adamant that the big development projects planned for their regions had to stop. Their impending lawsuits thus threatened billions of dollars of corporate investment.

The first real emergency came when a Quebec Superior Court judge, Mr. Justice Malouf, was about to grant the Cree an interlocutory injunction against the James Bay Development Corporation. By the time the order to halt construction came in November 1973, Ottawa and Quebec City had already decided to try to negotiate a settlement. The injunction's effects were quickly nullified by subsequent legal moves, but both governments were anxious to avoid further delays on the multi-billion-dollar project. Even before the conclusion of actions, the ten thousand Cree and Inuit of northern Quebec in November

1974 signed a treaty paving the way for corporate development in their traditional homelands.

The Cree and the Inuit were granted $225 million payable over twenty years, plus many special benefits in the fields of education, health, trapping, and so on, to be enshrined in various pieces of provincial legislation. They received 13 590 square kilometres of reserve land and as well as fishing, hunting, and trapping rights over a territory of 155 340 square kilometres subject to further development plans by the province. In exchange, the Quebec Cree and Inuit renounced for ever their rights to 1 035 600 square kilometres of northern Quebec — an area as large as Britain, France, and West Germany together — including the mineral resources of this country. Now a minority in their own land, they were pushed out to the fringes of their old kingdoms. As Hugh and Karmel McCullum have commented in *This Land is not for Sale,* "The Indians could keep the beaver, but the whites would keep the hydro, zinc, iron and timber. Some bargain."

The James Bay agreement was immediately described as a sell-out by most Native groups. It should nevertheless be said in defence of the Cree and the Inuit that their negotiators had been cornered in an impossible situation. The legal recourses available in the white man's system had resulted in a mockery of justice. Work at the construction site had not been stopped by the litigation except for a brief one-week interval in November 1973 before Judge Malouf's injunction was thrown into limbo by the appeal process. One year later, the appeal court finally overturned the injunction, six days after the signing of the agreement. Facing the possibility of a court battle lasting several years and a final ruling as ambiguous as the one delivered a few months earlier in the Nishga case, the northern Quebec Natives capitulated and signed the best agreement they thought they could get in the circumstances. The James Bay agreement became the prototype of what Natives did not want to happen again.

In British Columbia, meanwhile, Frank Calder was approaching the apex of his political career. In September 1972, the New Democratic Party had seized power from Social Credit in Victoria. The new premier, David Barrett, made the Nishga leader minister without portfolio responsible for Indian Affairs. Unfortunately, Calder's term in office turned out to be an unhappy one. Immersed in other reforms, the NDP lacked the determination to change the province's traditional stance on Native claims. And there were many Native leaders who had still not forgiven Calder for his 1969 stand in favour of abolishing the Indian Act; the local branch of the National Indian Brotherhood, the Union of B.C. Indian Chiefs, was particularly critical of the minister. Within government circles, many New Democrats also took a dim view of his special relationship with the federal Liberals.

Frank Calder stretched the political game to its limits, lobbying Ottawa directly to begin negotiation on the land claims at the same time that he faced increasing isolation within the NDP cabinet and the British Columbia Native movement. The contradiction between the man as a minister and as Native leader ended in personal tragedy. On 31 July 1973, Premier Barrett fired his minister without portfolio after an incident, an evening ride with a woman charged with impaired driving, for which Calder had not provided an explanation that satisfied his leader. The split from the NDP became a permanent one; in the next election, Calder ran for Social Credit, winning to serve one last term from 1975 to 1979. In November 1974, he had been replaced as president of the Nishga Tribal Council by James Gosnell from the New Aiyansh reserve. A new generation was coming to power to deal with the issue of land negotiations.

The new era was opened by a "Nishga Declaration" adopted at the 1975 Greenville convention. In it, the Nishga explained how they saw their relationship to the rest of Canadian society. They considered themselves as "citizens-plus," endowed with extra rights because of their ancestry. One of these rights was "self-determination":

> If Canadian society and Nishga society of which it is a part, is to be truly free, we as a distinct people and as citizens, must be allowed to face the difficulties and find the answers, answers that can only be found by determining our own social, economic, and political participation in Canadian life. Governments, both federal and provincial, must be persuaded that Nishga self-determination is the path that will lead to a fuller and richer life for Nishga people and all Canadians.

Frank Calder's switch to the Social Credit Party produced some visible results. In 1976 the provincial government created a new school district in the region of the Nass Valley. With a high school at New Aiyansh, the Nishga acquired an appreciable degree of control over their educational system. The curriculum was dictated by Victoria, but the Nishga children now had an opportunity to receive some instruction in their own language.

On 12 January 1976, the Nishga Tribal Council formally opened negotiations with representatives of the federal and provincial governments in a ceremony at New Aiyansh. The federal Minister of Indian Affairs, Judd Buchanan, spoke with great solemnity: "I intend to see your grievance settled. The patience of the great river from which you draw your strength will be rewarded." The Liberals, it should be noted, were in a minority situation in Ottawa until 1974; they needed the Nishga to keep control of the federal riding of Skeena. The provincial representative, too, had a political debt to pay; the Social Credit Party had just won at the polls and labour minister Allan Williams produced an amazing statement for the occasion, the closest the province of British Columbia has ever come to recognizing the necessity of land claim settlements: "The letter of invitation asking for us to be represented as the third party in the land settlement negotiations, and the fact that I am personally in attendance here today is to be regarded as an expression of the wish of the Government of British Columbia to acknowledge and accept its rightful place as full and necessary participant in these discussions — discussions which, I might say, have for too long been deferred."

Williams's commitment proved to be nothing more than post-electoral posturing. The exchange of official negotiating stands took three years, but when British Columbia made its answer known on 10 January 1978, the Nishga had to face a painful reality: the provincial government had not departed from its traditional attitude. In its position paper, British Columbia blamed Ottawa for the resurgence of the Indian question: "In recent years it appears that federal policy respecting native claims of aboriginal title has evolved from a positive 'no' to an equivocal 'maybe.'" The province reiterated its refusal to negotiate the land question.

> The Provincial Government does not recognize the existence of an unextinguished aboriginal title to lands in the Province, nor does it recognize claims relating to aboriginal title which give rise to other interest in lands based on traditional use and occupancy of land.

The position of the Province is that if any aboriginal title or interest may once have existed, that title or interest was extinguished prior to the union of British Columbia with Canada in 1871.

The Canadian position, also published on 10 January 1978, seemed on the surface to be more favourable to the Nishga. In contrast with the province's attitude, Ottawa held no misgivings about the negotiation process and was ready to deal with any points the Natives raised. The language of the federal document was phrased positively, as in its commitment "to participate in the protection and preservation of the Nishga culture." However, the stated goals of the government of Canada were a major source of disappointment for the Nishga:

> The federal government, however, while agreeing to negotiate with many claimants and recognizing their desire to share in the development and benefits of the areas in which they live, has made it clear that there is no question about the overriding sovereignty of the Crown in all areas of Canada, and that native land claims settlements must take into account the interest of all residents in the area concerned as well as the interests of Canadians as a whole. The settlement of the claim requires that an acceptable balance be reached between the interests of the Nishga people and the interests of the public at large. Social and political realities cannot be ignored in seeking a settlement. At the same time, the settlement cannot ignore the increasingly intensive utilization of land and natural resources that has developed in the Nass region. The development of a more intensive land and primary resource economy in Canada since the colonial period has been and remains the foundation of Canada's prosperity.

As in the James Bay precedent, there was no question of giving the Nishga control over natural resources. For the federal government, the main reason for the talks was to obtain a surrender of the Native's property title in order to make way for "a more intensive land and primary resource economy." In spite of its liberal coating, the policy of Canada was in line with the historical goals of colonization. From Ottawa's perspective, the negotiators were meeting to discuss, not the theft of the land, but the price of Native surrender. As a consequence, the federal government simply stated that it was "prepared to negotiate specific benefits for the Nishga people because of their traditional use of lands and resources in the Nass Valley, and to have such benefits confirmed in the settlement and implementing legislation."

The Indians had a more global approach to the negotiation process. Their position had already been stated in the "Nishga Declaration" of January 1976: "What we seek is the right to survive as a people and a culture. This, we believe, can only be accomplished through free, open-minded, and just negotiations with the provincial and federal authorities, negotiations that are based on the understanding that self-determination is the 'answer' that the government seeks to the 'difficulties' as they apply to the Nishga people." By using the term "self-determination," the Nishga were stressing the fact that their claim was not a question of "benefits," but a question of power. This became clearer in a 27 April 1976 position paper on the tribal council's negotiating objectives: "The Tribal Council wish to negotiate with the two levels of government towards the acquisition of self-government for the Nishga people in Naas Valley. It is abundantly clear that to accomplish this, there will have to be certain statutory amendments to the legislation at both levels of government and, in particular, the federal Indian Act."

The difference between the Indians and both governments was a major one: "The Nishgas have no interest in selling their land in exchange for extinguishment of title. This definitive statement clearly means that unlike the James Bay situation, the Nishgas wish to maintain their ownership of the land (or 'aboriginal title') even after the negotiations with the two levels of government are completed." They saw this request as a necessary condition for local control over the economic development of their region: "The Nishgas wish their total land claimed as their domain, and they wish complete unrestricted rights to hunt and fish on their land without government intervention." The Nishga did not systematically oppose any development project; they wanted to have the final say in negotiations between governments, private interests, and themselves. Their emphasis on local control over decisions which affected their lives clashed with the interests of the real powers behind the Canadian government. As was to become apparent, the reason for Ottawa's convoluted stance was to allow the opening of Native land to private companies. Corporate power was not going to wait for the conclusion of the government's pretended efforts at negotiation before moving into the act.

CANADIAN APARTHEID

The history of the Indian people for the last century has been the history of the impingement of white civilization upon the Indian: the Indian was virtually powerless to resist the white civilization; the white community of B.C. adopted a policy of apartheid. This, of course, has already been done in eastern Canada and on the Prairies, but the apartheid policy adopted in B.C. was of a particularly cruel and degrading kind. They began by taking the Indians' land without any surrender and without their consent. Then they herded the Indian people on to Indian reserves. This was nothing more nor less than apartheid, and that is what it still is today.

Thomas Berger, 1 November 1966

Apartheid is a bad word. It describes a system of oppression by which society is compartmentalized on racial grounds, and a segment of the population — in the South African original model, the majority — deliberately set apart, geographically, legally, economically, so that it becomes for most purposes invisible in its reality. Is it fair to use such a word for the situation of the indigenous peoples of Canada as the lawyer for the Nishga did in 1966? Is a parallel between the two systems too far-fetched?

When governments decided to enclose their Native populations inside reserves, they faced a delicate problem: they had to provide legal definitions of who was a Native and who was not. The answer to this question is at the base of the system codified in the Indian Act, a system the main elements of which have remained virtually constant for more than a century.

Who is an Indian? The answer, for a Nishga like Harry Nyce, is quite simple. "A Nishga is always a Nishga when he is born. Only a Nishga mother would know who her family is, and no one has any jurisdiction to make any other claim. Should a Nishga mother, a Nishga woman, adopt a person, it's only by adoption that the child becomes a Nishga. But a born Nishga belongs to the Nishga tribe as identified by the mother." The Nishga, like any other human group, know their own. Since the imposition of the reserve system, however, their views have been in direct conflict with the laws of Canada, where, under the Indian Act, a Nishga is simply "a person who pursuant to this Act is registered as an Indian or is entitled to be registered as an Indian."

Who is an Indian? To ask the question in legal terms is in itself discriminatory. One would not dream of enshrining in a law a definition of the Québécois, the English Canadian, or the New York Jew. People do not need legislation to know their origin or place on this earth. They know who they are, period. In Canada, however, the lawgiver has not shied away from the murky half-truths of racial definition. For him, an Indian is a person registered on an "Indian Register." In the federal Department of Indian Affairs, there is a civil servant called "the Registrar" whose task is to keep a record of certain people — a racial record — and whose decisions are, by law, "final and conclusive."

The Nishga, like any other Native group, live a painful contradiction. Many members of their society, often prominent members, are denied their "indianness" and remain forever, in the eyes of the authorities, outsiders trespassing on reserve land. Harry Nyce has described the situation:

We have first cousins. In Canyon City, the Wolf tribe is the head of the Canyon City area. And the next in line in the Wolf tribe who is now in power, the end of the line is Peter Squires. But he is half-breed, half Nishga, half white. And from there, he is refused housing, he is refused any privilege like any other person or Indian person as identified in the Indian Act. And therefore, there is a conflict. Peter by right, as a Nishga, because his mother is a Nishga, should be able to be helped in housing or in other aspects of family life within the context of Nishga law.

This denial of native realities is a major disfigurement in the Canadian statute book. The act systematically ignores any concept of law or social organization the Natives might have developed on their own. Nishga, for instance, transmit property, family titles, and clan privileges through the mother's line, an idea utterly foreign to the Indian Act, which imposes a Judeo-Christian patriarchy on all groups. As the law now exists, a person must have an Indian father to be considered an Indian. In cases of illegitimacy, the state allows the mother to pass her Indian status on to her child, unless someone challenges her by claiming that the father is a non-Indian. In this event, the Department of Indian Affairs has the delicate statutory obligation of investigating to establish paternity. A white woman who marries an Indian becomes, by law, "Indian," but an Indian woman wedded to a white man loses her official status. The Canadian government has recently promised to eliminate this remnant of sexism from the act, but the department will still have the right to define who an Indian is. And whatever is done now, more than a century of sexist law has already caused irreparable harm to Native societies by erasing thousands of individuals from the official register.

Until the postwar reform, the Indian Act specified that the Indian was "not a person." Barred from the polling station, from the banks, and from the bars, he was comparable in status to a minor. The restrictions played a crucial role in keeping Native people at a low stage of economic development. Nishga Harry Nyce's father, for example, "purchased a gillnet boat. He did not have financial help, collateral. He had to go the the Department of Indian Affairs to have his qualifications documented. He had to go to the fishing company to obtain their backing, and he had to have the permission of the Superintendent of Indian Affairs in the Rupert District to borrow money or to get in any kind of financial transaction."

Nowadays an Indian can borrow money by himself. But he still faces the problem of collateral. He does not have clear title to his house or his land on the reserve. Natives have tried to circumvent this difficulty, but they still face a handicap in their dealings with the banks:

Before, your house belonged to the band council, and from there, it belonged to Her Majesty, the government in effect. But there was a policy made back in the early seventies that identified specific areas. A band council would have a survey done of the reserve area where the residents live, and each plot of land where each individual lived would be marked by latitude, longitude, and all of this stuff, and the band council would then issue a band council resolution stating that such and such property belonged to the member of the band whose house sat on the particular plot. . . . We cannot use anything on the reserve as collateral, because of that restriction. . . . It puts you in a situation where, just for the purchase of a car, you'd have to work over a period of three to five years to get enough of a down payment. And then you'd have to find some other area to cover your balance. But you couldn't use your house, or you couldn't use your boat or whatever, as it is on reserve.

In the process of registering individuals, the Indian Act atomizes native societies. The Indians are grouped into "bands," units roughly corresponding to villages. The term "band" has a vaguely derogatory connotation and usually applies to loosely knit groups — a band of thieves, for example — lacking in many of the virtues of civilized society. By assembling the natives into "bands," the lawgivers have made no provision for the historical, linguistic, and political units recognized by the Natives themselves. Under the Indian Act, such nations as the Dene, the Nishga, or the Iroquois, do not exist.

And like other groups, the Nishga have not only a highly conscious nationality, but a distinctive political system as well, as Chief Rod Robinson has stressed:

We're matrilineal. I belong on my mother's side. And when my great-uncle died, he was a great chief, I was in line for that title. Therefore I had to put a potlatch. And I had to be worthy, I had to know the history of our people. I have to know the laws of our people, our culture. I have to be conversant in our own tongue, as well as English, for communications. And I have to be a peacemaker. . . . But along with that, title of the land also passes to me. A certain portion of the Nass Valley passed on to me.

A Nishga chief, as head of a "house" or "wilp," holds title to a portion of the territory and all its resources in the name of all members of his group. Under the traditional system, decisions are taken within the clan in accordance with a well-established hierarchy of duties and privileges. Every Nishga village has four clans, and each clan has a hereditary chieftain. The chieftains do not constitute an aristocracy in the European sense; their authority derives from consensus within the clan, and if individuals are found to be unworthy of their titles, others are asked to take them over. The ranks of leaders have to be recognized periodically at various meetings; in other words, the old potlatch is not dead . . .

> Potlatch is on a grand scale of the initial move where recognition of an emerging chief comes. The initial stages of feasting are called "yukw." This is where you have practised the law of the Nishga. You are being introduced into our structure, the law-making structure. That's the initial stage. And when you do that so many times, you are being tested right then. And after a while, then, you reach the grand scale, as referred to now as potlatch. In plain language, what it is, it is a giant feast. It's a feast where all the people come together and the gifts are given out from one family, like when I took over this name. It's a giant feast where all the people come together and witness the transfer of name and place.

The Indian Act ignores all traditional political structures. The European concept of "chief" as imposed by the law does not correspond to the Natives' own definition of the function, since it implies a situation in which certain men give orders and others obey with no participation at all in the decision-making process. The idea that indigenous societies are divided into "chiefs" and "braves" is a white idea. How do the Nishga live the contradiction? Harry Nyce of the Canyon City band has explained:

> I was chief-councillor of my band. I was elected because of my education background and also my experience. However, I publicly said that I was not the decision-making person. I was only elected to oversee the funds coming from the Department of Indian Affairs to our band, and then from there work with the hereditary chiefs in the band to see that various functions in the band operate smoothly according to their wishes, not mine. And also the band council as a whole has the same attitude.

With the postwar reform the federal government encouraged routine management of band affairs by band officials. Blatant paternalism, it was said, had become a thing of the past. Some bands, like the New Aiyansh band, have been granted the status of "advanced stage of development" under Section 83 of the Indian Act. This allows them to make by-laws and raise money, but every decision must still ultimately be approved by the Department of Indian Affairs and cannot run counter to official policies or regulations. One of the main reasons in favour of band autonomy is that it is less expensive for governments, a point made explicitly by the 1946 joint Senate–House of Commons committee, and one imbedded in the tenacious memories of the bureaucrats. Contemporary moves in the direction of band autonomy will not necessarily spell the end of federal control, as is indicated by a confidential document on Indian sovereignty prepared for the minister in 1979 which stressed that "the Department's strategy should be to 'sell' the tribal government proposals as a means of achieving many of the practical aims and objectives (but not accept the sovereign, self-determining rights of the sovereignty argument) while at the same time maintaining . . . the constitutional and legal status quo." In other words, let the Natives play with some activities of a quasi-municipal nature while being kept away from the real world of power.

The ultimate act of paternalism — weighing how much pocket money a child has deserved — is still at the core of the Canadian system. On the one hand, Indians are not required to pay income tax for their activities on the reserve; on the other, they are kept dependent for their collective needs on a regime of social assistance in which government determines the funds available and controls their general allocation. Nishga like Percy Tait believe that the balance sheet is not in their favour: "Most of us are gainfully employed in the logging industry and in the fishing industry. So we pay our own way. We get a grant from the government. But it is far below the amount of money that we pay into the coffers of the government through income tax." Although the tax received from the Native population might be negligible on some reserves, the revenue accrued from exploitation of Native territories is most decidedly not. The land is rich, but the people on it are poor, as Chief James Gosnell has testified.

If you look at our villages, nobody has to tell you that it is an Indian village. You can tell with your own eyes, because we live in mud. Every other community throughout Canada is all paved; towns are paved. You take a good look at any Indian village, none of them — maybe one or two I think in British Columbia — but we live in mud. We are getting tired of living in mud like pigs yet our natural resources are going out of the Nishga Valley every day, twelve months of the year, fish, minerals, timber.

Historically, the aim of the Indian Act has been to keep the Indians in check — broken remnants of forgotten nations on small patches of reserve land. At the same time, however, Canadian governments have promoted the idea that the treatment chosen for the Native was really for his own good. The system held promise of promotion for those who were truly worthy. It is known as "enfranchisement," and although it has fallen into disuse, not to mention disrepute, it is still there in the Act. Becoming officially non-Indian by departmental fiat, the new non-Indian Indian who applied would then claim a part of the band's lands and assets corresponding to his share. As Harry Nyce has described it,

> When enfranchisement back in the forties came about, certain changes were granted to individuals from the reserve, like moving outside. Many relinquished their indianness. The privilege of going to the bar, down to the local pub, was one. And there were other restrictions, like being able to move around the province, around Canada without being stopped and asked where are you from, what are you doing. It felt like a Gestapo type of questioning. Some people, in order to get away from it, felt that they had to enfranchise themselves, to get out of the Indian Act and to get away from the indianness. . . . But they are still recognized as Nishgas by blood, and because of the traditional traplines, traditional fishing areas in the valley, they hold that.

This peculiar form of legal suicide has disappeared from modern Native behaviour. The mere presence of "enfranchisement" in the present Indian Act, however, is still proof that in the eye of the legislator, Indian status is a handicap that can be overcome only by assimilation, a denial of one's nature. No Indian, no problem.

The legal weeding out of thousands from the official Indian list has been disastrous enough, but the policy of separating Native children from their parents has had even more devastating effects on the Native communities. The Act makes it an obligation to send Indian children to school. Until recently, and this is still the case for some tribes in remote areas, the department has encouraged the transfer of students between the ages of 6 and 16 to church-run residential schools, depriving them of their original cultures for the crucial formative years. As Harry Nyce has remembered:

> There is an epidemic of tuberculosis in our area, and when my parents decided to move to Prince Rupert for us to get educated in the public school system, my mother was hospitalized along with a younger brother and my older sister. So that left three of us. We were sent to residential school in Edmonton. It was a church-run school. Recently coming from the Nass, I spoke my language fluently, understood everything that was said. But arriving in Edmonton residential school, I was punished for speaking the language. Because I didn't understand what was happening, I was asking, I believe it was a cousin or another Nishga, in the room, I recognized and asked him, what's happening, or what are the rules, or what are we supposed to do, in Nishga. And I was taken out and punished for having spoken the language. . . . It was the Department of Indian Affairs' decision [to send him there]. They broke the family up so the contamination, whatever, tuberculosis, wouldn't keep up on the family. But that was the extent of their expertise, I guess. Having experienced that, I come to the realization that the policies made by the Department of Indian Affairs came with this attitude of separation, and they alienated us from our culture. . . . Most of us lost our language. I'm fortunate that I kept mine. I'm one of the stubborn ones that kept my life despite the punishment.

Nyce, a man in this thirties, was fortunate enough to keep his roots. But a century of the Indian Act has created generations of cultural misfits who cannot speak the language of their forefathers and have lost the keys to themselves, their nations' customs. The generation gap and the economic morass prevailing on most reserves place dangerous stress on Native societies. Unable to adapt to local conditions or find jobs, many young people move to big cities. Those who fail again end up swelling the ranks of the destitute of Canada's skid rows.

The damage caused to the Native social fabric is eloquently reflected in the statistics. Although status Indians represent only 2.3 per cent of the overall British Columbia population, or around 5 per cent if non-status people are included, 18 per cent of the inmates in provincial jails are Natives. Across Canada, with the percentage of Native people at 1.1 per cent, 9 per cent of federal inmates are Natives. In British Columbia, young Indians make up 35 per cent of all adolescent suicide cases, and 36.7 per cent of the children apprehended by the provincial welfare authorities are native Indians.

Having deprived Native nations of their economic means of subsistence and their moral faith in themselves, Canada can now indulge in one of her major specialties, "social concern." The apprehension of Indian children is a phenomenon that has grown up in the postwar era. To the social workers, the removal of Indian children from their families is no doubt justified in terms of the individuals' well-being. The children are relocated in white foster homes on the pretext that their parents are, from the white society's viewpoint, unfit — meaning too poor, unemployed, sick, separated, or alcoholic. For the Indians, however, the intervention of child welfare authorities is just another form of genocide. The Nishga, for their part, have maintained one of the healthier Native societies in British Columbia, not as affected as others have been by the social workers' zeal; and yet many Nishga children have been apprehended outside the Nass Valley.

In 1981, a 23-year-old Nishga woman, away from the valley since infancy, gave birth to a baby girl while she was under methadone maintenance treatment. As a result, the child came into the world with a methadone addiction. The provincial Department of Human Resources stepped in, and the mother, who had been addicted to heroin since age twelve, lost custody of her child. Her relatives in the Nass Valley decided to intervene. The baby's uncle and aunt, two Greenville residents, applied for permanent custody of the girl, arguing that their niece should be raised within her Native heritage. They also stated that the region offered enough medical facilities to look after her condition. On 4 August 1983, the B.C. Court of Appeal rejected the application. Judge A.B. Macfarlane's ruling illustrates the magnitude of the cultural gap: "The ties to the Nishga people are of importance. That is not in dispute. Education and training in the Nishga community and experience would be invaluable to D.J. The value of that, however, must be measured against the detriment of placing the child in a position which would make her vulnerable to the mother's unstable character and reputation." The family and the Greenville band are appealing to the Supreme Court of Canada. Their action is taking place in a definite context. The Nishga people try to keep track of their membership, and recognize the importance of maintaining a strong link with relatives outside the valley. There is, for instance, a chapter of the Nishga Tribal Council in the Port Edward–Prince Rupert area, where fishing and canning activities have attracted many families. Recently, the council also opened a new chapter in Vancouver, where many Nishga reside.

In spite of the systematic dismemberment of their society, many city and "non-status" Natives have managed to retain contact with their cultures of origin. Some of them, militants or artists, now play an important role in the Native renaissance. Efforts at reviving the Native world will lead nowhere, however, if the people in it are not provided with an adequate economic base. Those who have not budged, who have stayed in their homelands and refused to be recast in the Anglo-Saxon mould, have been relegated to a dead end on the reserves, minuscule, muddy territories that are Third-world enclaves in the megalopolis of capitalism.

One of the greatest dreams of Canadian politicians has always been to see the Indian disappear as a distinct group. In 1969, Liberal Prime Minister Pierre Elliott Trudeau unveiled the ultimate plan:

> So this year we came with a proposal. It's a policy paper on the Indian problem. It proposes a set of solutions. It doesn't impose them on anybody. It proposes them — not only to the Indians but to all Canadians — not only to their federal representatives but to the provincial representatives too and it says we're at the crossroads. We can go on treating the Indians as having a special status. We can go on adding bricks of discrimination around the ghetto in which they live and at the same time perhaps helping them preserve certain cultural traits and certain ancestral rights. Or we can say you're at a crossroads — the time is now to decide whether the Indians will be a race apart in Canada or whether it will be Canadians of full status.

For a prime minister who had always flattered himself as enlightened towards the nations of the Third World, the state of the Natives was a blemish on Canada's record. Taken at face value, his offer was nothing but generous; the last vestiges of official discrimination would be erased, and the indigenous peoples finally invited to join the great North American melting pot. Nonetheless, most Native organizations declined it. This is not hard to understand, since what Trudeau proposed was ultimately the disappearance of their nationalities and cultures. Given the choice between nothing, that is to say assimilation, and almost nothing, the reserve system, they opted for retention of the Indian Act in its present form, and the little protection they still had.

The problem as presented by Prime Minister Trudeau was, of course, based on false premises. The Indian Act is not the cause of discrimination: it is the legal expression of the theft of the land and resources without which Native societies have no future. The Canadian government would have solved nothing merely by abolishing the Act. The proposal would not have put an end to the Native misery; it would only have pushed them from one ghetto to another, from the reserves into the realm of moral and social decadence experienced by many of city and non-status Natives. Without an economic basis for their development, Native people would have remained what they already are — non-participants in the Canadian dream — with the additional handicap of having lost their identity. The real question, the only question, is the original and continuous despoiling of their rights and lands. The solution lies in settlement of the land claims, an objective that interests Native leaders much more keenly than endless discussion on reform of the Indian Act.

Canada is not the only country in the world where the Native people have been methodically removed from their lands to make way for immigrants and profit-making ventures. The list of such expulsions is unfortunately very long. Among the most violent cases have been the Indians of the United States, the Tasmanians of Australia, or the Amazonian Indians of Brazil. The British ancestors of the Canadians sometimes resorted to physical extermination of the Indian population. On the island of Newfoundland, the Beothuk were completely extinct by 1829, in part because of a bounty system that encouraged systematic massacre. In British Columbia, nine Vancouver Island villages were destroyed by the navy in 1864. In that same year, the Chilcotins rebelled against white encroachment. When it was learned that the settlers were dispatching a military expedition, many of these interior Natives fled into the bush and starved to death. Repression of indigenous people has spread through a great number of countries and across ideological boundaries — the South African blacks, the Ainu of Northern

Japan, the Tatars of the U.S.S.R., the Arabs of Israel, the Kanaka of French New Caledonia, the Indians of Latin America, the Lapps of Northern Scandinavia . . .

Naked violence is not the only means of oppression. Canada's answer to the Native question differs from others in its methods, not in its nature. The Indian Act and the reserve system place the country in a special category of states that share two main features: certain groups of citizens have been set apart by law on a purely genetic basis, and the original inhabitants have been removed from most of the land. Canada, Israel, and South Africa are all colonization experiments where it was decided at an early stage to eliminate the aboriginal people as nations. In each, there is racial legislation restricting the activities of certain groups. In Canada, Indians are enclosed within well-defined boundaries, in a legal category by themselves. In Israel — a state where full citizenship is based on a notion of race, Jewish ancestry — the remaining Palestinians are second-class citizens in most aspects of daily life: freedom of movement, political and professional organization, education, social services, housing, and land rights. In South Africa, society is divided into four official categories — black, white, coloured, and Asian — and the restrictions cover the same areas as in Israel.

The intensity of personal oppression varies considerably, of course, from one example to the other. But there is one feature that remains the same in all three: the native population has been herded on to reduced territories in order to make way for others. Although they are not officially called "reserves" or "reservations," the lands left to Israel's Arabs are ghettoes on an equal footing with those of the Nass. Some properties are sold, others simply confiscated; whatever the method, the areas allocated to the Arabs are constantly shrinking.

In South Africa, the white minority has seized 85 per cent of the country and the black majority is now officially foreign on most of the territory. The white regime has created puppet "republics" with absurd boundaries and names like Bophutatswana, Kwazulu, or Transkei, in the poorer parts of the country. The Tswana, the Zulu, or the Xhosa who live in the suburbs of cities like Johannesburg have suddenly lost their South African citizenship. Forming a reserve of cheap labour in delapidated townships, they have been given the status of migrant workers with no right of permanent residence in the zones set apart for the only real "republic," the white state.

Canada, a country which boasts of its progressive attitude on the international scene, is not usually associated with the racist regimes of the world. How could one compare the situation of an Indian, even on a reserve, with the fate of an Amazonian hunted like an animal from helicopters, or the plight of a black worker stuck in Soweto? After all, Indians enjoy the same civil rights as the rest of their fellow Canadians: they can move freely, settle outside reserves if they wish to do so, marry across ethnic boundaries; they can even vote.

The liberalization of oppression, and the apparent equality granted to the Indians, do not amount to a difference in nature between the Canadian reserve system and other forms of apartheid; they are simply evidence of the fact that the elimination of the native population is more advanced in North America than elsewhere. The only difference is one of numbers. Threatened by hostile African nations, unsure of their own explosive racial mix, the white South Africans have protected their minority situation by turning the whole country into a forced labour camp. In a way, the Israelis are better off: at least they are a majority within the borders of Israel. However, their fundamental problem — what to do with the original population — is compounded with each new military victory.

In North America, the balance of power clearly favours one side. The Natives lost a long time ago; drastic measures are no longer needed. South Africa and Israel still need naked violence to contain their native populations. In Canada, however, the system becomes softer as it gets closer to extinguishing the original nationalities. Today's objectives are to protect the continuous plunder of the country's resources and enclose those who still resist in a legal and territorial ghetto from which they are helpless to interfere. Canadian apartheid can afford to be understanding, concerned, and open to reform, because it has almost succeeded. And maybe, one day, if the governments have it their way, the original inhabitants of the land will forget that they used to be Indians.

ERA OF THE MULTINATIONALS

The story of the log supply for the Prince Rupert mill is a story of the opening up of virgin land. It began in 1948 with the granting to the company of the original Forest Management Licence No.1 (now renamed Tree Farm Licence No.1); actual logging was undertaken in 1950, in preparation for the start of mill operations the following year. The territory covered by the licence boundaries ... totals over two million acres. It lies in the watersheds of the Nass and the Skeena, two of the major rivers of British Columbia, but until ten years ago the area was all but unpopulated, with fishing and trapping as the only activities.

Columbia Cellulose Company annual report, 1960

Once upon a time there was a beautiful virgin princess whom a spell had cast into sleep in the middle of the forest for years and years and years. But one day in 1948, a prince charming who happened to survey the country found the sleeping beauty and awakened her from her millenial rest. The prince's name was Columbia Cellulose, and, when they wed, the sleeping beauty, known as Nass Valley, brought her new master a dowry of eight thousand square kilometres, equal to a third of the State of New Hampshire or a fifth of Switzerland.

From the standpoint of white power, the opening of the Nishga valley to forest industry was a fairy tale indeed. The place was "all but unpopulated," its three thousand inhabitants unworthy of serious mention with their marginal "fishing and trapping" activities. Invariably, big business tries to colour profit making with a tinge of moral necessity. In the case of Forest Management Licence No.1, the development of "virgin land" was a moral call-up for corporate power. Suddenly, the takeover of the land by O'Reilly and his accomplices seventy years before had found its justification; the land taken from the Indians had been held wisely against the happy day when someone more competent came along to "develop" it.

Nishga colonization entered a new era with large-scale exploitation of the national resources of their lands. The tree farm licence given to Columbia Cellulose, a subsidiary of the U.S.-based Celanese multinational, was like a permit to print money. Exclusive rights over an immense tract of country entitled the company to cut the timber it wanted all but free of any interference. For unlike the neighbouring American states, British Columbia had a policy of granting logging licences without competitive bidding; territories that were supposed to belong to the public domain were transformed by the stroke of a pen into private fiefs whose landlords had a virtual monopoly on employment in adjacent communities.

From 1948 to 1964, Columbia Cellulose built up a total holding of 7284 square kilometres, more than a third of it on Nishga land. The pattern of its activity was typical of colonialist enterprise. Valleys and hills were clearcut; the timber was trucked on unpaved roads to Terrace on the Skeena or else floated down to the harbour of Prince Rupert, then sawed or transformed into pulp for export to the United States, Japan, and Europe. At first, Columbia Cellulose concentrated on the areas closest to the mills and the most accessible nearby districts. In the space of a few years it had created a barren no man's land around the town of Terrace and was having to venture farther and farther afield to keep its big plant supplied. After ten years logging the forests of the Kitsumkalum Tsimshian to the north of Terrace, the multinational's subsidiary decided to enter its fiefdom of the Nass.

In 1958, the company extended a 105-kilometre unpaved road into the heart of Nishga country, linking the valley for the first time to the British Columbia highway network. The intrusion triggered many changes, especially as white workers and their families flooded in. Moving from camp to camp with the logging pattern, the newcomers were not for the most part coming to stay. Of the seven hundred the company could draw in peak periods, only sixty had settled by 1975 on private land, mostly around "Nass Camp," a site close to the reserve of New Aiyansh.

For the Nishga, the arrival of the forest company offered a new market for employment, and about three hundred of them were hired. In a 1975 study on the potential impact of a proposed railway on the area, however, sociologist Bill Horswill found that these opportunities had not radically altered the Nishga way of life.

> While a substantial number of the Nishga men from New Aiyansh, Canyon City, and Greenville communities depend upon logging today for their livelihood, an even more significant number of Nishgas still earn their living as commercial fishermen each season on the coast. In fact, the Nishgas own their own fleet of commercial fishing craft, involving a substantial capital investment and annual income for them and their families.

Unlike the Nishga whose economic life hinged on the perpetual renewal of resources, the forest industry, behind the misleading label of "tree farming," carried out what amounted to a scorched-earth policy. Once cut, the most valuable trees of the primary forest did not grow back. Reforestation did not keep pace with logging, and the original groves were replaced by dense bush of less valuable species. Col-Cel's problems were worsening: the farther loggers had to go, the greater the difficulties of finding good timber and transporting it. The proportion of pulpwood increased.

The story of Tree Farm Licence No.1 was therefore a headlong rush to ultimate desolation. In 1948, Columbia was granted an annual allowable cut of 41 000 cubic metres. In 1964 this quota was upped to over a million, and the annual cut had passed the two-million cubic-metre mark by 1970. To justify this waste, the provincial government pretended that quotas were being calculated on the basis of the eight thousand square kilometres included in T.F.L. No.1, whereas the annual cut was actually taken in the much smaller area close to the roads and the Terrace plant.

In spite of its untrammelled freedom and vast forest domain, Columbia Cellulose's performance was consistently disappointing. From 1966 on, the company lost money in every year but one, and by 1973 its deficit had climbed to $120 million. It slowly emerged from the figures that the company's management was inept; inventories of good timber had been grossly overstated, and in many areas where trees were supposed to be of good quality the workers found only over-mature logs of poor value. The unconditional nature of its tree farm licence made it possible for the company to paint an enthusiastic picture for its lenders, but the truth was that by pushing logging operations into ever more remote districts, management was simply deepening the deficit. According to sources close to the industry, a further problem was the Celanese Corporation's practice of transfer pricing — of siphoning off part of Columbia's revenues to other subsidiaries, which bought its wood products at prices set below true market value. This manoeuvre, quite common among multi-national corporations, was indicative of the level of the firm's commitment to the economy of the region.

In 1973, the match of the prince and Sleeping Beauty ended in divorce. In Victoria, the New Democrats, who had recently come to power, were caught in a classic political bind: if they did not intervene, a whole region would be put on the unemployment rolls. The acquisition of Col-Cel by the province of British Columbia was not the result of any "socialist" strategy, contrary to what the rightist opposition claimed at the time. It was not the intention of Premier David Barrett to nationalize the forest industry or launch a frontal attack on the giant multinationals that dominated the primary economic activity of British Columbia. Corporations like MacMillan-Bloedel, Crown-Zellerbach, and Rayonier were untroubled by the move. Following in the footsteps of other social democrats around the world, the Barrett government was nationalizing, not a key industrial sector, but one deficit-plagued venture.

The deal signed in June 1973 transferred Columbia's ownership to a Crown corporation, Canadian Cellulose, or Cancel. Having failed to find a private buyer for its assets, the Celanese Corporation erased a $73-million Col-Cel debt from its books and guaranteed the rest of the money still owed, $70 million, plus $14 million in bank loans. Resources Minister Bob Williams stated that the acquisition had not cost the province anything, to which the former Social Credit premier and now opposition leader W.A.C. Bennett replied: "Nothing for nothing is what it is."

When the right-wing coalition of Social Credit regained power in 1976, the new government led by W.A.C. Bennett's son William decided that even a marginal government presence in the forest industry constituted a dangerous precedent. In 1979, the Socreds denationalized Cancel in a scheme that cost thousands of private citizens their savings and the province's taxpayers their investment in a Crown enterprise. The provincial government transferred its assets, 81 per cent of Cancel's capital, to a newly created private company, the B.C. Resources Investment Corporation, which also received the shares of other resource companies acquired by the New Democrats. The distribution of five free BCRIC shares to each voter undoubtedly helped the Socreds squeak through the election of that year. Inspired by enthusiastic statements from the premier, British Columbians also paid $465 million for BCRIC shares, the largest public response of this kind in the financial history of Canada. When the smoke cleared, many amateur investors who had borrowed to buy extra shares discovered to their dismay that BCRIC was not such a good investment. Over its first four years, shares purchased for six dollars each fell to around the three-dollar mark. It would be hard to predict the future of BCRIC stock, but one thing is certain: its forestry component, now renamed B.C. Timber Ltd., will face enormous problems in a few years when the good timber has all been cut. The northern coastal environment is a fragile one. Under ideal conditions, it would take about eighty years to regenerate a forest of marketable value with the same species as in a virgin ecological system — western hemlock, fir, sitka and white spruce, red cedar, and pine. With present practices, nature will not fully recover for some four hundred years. As a facetious forester might say, timber, like oil, is a renewable resource — given enough time.

The first condition for healthy growth is the state in which the ground has been left after harvesting. In the rain forest, soil is thin and vulnerable, especially on slopes. A recent study by the B.C. Forest Service's Prince Rupert district, which includes the Nass area, indicates that careless logging practices are widespread:

The following conclusions based on selected clearcut samples and observation are applicable to soil disturbance associated with yarding in the Prince Rupert Forest District.

1) Average total soil disturbance for the various logging systems: access, tractor with arch — 89.9%, crawler tractor — 65.1%, rubber tire skidder — 59.8%, and highlead — 47.4%.

2) Mineral soil exposure: access, tractor with arch — 54.2%, crawler tractor — 43.8%; access (truck) — 30.7%, rubber tire skidder — 22.1%, and highlead — 17.0%.

3) Deep disturbance: crawler tractor — 33.8%, access, tractor with arch — 30.7%, access (truck) — 30.7% rubber tire skidder — 22.1%, and highlead — 8.8%.

Soil disturbance, erosion, insufficient or nonexistent cleaning of logged areas, lie at the root of the deforestation problem. A second crucial factor is the companies' poor record in the field of "tree farming." From 1952 to 1981, Tree Farm Licence No.1 produced 25.8 million cubic metres of logs. If one is to believe official records, this was done with the greatest care for conservation. According to the 1981 annual report submitted to the B.C. Forest Service, of the 78 541 hectares that had been denuded, only 15 134 were "not satisfactorily restocked." Allowing for fire and insect damage, an "NSR" ratio of 19 per cent is a good record.

A visit on the field, however, alters the picture radically. Official reforestation is supposed to happen in two ways: by planting new seedlings or by leaving enough small trees on the ground to ensure natural growth. Both methods require occasional thinning and elimination of the faster-growing unwanted species. If the topsoil has been damaged, if the seedlings are unhealthy, or if clumping is allowed to occur, coniferous trees do not develop and there is thus no reforestation. There is evidence that such a state of affairs exists on a large part of T.F.L. No.1.

The main timber-producing area of the Nishga country lies within two hundred kilometres of the mouth of the Nass River. In this section of the valley, Col-Cel, Cancel, and now, B.C. Timber, have logged 15 461 hectares that are supposed to be restocked. A recent survey shows that only 6 per cent of the area can actually be considered to be restocked. The bulk of the "tree farm" is in fact plagued by erosion, deadwood, clumping, and brush competition, and will not produce a harvestable forest in anybody's lifetime. The situation is particularly acute in the 11 660 hectares that were supposed to be restocked by natural process, where only 285 hectares, 2 per cent of the land, are on the road to recovery. In the "artificially" restocked section, 3801 hectares, the rate of success is still poor at 17 per cent.

The failure of the reforestation efforts is especially worrying in the bottom lands of the Nass, between the end of the lava bed, near Canyon City, and the sea. This area, which used to carry the giants of the rain forest, is now covered for the most part by a bush of minor species — red alder, cottonwood, and red osier dogwood — and there is little sign of the high-quality timber supposed to be growing back. Of the 2684 hectares logged in this section and, at least on paper, "restocked," 74 per cent of the sites, or 1972 hectares, suffer from heavy brush competition.

The Nishga people are rapidly realizing the magnitude of the catastrophe. In 1976, the tribal council presented its own plan of forestry management for the area. Its premise was that proper care of the resource could not be obtained from absentee landlords. What had been lacking through the years was the long-term commitment to the area that only the people who lived in the Nass Valley could provide. The core of the proposal was a transfer of authority from the provincial government to the Nishga nation. The council was convinced that it could rationalize the exploitation of the resource by building a network of paved roads to be financed by a levy on the timber harvest. The Nishga were aware that the valley's logging operations were supporting a vaster region. They decided to act responsibly by promising co-operation with the industry. They proposed to fix the yearly allowable cut that they would accept on their territory at 600 000 cubic metres. This was an enormous figure, but the Nishga felt that they had to alleviate the fears of the industry and guarantee the mills of the region the huge quantities of wood they required. The wisdom of suggesting such a substantial allowable cut was questioned by one industry analyst, Richard Overstall, who charged that the Nishga report was

not tackling the question of why the forest service, with the same good intentions and professional expertise available to the Nishgas, has been unable to enforce sound sustained-yield forest management in the northwest for the past thirty years. An analysis of this failure is fundamental to any efforts to reverse the highgrading and overcutting of the prime timber that will leave the Terrace-Hazelton region without an economical sawlog harvest in less than a decade.

The 1976 forestry proposal was not a satisfactory document, and the Nishga themselves eventually decided to modify their approach. After all, their experience in the field had been acquired working for the same companies that were at the root of the problem; it was no wonder that they had at first accepted the basic corporate thinking on allowable cuts. Since then, the tribal council has come to the realization that if present practices are allowed to continue, the resource base will be destroyed before the end of the century. A new forestry paper expresses stronger concern for future generations. With proper care, the resource should be renewable, and its dividends under Native management could be a definite asset for the development of the Nishga nation. Corporations can afford to cut and run; peoples cannot.

Huge as it was, the forest-products company remained a single enterprise. In the early 1970s, however, technicolour corporate and government plans for new-frontier development in the region assumed gigantic proportions. The key to the future was to be a railway link with the Yukon and possibly Alaska through Nishga territory. The vision was breathtaking: 11 million hectares of virgin forest to be opened up for logging, the Groundhog anthracite fields of the upper Nass, 200 or 300 million tonnes of undeveloped copper in the basin of the Stikine at a time when the Chilean socialists were nationalizing their mines; asbestos near the Yukon border, and beyond, farther north, the possibility of a real pipeline on rail. The time was right. Given the energy crisis and the worldwide explosion in oil prices, prospecting, drilling, and pumping had suddenly become feasible in the remotest areas. The crude oil from Prudhoe Bay on Alaska's Arctic coast would not have to pass through the complicated delivery system of a pipeline to the Pacific, then tankers to Louisiana through the Panama Canal, if only a railroad connected the fields to the continental network. The plan could also include the Mackenzie Delta natural gas from the Canadian Arctic coast, and even the oil lost under the ice pack in the Beaufort Sea. A territory of 1½ million square kilometres lay waiting; 125 000 people would be funnelled into this vast empire over the next twenty years.

The vision was grandiose and it was also very expensive. There were the roads and towns to be built, and above all, the 1600-kilometre rail link. Private enterprise was ready for new ventures in forestry, copper, coal, asbestos, and oil and gas, but there was no question of these companies embarking on such a dangerous financial proposition as a rail line; the risk here would have to be shouldered by the public sector. In 1972, a timely report from the Hedlin Menzies consulting firm surfaced in the upper reaches of the Canadian Department of Transport:

> Dramatic development for the mineral and forest wealth of northern British Columbia and the Yukon is foreseen for the 1970s and 1980s. Realization of this vast potential will depend in large part on a major expansion of the region's transportation capabilities. Building a new thousand-mile northern railway to tap these resources offers a singular opportunity for meeting these basic transportation needs and for stimulating the development of Canada's Northwest. Despite the area's extensive mineral promise and the fact that over twenty per cent of Canada's softwood timber is located in the region, the Northwest currently generates less than two per cent of Canada's mineral and forestry production. Within two decades this picture could be radically changed; growth in the region's annual timber harvest could represent ten per cent of Canada's total current forest production, while the increase in annual mineral sales from the region could amount to twelve per cent of present Canadian mineral sales.

Stated in terms of regional development, the policy floated by the transport department sounded highly positive, but the truth was that without massive subsidies and tax exemptions, without the giveaway of immense public territories and the assumption by the taxpayers of ruinous infrastructure costs, the railway project made no economic sense. If it was to become a reality, the corporate dream had to be sold to the politicians.

The first statesman to grab at the great northern dream was W.A.C. Bennett, who had been premier of British Columbia for two decades under the conservative Social Credit banner. Bennett was not afraid of visions; indeed, he had had a recent happy experience of just such a dream in the Columbia River agreement that would serve the energy requirements of the United States so eminently well. He was joyously continentalist in his approach, and wedded with resolution to the idea of his province as a reservoir of cheap natural resources.

> It was apparent [in the late sixties] that the North would become a dramatic arena of economic activity. The only possible British Columbia involvement in this modern-day gold rush was through

the railway. The United States cannot and should not depend on water as the sole link to the ever-increasing vitality of Alaska. The shipping lanes, relatively insecure in time of peace, carry a positively ominous danger in the threat of military conflict and the potential appearance of enemy ships and submarines. From a security point of view, the British Columbia Railway potential to the Americans is attractive to the point of no rebuttal. From an economic point of view, "steel on steel," rolling freight, is still the most inexpensive, secure, and convenient mode of bulk transport.

Such a stand was not surprising in a politician of the right, but it was disconcerting for some, after Bennett's 1973 electoral demise, to see the railway dream appropriated with no apparent misgivings by his social-democratic successor David Barrett. On 23 July 1973, the government of the New Democrats signed an agreement with Ottawa for the development of the Northwest, an initiative taken without involving the region's population. Its main element was the construction of a railway towards the Yukon border with a spur line along the Nass Valley. Most of the project was to be built by a provincial Crown enterprise, B.C. Railway, while Canadian National, the federal rail corporation, was put in charge of the 424-kilometre line along the Nass. This last section avoided the detour by the city of Prince George and represented a 500-kilometre shortcut in the route from the north to the Pacific coast.

Federal Liberals and provincial New Democrats cited the allurements of their plan with obvious glee: new copper, coal, and asbestos mines; the construction of two big sawmills in Nishga territory, and, eventually, a permanent link with the Yukon and Alaska. The cost of the project was estimated officially at $325 million, a figure that was obviously too low. To justify sinking public funds into the scheme, the Trudeau and Barrett governments promised benefits of $495 million in less than twenty-five years from new income for the railways and new taxes paid by industry.

The plan was not well received by the local population. The union movement was particularly critical. An ad-hoc committee, created earlier by the Kitimat-Terrace and District Labour Council and supported by the Prince Rupert unions and the B.C. Federation of Labour, organized the protest against this modern-day version of the gold rush. V.O.I.C.E. (Victims Of Industry Changing Environment) dissociated itself from the workers' "traditional friend," the New Democratic Party, while trying to articulate a democratic alternative to the scorched-earth model of development. To the Natives, the project was just as unpalatable and proved the duplicity of governments once again. The Canadian National spur line was to be built across Nishga territory and the communities planned around the new sawmills would turn the Nishga people into a minority on their own land. All this was happening just after the verdict of the Supreme Court of Canada and when the federal government was publicly stating its willingness to settle the land-claim issue through negotiation.

Superficially, Trudeau and his ministers seemed ready to enter into talks with anybody — the Inuit of the Arctic, the Cree of James Bay, the Dene of the Northwest Territories, or the Nishga of British Columbia; but behind this apparent good will and desire to atone for past offences, there had been no fundamental change in attitude. While negotiators tried to lure Natives into believing that they were at last being listened to, gigantic projects were leaving the drafting boards: hydro-electric dams near James Bay, pipelines for the Mackenzie River Valley, oil drilling in the Arctic Beaufort Sea, railways to the Yukon and Alaska. . . . The public speechmaking about settlement of Indian grievances obscured the real goal: the urgent appropriation of immense territories, still inhabited by Native groups, containing vast amounts of oil, copper, coal, timber, natural gas, uranium, molybdenum, asbestos, and other valuable substances.

In Victoria, Frank Calder had fallen out of favour with Premier Barrett and the party's right wing controlled all the economic portfolios; there was no question of dropping the Nass Valley rail project. In 1974, the Nishga Tribal Council advised Canadian National that surveyors would not be permitted on its territory as long as the land question was unresolved. At first, the federal corporation began work along the valley of the Kitsumkalum in the vicinity of Terrace, but before the Nishga installed a roadblock it announced its intention to comply. In July, a CN official said that if there was no agreement before surveyors reached Mile 35, the border of Nishga territory, the railway would inform Ottawa that it could go no farther.

The ease with which CN bowed to the will of the Nishga was suspicious. Taking the statement at face value, the press carried headlines announcing that the Nishga were preventing the project from proceeding. In fact, the decision to halt the Nass Valley rail project had already been made; the Nishga were just a convenient scapegoat for the company. Two years earlier, Canadian National and B.C. Railway had produced a secret report seriously questioning the economics of the project. A line along another route, the Kispiox Valley, would cost half as much and bring in twice as much revenue. The only reason for sticking to the Nass was political, to let Canadian Cellulose expand into the hinterland and subsidize its operation by a rail deficit.

Other criticism issued from an unexpected quarter. Canadian National had commissioned a study of the project's ecological and human impact, but the expert it hired, sociologist Bill Horswill, committed what was an unforgivable crime in the soft-spoken world of technocracy. Instead of producing the usual uncontroversial report, Horswill was highly critical of the proposed rail line. The Nishga, he stressed, had to some degree maintained an economic system that was in balance with the resources of the valley. He foresaw that construction of the railroad would bring radical change to the Native society.

Apart from the obvious disadvantages of any uncontrolled economic and population boom, like increased crime, alcohol and drug abuse, special mention should be made of some of the less tangible social costs related to forced change. For instance, the demoralizing sense of relative deprivation which the rural northern resident (Indian and non-Indian alike) begins to experience with the arrival of his affluent and more ostentatious "southern" neighbours spawns a deep-seated sense of self-doubt, inadequacy, and resentment. This is acutely felt in the face of pressures brought to bear upon the family bread-earner by way of his children's changing expectations and materialistic standards through daily competitive contact with the new majority school population. With basic decision-making increasingly in the hands of absentee, urban officials and corporate interests, the local residents are likely to undergo a growing feeling of alienation from the important decisions which affect their lives and determine their future. Similarly, in the face of rapid, unplanned, and exogenously imposed social change most people become victims of "anomie," the emotionally and morally devastating experience of losing one's traditional values and beliefs, yet without gaining a meaningful new set in exchange. It is these less tangible by-products of rapid development which usually lead to the more visible social problems of alcoholism, family breakdown, and welfare dependence.

Horswill's conclusions were not based simply on premonition but on direct observation of a process of social decay that was already well under way in Terrace itself. His report was quickly buried by CN, and the final impact study bears no resemblance to his document.

The Yukon railroad was never built. It was defeated, not by opposition from unions and Natives, but by sheer economics. The idea of a "pipeline on rail" so stoutly championed by Premier W.A.C. Bennett and his successor David Barrett had been dropped meanwhile by the business community. Instead of using a costly continental route, the oil companies had decided to pump Alaska crude by pipeline to the Pacific port of Valdez and ship it from there to market by supertanker. A plan had also been developed for bringing oil tankers right into the Beaufort Sea and running pipelines from the Mackenzie Delta and the Canadian Arctic down into the industrial heartlands of the south and east.

The opening of northwest British Columbia to the mining industry was postponed as well. The world price of copper had started to fall by 1974, and the multinational corporations had reoccupied the copper mines of Chile after the assassination of Salvador Allende, the country's socialist president. The development of the Stikine copper fields was no longer on the agenda. As for the timber resources of the Nass and the Groundhog anthracite deposits, they were not attractive enough to justify the construction of a rail line. Under state ownership, Canadian Cellulose was reorganizing its operation and making better use of wood chips from its sawmills, while the coal companies, acting for Japanese interests, were now looking into a more promising area, the vast fields available for strip-mining on the eastern slopes of the Rocky Mountains.

The politicians were the last to put the project to rest. In May 1974, NDP resources minister Bob Williams was still accusing the Nishga of "harassing" the government by fighting the rail line. In November of the following year, in the middle of a bitter election campaign, the Canadian government did Premier David Barrett a favour by signing a meaningless agreement on the sharing of construction costs. During the campaign, the Social Credit leader William Bennett Jr. attacked the railway dream as an "act of despair." The New Democrats were thrown out of office and the grand plan was heard of no more.

The post-mortem on it was written by a 1978 royal commission of inquiry which revealed that the main company supposed to build the Yukon line, B.C. Railway, had accumulated a $700-million deficit. A few years earlier, Social Crediters as well as New Democrats had been urging that the costs of the rail infrastructure needed to insure the profits of private enterprise be borne by the public; now that the corporations were no longer interested, William Bennett abandoned the dream the commission described as "a disastrous plunge into the North." The Nishga people had escaped a new invasion. But for how long?

AMAX — DOLLARS V. PEOPLE

Molybdenum is a precious commodity. Used in the manufacture of high-quality steel, this rare metal is greatly in demand by the aeronautical and armaments industries. More than half the world consumption of molybdenum is supplied by the Connecticut-registered AMAX Corporation. In the spring of 1981, AMAX of Canada Ltd., a wholly-owned subsidiary of AMAX Corporation, opened a new mine at a site named Kitsault on Nishga land. One of the technical problems encountered was the disposal of wastes. Instead of building tailings ponds, the company saved $23 million and opted for a very simple solution: a pipe, starting at the refining mill and ending fifty metres below the surface of the sea. For a year and a half, until the world recession shut the mine down temporarily, AMAX was dumping 12 000 tonnes of tailings every day into Alice Arm, a Nishga fjord. Over the twenty-six years of the mine's expected life, this would mean some 100 million tonnes of tailings. With levels of 400 grams of suspended solids per litre, the wastes discharged by the Kitsault molybdenum mine have a concentration that is 8000 times greater than the allowable limit established by the Parliament of Canada. Copper, zinc, cadmium, mercury, radium-226, uranium, arsenic — the "soup" coming out of AMAX's pipe is indeed quite thick. But it is all legal.

Theoretically, such massive pollution is forbidden by law, but Cabinet can change the rules of the game simply by passing an order-in-council. This was done in AMAX's case at the oddest time, in the middle of a federal election campaign which ended with the defeat of the Liberal government led by Pierre Trudeau. On 10 April 1979, order-in-council SOR-79-345 freed AMAX from the normal regulations. The local population was not consulted. The only notices were printed in the legal columns of two publications that are not read in the Nass Valley, the government's *Gazette of British Columbia* and the Prince Rupert daily. As for the site of the mine, it was on land confiscated decades earlier. There was no requirement in law that the Nishga be approached on the matter. They did not find out what the government had done until ten months later, in February 1980. Once again their territories had been disposed of without their consent, and a new threat, the pollution of their fishing grounds, had been added to their lives.

The story of pollution permit SOR-79-345 is a fascinating tale of interaction between the political sphere and corporate power. Most of what is known has been uncovered by the efforts of a New Democratic MP, Jim Fulton, and a journalist, Geoff Meggs of *The Fisherman*. For years now, the federal government has refused to release the full AMAX file, and important aspects of the decision process are still unexplained.

The "Metal Mining Liquid Effluent Regulations," that prohibit the unconfined disposal of solid tailings into waters frequented by fish, were approved by the Canadian government on 24 February 1977. By June of that same year, AMAX had already approached Ottawa's Environmental Protection Service to discuss a possible exemption for its planned Kitsault mine. It even appears from leaked documents that AMAX played an active role in the drafting of its own pollution permit. Between July 1978 and April 1979, there were at least fifteen instances of communication between the company's lawyer, Robert Granger, and various officials of the government from the Department of the Environment to the Privy Council. On 22 November 1978, a full six weeks before AMAX made official application for the pollution permit, Granger got a copy of the draft regulation. His law firm, Aird & Berlis, included among its partners a prominent Liberal personality and that party's national treasurer, Senator John Black Aird, who was at the time also the sole

Canadian member on the AMAX Corporation's board of direc-
tors. With his party back in office in 1980, Aird resigned his
previous functions and accepted the prestigious appointment as
lieutenant-governor of the province of Ontario.

Jim Fulton rose in the House on 27 October of that year to
charge that order-in-council SOR-79-345 was "a result of a
back-room cabinet deal between the Liberal Party and the
AMAX Corporation." In a question to the finance minister on 16
April 1981, he became more explicit: the AMAX permit had
been

> granted during the 1979 federal election, unknown to the House.
> Until September 12, 1980, John Aird was on the board of AMAX.
> On September 15, 1980, he became the lieutenant-governor of
> Ontario. His connections with the federal Liberal party are well
> known. Was there any direct or indirect communication of any
> kind between John Aird and members of cabinet or their staff
> regarding the permit of AMAX Limited at Alice Arm?

By October, the government had still not complied with Fulton's
request to produce whatever correspondence, if any, had taken
place between John Aird and ministers of the Crown. The MP
now charged that

> AMAX ... has an international reputation as a plunderer of
> resources and an outfit that pays little or no attention to environ-
> mental concerns. ... Canada is not left untouched. On 4 June
> 1980 Mr. Aird was appointed lieutenant-governor of Ontario. He
> was replaced on the AMAX board by none other than the former
> president of the United States, Gerald Ford. Aird was also the
> chief national fund raiser, or perhaps as we in the House better
> know it these days, the bagperson, for the Liberal Party. He has
> held that position for some time for the national Liberal Party. ...
> Peter Newman in volume I of *The Canadian Establishment* quoted
> Mr. Aird's views on making deals, as follows: "For instance, if
> you're in a town where there's a Royal Bank and you go and tell
> the manager you are a director of the Bank of Nova Scotia, you're
> going to be looked after."
> We know who has been looked after in the AMAX deal. Mr. Aird
> was also a member of the Permanent Joint Defence Board.
> Molybdenum, an important mineral used in the industrial arms
> race, is produced by the AMAX mine at Alice Arm.

Fulton's inference of political patronage has been regularly denied by the federal government. Lieutenant-Governor Aird has not commented on the AMAX controversy thus far but he did volunteer the following statement in a letter to the Canadian Broadcasting Corporation, parts of which were read on the 4 July 1982 edition of the radio public affairs program, "Sunday Morning":

> In the late 1970s, partners of mine in the Aird & Berlis firm undertook legal work for the AMAX group, and one of the engagements concerned the Kitsault mine. The firm was instructed to assist in obtaining a regulation under the Fisheries Act allowing the operator of the Kitsault mine to deposit tailings from the mill into Alice Arm, with the result that the Alice Arm Tailings Deposit Regulations were published in full in the *Canada Gazette* on April 25th, 1979. I did not participate in any manner in the work done by the Aird & Berlis firm relating to the Alice Arm tailings deposit regulation.

Nothing in the official reactions addresses the question of how AMAX convinced the Canadian government to disregard its own pollution laws. The decision must have been taken at a high level, and for very compelling reasons. Then fisheries minister Roméo Leblanc took the brunt of the opposition attacks, refusing steadfastly to refer the matter to an independent commission armed with powers of subpoena. It now seems from leaked documents, however, that he was not made aware of the contents of the permit before March 1979, a few weeks before final approval by Cabinet and several months after the main body of the document had been drafted. A 27 September 1978 memorandum from Dr. Cam MacLeod, head of the Fisheries Habitat Protection Branch, sheds some light on the mystery:

> I would like to emphasize that the minister will not be easily convinced to take this action. Unless there is evidence that demonstrates that unconfined marine discharge of tailings can be practised with no negative effects on existing or potential fisheries, Mr. Leblanc is unlikely to approve an exemption from requirements necessary to protect these resources. To do otherwise would be interpreted as a softening of the minister's existing policy on protection of fish habitat, a step he would be opposed to take, particularly in view of the sensitivity of the citizens of B.C. to environmental and fish habitat protection issues.

If Roméo Leblanc was unlikely to approve the exemption, then who pushed the pollution permit through the bureaucracy and on to Cabinet? At least one thing seems certain: four months before AMAX's official application, some ministers were closer to the dossier than their own fisheries colleague was. According to a report produced at the deputy-ministerial level of the Department of the Environment,

> on September 18, 1978, AMAX officials met with Mr. Len Marchand, Minister of State for the Environment, and Mrs. Iona Campagnolo, Minister of State (Fitness and Amateur Sport) who was the member for Skeena at the time. The AMAX officials wanted to determine the procedure to obtain an authorization under the Fisheries Act to deposit tailings into Alice Arm. . . . Attending the meeting were Mr. A. Born, president of Climax Molybdenum [later AMAX of Canada] and lawyers Mr. H.C Milham, Vancouver, and Mr. R.N. Granger, of Aird & Berlis, Toronto. Mr. MacLatchy attended for EPS [Environmental Protection Service] Ottawa.

Iona Campagnolo, whose constituency included Alice Arm, became president of the Liberal Party of Canada in 1982. According to journalist Geoff Meggs, the former minister is not certain that she did attend the meeting between AMAX's president Allen Born and environment minister Marchand.

> Campagnolo said she does not remember the meeting and doubts she was there. She said she remembers only one meeting she had with AMAX officials that occurred in Vancouver well before the 1978 gathering. She cannot remember who she met. "In general, they were talking about AMAX's possibilities of opening," she said: "There was no discussion of tailings at that time." She "rode herd" on the scheme, she said, because "we knew it was a controversial project." Campagnolo said she urged the AMAX officials to consult with the Nishga and win their support, but "there was a brushing aside of discussions with the Nishgas."

At this point, the trail of Liberal personalities peters out. As environment minister, Len Marchand was responsible for the drafting of the pollution permit. It is hard to imagine, however, that a junior minister would have taken it upon himself to grant such an extraordinary exemption to the law, especially when it was obvious that the permit ran counter to the stated policy of fellow minister Leblanc. Who gave the green light to the deal, and for what reasons? We still do not know.

Puzzling through the AMAX controversy, one gets the impression that the Alice Arm file was stamped with a secret seal of approval from the start. The permit was drafted quietly in close collaboration with corporate lawyers before formal application had been made. Equally disturbing is the fact that the established policy of the Department of Fisheries — "protection of fish habitat" — carried little if any weight. Leblanc, who was "unlikely to approve an exemption," was kept uninformed; moreover, it has now been established that the "review" process of AMAX's plans was a farce.

In the course of the summer and fall of 1978, the unfiled application was scrutinized by an interministerial screening committee of five scientists — a normal procedure under normal circumstances. Four of the five had serious reservations about the dumping of tailings into Alice Arm. Dr. Pat Nasmyth of the Institute of Ocean Sciences recommended against granting any permit before further studies had been carried out:

> We did not do any actual field work. We were presented with a study which had been done for AMAX, aspects of the physical oceanography, the biological impact, the chemical results of the operation of the mining area. My feeling then and now was that the information was limited in scope and was rather superficially analysed, that some of the conclusions could not be supported by the available facts.

In a 6 November 1978 memorandum, a second expert, Michael Nassichuk of the Department of Fisheries and Oceans, also opposed the project: "The discharge of tailings from the proposed mine at Alice Arm is unacceptable and should be opposed. The heavy metals associated with the tailings discharge will result in the elevation of heavy metals in sediments, algae, invertebrates, and fish within Alice Arm, possibly to levels which exceed the recommended maximum for human consumption." A third, Darcy Goyette of the Environmental Protection Service, expressed other concerns: "Tailings will spread throughout most of Alice Arm, both into the estuary of the Kitsault and Illiance River, and seaward into Hastings Arm. Deposits will likely develop outside Alice Arm." And Don E.C.

Trethewey of the Canadian Wildlife Service wrote that "it is not for us to compromise our responsibilities to the resources we have a mandate to safeguard. Therefore, I also support Mr. Nassichuk's opposition to the project."

The fifth member of the review committee was also its chairman. Rick Hoos of the Environmental Protection Service was the Vancouver contact for John MacLatchy, the Ottawa legal advisor who did most of the drafting in conjunction with AMAX's lawyer Robert Granger. Overriding his four colleagues' objections, Hoos submitted a final report in favour of the project. This prompted an angry reaction from Trethewey, who, in a letter of 11 December 1978, took a dim view of a procedure which he termed "highly irregular and completely unacceptable": "I regard any revisions or so-called 'fleshing out' after the fact . . . of the present report to be attempts to play down the importance of ecological concerns [and] justify a decision that was made on other than ecological consideration." Hoos himself, by then environmental co-ordinator for Dome Petroleum, explained his attitude in a 1982 interview with the CBC:

> The way I looked at it was, unless there was absolute proof there is some harm, there was simply no information, no proof at all to suggest that there would be a problem. If people do want to be critical of myself, it's probably because I am prepared to take a stand, to make decisions, and to not necessarily have a truckload of data if a carload of data will do the job.

Or if the right people will do the job. In the Nishga case, AMAX's approach has been heavy-handed — typified by secret lobbying, direct contact with government, ignorance of local concerns, and disregard for the Native point of view. Yet it should not be concluded from this that multinational corporations always resort to the same type of behaviour when dealing with Native lands. Depending on the circumstances, a company like AMAX can be "a good corporate citizen," actively seeking the collaboration of all concerned, or, at the other end of the spectrum, rely on sheer force. Throughout the world, AMAX has exhibited remarkable qualities of adaptability. These have emerged in four very different locations: Namibia, Australia, southern Montana, and Washington State.

First, a bit of history. AMAX's origins go back to the American Metal Company created in 1887 to export U.S. lead and copper to European markets. After the Second World War, Amco ran into a bargain on expropriated German copper mines in the territory then known as South West Africa, now South African-occupied Namibia. In 1957, it merged with Climax Molybdenum, another U.S. corporation, to become American Metal Climax; the company was renamed AMAX in 1974. Today, its activities span several continents and a wide range of mineral and energy resources — molybdenum, coal, copper, zinc, lead, tungsten, potash, and oil. The corporation is the third U.S. producer of coal and the largest producer of molybdenum in the world. By multinational standards, AMAX is a modest giant: in 1980, with annual sales of almost $3 billion, it held only 169th place among the biggest U.S. corporations. Nevertheless, its corporate connections link the company with some major financial, industrial, and political institutions in the United States. And since 1975, AMAX has been closely associated with one of the most powerful corporations in America, Standard Oil of California, which owns 21.7 per cent of its stock.

The Namibian situation is the clearest case of disregard for native concerns. There, with another U.S. corporation, Newton Mines, AMAX controls 60 per cent of Tsumeb Corporation, the country's main copper mine. Tsumeb relies for its manpower on a system known as "contract labour." Under apartheid, black tribesmen are restricted to reduced territories called "homelands" which they cannot leave without a special pass; one way to escape from endemic famine is to sign a twelve- to eighteen-month "contract" with an outside employer like Tsumeb. In their exclusively masculine compounds surrounded by walls and barbed wires, the workers are virtual slaves, unable to seek employment elsewhere without violating their "contracts" and the pass laws.

Corporations like AMAX operate in defiance of international law. In 1971, the United Nations, at the request of its Security Council, declared South Africa's occupation of Namibia to be illegal. In 1974, the general assembly of this world organization issued a decree for the protection of Namibia's natural resources, forbidding any mining activity there without U.N. authorization. AMAX and the American government have systematically ignored this decision on the pretext that the South African presence constitutes a de facto administration.

On 24 February 1974, AMAX issued a pamphlet explaining its activities in Namibia. Its basic theme was the fundamental innocence of private enterprise. The reasoning was impeccable: the company did not meddle in the domestic affairs of the territories where it operated; the South African policy of apartheid was the sole responsibility of the local authorities; as a law-abiding corporate citizen, AMAX had no alternative but to apply the regulations of its host country. The alibi was perfect. The multinational company left politics to the politicians.

The doctrine of corporate innocence would explain why, in the Nishga case, AMAX has never been held accountable for the events leading up to approval of its pollution permit. And another interesting example of interaction between this multinational and the political environment is to be found in Western Australia. There, a group of aborigines called the Yungnoras had managed to recover part of their traditional territory after the Australian government bought a 384 000-hectare ranch near the town of Noonkanbah on their behalf. The experiment was lauded as one of the rare success stories of development among aboriginal people, but the Yungnoras learned in 1979 that they were not the masters of their own land after all. The state of Western Australia had given AMAX Explorations, a wholly owned subsidiary of AMAX Corporation, the right to drill for oil right in the middle of the ranch. The chosen site was at the foot of a bluff known as Pea Hill which the aborigines revered as the domain of the Great Goanna, spirit of the Dream Time and guardian of the land, whose protection was essential to the survival of the tribe. For the authorities, the story of Great Goanna was just a laughable matter. Had they made the parallel with other religions, however, they could have seen that the desecration of Pea Hill was as serious as trying to drill for oil at the foot of the Wailing Wall, on Saint Peter's Square, or in the middle of Mecca.

In August of 1980, the government of Western Australia organized a quasi-military expedition to break the blockade of the drill site by a handful of aborigines and defuse the boycott of AMAX by the entire Australian labour movement. The authorities chartered fifty trucks, whose owners were issued false licence plates to avoid further union retaliation and driven by "scabs" who received more than $3,000 each for the 2500-kilometre journey from Perth to Noonkanbah. There was a big detachment of armed policemen to escort the convoy and an airplane to "protect" it. This operetta army easily overcame the protesters, who put up no resistance; twenty Yungnoras were arrested in front of the fence the government had installed.

The case of the Montana coal deposits followed a similar pattern of direct dealings with government, but was also significantly different in terms of the success of native resistance. It is estimated that between seven and thirteen per cent of known U.S. coal reserves are located beneath Indian reservations. In the wake of the energy crisis of the early 1970s, the American government leased 1100 square kilometres of tribal lands to private interests. The land grab was made possible by two laws, the 1920 Mineral Leasing Act and the 1938 Omnibus Tribal Leasing Act, which allowed the federal authorities to lease Indian territories in the name of the natives. AMAX was one of fifteen multinationals to benefit from the move. Its leases were in southern Montana, where five companies were to supply four major power-generating plants with coal near the town of Colstrip. The plan called for strip mining 56 per cent of the tribal territory of the three thousand Northern Cheyennes.

By 1973, many Cheyennes had realized that in addition to a massive pollution problem, their nation faced the likelihood of the irreversible destruction of its lifestyle and culture. The Northern Cheyenne Tribal Council began a court action on the grounds that there had been thirty-six violations of the contract procedure. The council also used its legal powers to designate the reservation as a "Class I Air Quality Area," a move that blocked the construction of thermal plants. After a standoff lasting some six years, the parties agreed to a compromise. In 1981, Washington gave the companies, including AMAX, the option of acquiring other coal deposits on non-Indian public lands, and the Northern Cheyenne received a $3-million settlement in return for dropping their lawsuits. The Indians had managed to save their land.

In all these cases, AMAX's goal has been to gain access to natural resources. For this, deals between the company and governments, excluding the aboriginal inhabitants or workers, have been the best and fastest means of establishing control. Experiences such as the one with the Northern Cheyenne, however, have taught the AMAXes an important lesson about our changing times: it can be more rewarding to show concern for the Native people's well-being, and more expedient to seek active co-operation with their leadership. This was the strategy AMAX used in dealing with the Colville Indians of the State of Washington, who sit on one of the richest molybdenum deposits in the world at Mount Tolman.

The mining was opposed by a small group of Indians and white residents of the area, the "Preservation of Mount Tolman Alliance," which argued that the mountain was a native sacred ground and the industry would do permanent injury to the Colville way of life. After forty years or so of mining activity as planned, Mount Tolman would no longer be a summit rising 1700 feet above the surrounding area but a gap 1200 feet deep, two miles long, and a mile wide; the tailings would fill two nearby valleys. In this case, however, instead of antagonizing the tribal council, AMAX bought a 1974 mining option for $17 million in hard cash. Part of this sum was distributed to the six thousand members of the tribe, each of whom received a direct payment of $1,000. And the company proceeded to head off all potential avenues for native discontent. It financed the printing of a glossy monthly newspaper, a number of social programs, and scholarships for young people. The deal was approved by a referendum in which only 875 of the 3500 eligible tribal voters cast their ballots. Some 567 Colville Indians voted for the mine and 308 voted against it. The "Preservation of Mount Tolman Alliance" was no match for the slick and highly efficient multinational. By waving a $5,000 cheque in front of every tribe member for each year of mining operation, AMAX was able to convince a majority of voters — though a minority of the tribal membership — to mortgage the future of their nation.

When the time came to sign the final agreement in December of 1981, however, AMAX cancelled the whole project because of the world economic crisis and a fall in molybdenum prices. The irate Colville leadership was abruptly deprived of its millions. The harmonious development of Indians and industry, the corporation's social responsibilities, everything went by the boards as soon as the hard laws of supply and demand wiped out the prospect of profit.

The American experiment is of prime importance to the Native people of Canada. In the United States, the Indians generally have larger territories, including sub-surface and water rights, and enjoy a greater degree of autonomy than do their Canadian counterparts. In order to gain access to the resources, multinational corporations have fostered the emergence of an Indian bureaucracy favourable to their aims. For this purpose, a Council of Energy Resource Tribes was created in the mid-1970s with generous federal grants and immediate support from big companies such as power utilities. This C.E.R.T., to which the Colville leadership belongs, acts as a catalyst for pro-industry forces on many reservations and even some Canadian reserves. One of the most tragic stories of partnership between Indian managers and private companies is probably that of the Hopi-Navajo tribal land in the southwestern United States, where six thousand people have been displaced to make way for coal strip-mining operations. Some eight thousand Eastern Navajo are also scheduled for relocation.

The multinationals' intrusion into Indian societies has caused a deep rift on the U.S. reservations. The fact is that some "tribal governments" offer natural channels for the exploitation of the Indians by their own people. Imposed by the 1934 Indian Reorganization Act, these structures are seen by many as expressions of a foreign power. The division between "business Indians" and "traditionalists" is probably now a permanent fixture of U.S. native politics. A similar divergence is already perceptible in Canada, especially where one of two conditions is present: the Natives are likely to inherit large territories as a result of their land claim, or an existing band is sitting on a very valuable piece of real estate.

So far the Nishga people have remained united, resisting the exchange of their birthrights for a speedy and destructive type of development. Behind projects like AMAX's, they see not industrial progress and jobs but the end of a style of life they cherish. Chester Benson of Kincolith voiced a general feeling of loss and helplessness in 1981:

In the fall time we go up there [Alice Arm] to get our sea food. Cockles, some pick up mussels, we go after wild ducks, black ducks, they feed out of the mussels, geese is there, and the bear right now they're comin' out in the spring. We get them throughout May. Now they're dumping. I don't know what we're gonna do about it. For AMAX scientific group, or whatever it is, I wouldn't believe in them myself, because our grandfathers and our great-grandfathers have lived in that same place for thousands of years, and that's the only place we get salmon. You know we cure them, smoke them and fillet them, you know, for lot of uses. We salt them, smoke cure.

Last year, I went with my brother here, and we had about five representatives of five houses, and that consists of about thirty or forty people you're feeding from one boat. And we picked there for about five days. We worked from bed to bed at the big runoff.

We get our wild ducks and seals, sea lion. And when they mentioned what we heard about the salmon migrating in and out of there, they do migrate in and out of there. And they wouldn't answer the question when they said, well, how do you know that there is still migration of salmon? They don't know because they had to close the inlet for so many years now ...

My father has on the right of the head of the inlet a whole valley, like goes thirty miles back in a triangle. That's his trapline right to the water line. And mine is on the left side going up right behind Kitsault, where the town site is, five miles wide and thirty miles up. Not only the salmon is going to be contaminated. Also there's other animals, fur-bearing animals, you know, like the minks. They come down to feed on the mussels, ground food from the bottom of the sea, sea otters, you can imagine how much a million, how much of our fur-bearing animals is gonna go out of existence ...

My dad and I have one smoke-house standing there still. We built it a few years ago. And our house, well it rotted and it went down to snow. So over the last three or four years, now, we haven't lived out there, on that account. But throughout all the years ever since I was a small child, I'm now fifty-seven years old, and you can figure how many years between, all the years that my father has fed me out of that inlet, and I have fed my children out of that inlet, and Stewart here, Doolan the councillor, he has fed his relations and his children out of it.

Chester Benson and the rest of his people are confronted by the calm insistence of AMAX's president, Allan Born, that "the marine disposal, in the opinion of expert marine consultants and federal and provincial governmental officials, will have no detrimental effect on the marine life in the area and will not harm the salmon fishery." AMAX and the government of Canada have yet to acknowledge even the possibility of adverse ecological effects at Alice Arm. As noted by one of the four dissenting official experts, Dr. Pat Nasmyth, the scientific data on which the decision to issue the permit was allegedly based came from a study commissioned by AMAX itself, a document Dr. Nasmyth described as "limited in scope." According to a statement made by Jim Fulton in the House of Commons, the multinational paid its consultant John Littlepage approximately $1 million to prepare its case. Littlepage asserted that the tailings would probably settle to the bottom of the fjord without mixing with surface waters or being carried out to the open sea. AMAX's consultant also stated that the waste was nothing more than "sand," and that at any rate the Nishga consumed none of Alice Arm's resources.

Even if this "carload of data" looked better than a full "truckload," the federal government could hardly claim ignorance of the effects of dumping mine tailings in the sea. As early as 1977, the Canadian Department of the Environment knew of some of the possible consequences from studying a comparable situation. Its scientists had sounded a warning about a copper operation at the north end of Vancouver Island where the Utah Mines Company had been dumping wastes into a fjord since 1971. There, too, the material was supposed to settle to the bottom, but in a 1980 follow-up report, another federal expert, Michael Waldichuk, found that "tailings are resuspended by tidal turbulence and upwelling at the junction of Rupert and Holberg inlets." The ecological impact was serious, as "bottom organisms are being smothered and benthic habitat obliterated in the inlet trench." Further, "according to Mr. Frank Walter, Chief of the Quatsino Band, the Indians have ceased to make use of this resource because waters are 'muddy' in Quatsino Narrows and there is concern among the Natives that seafood contaminated by the mine tailings may be unsafe to eat."

It was at last revealed in the spring of 1981 that the same Michael Waldichuk, an oceanographer, had also been asked for advice by Ottawa before the AMAX plan was formally approved. His response was extremely guarded in a 7 November 1978 memorandum.

> The danger of setting a precedent by allowing tailing disposal into Alice Arm at this time undoubtedly exists. However, stopping disposal of tailings into Alice Arm in order to avoid such a precedent has to be a policy decision. It cannot be supported on environmental grounds with the available information. Each case must be considered on its own merits. As I said in the outset, our long-term goal should be elimination of unconfined tailings disposal into coastal waters and development of environmentally more acceptable mine-waste disposal systems.

Dr. Waldichuk stated further in a newspaper interview that he was never consulted about the objections of the four experts on the review panel, and that he was unaware of their work.

One of the assertions made by Fisheries Minister Roméo Leblanc was that the Indians had known all along that AMAX planned to open the Kitsault molybdenum mine. As mentioned above, Iona Campagnolo, then MP for the district, had the contrary impression that "there was a brushing aside of discussions with the Nishgas." Leblanc detailed his claim on 13 May 1982 to Parliament's Standing Joint Committee on Regulations and other Statutory Instruments:

> There were four officials of my department present at the Nishga Tribal Council meeting of November 1978 at Prince Rupert. Of these, two had personal private conversations with Nishga commercial fishermen who had fished in Alice Arm. We have only been able to contact one of these two (the other no longer being in the employ of the department). He advises that both he and the other officer had the said conversations. He spoke with five such individuals, one of whom was Mr. James Gosnell, president of the Tribal Council. The objective of these discussions was to raise with these individuals the topic of the reopening of the mine and the proposed tailings deposit and to obtain information on the fishery resource utilization and potential of the area.

The Nishga leaders have always maintained that they were not informed of the AMAX plan before its approval by the Canadian government in April 1979. But it is not a matter here of choosing between the word of the minister and that of the Natives. A Prince Rupert journalist, Cam Ford, located the two officials mentioned in Leblanc's statement. He reported in a CBC broadcast of 31 May 1982 that the conversation referred to had occurred informally during a coffee break. Moreover Burle Kurtz, the fisheries officer who spoke with Chief Gosnell, denied that he had explained the Alice Arm project to the Nishga. Gus Jultema, Kurtz's supervisor at the time, told Ford that the mine's application was mentioned only when some fishermen asked why the officers were so curious about fishing patterns in the area. The topic of the day had been fish, not tailings. So much for the alleged official notification.

When the Nishga did find out what had been decided behind their backs, they hired their own consultant to challenge the opinions of the experts who had sided with the multinational. In October 1980, the McCart report concluded that the tailings were not mere "sand," there was a real danger of contamination of the Natives' food chain, the wastes could spread over a much larger area than orginally forecast, and the Nishga were indeed consuming seafood and mammals from Alice Arm. In fact the Nishga diet was higher in seafood than any other on the North American continent. According to a 1977 study by the Canadian fisheries department, the people of the Nass were catching 16 800 salmon a year for their own consumption, and the McCart report stated that they were getting from 70 to 80 per cent of their animal protein from their fishing activities.

The preservation of Alice Arm quickly attracted a broad coalition of concerned groups to support the Nishga cause. They found allies in all the churches, the B.C. Federation of Labour, fishermen, various ecological organizations, the New Democratic Party, and even, although more discreetly, some Conservative members of Parliament. The tribal council tried without much success to challenge the pollution permits in the courts — provincial permits had been issued after the federal go-ahead.

Another symbolic battle was predictably lost in May 1981 when a Nishga delegation led by James Gosnell and Rod Robinson went to New York to plead the Native case at the AMAX shareholders' meeting. The Anglican church of Canada had acquired a thousand company shares and given the Nishga proxies to defend a resolution calling for a halt to the dumping. Among those whom the Nishga attracted to their cause was Alice Richard, daughter of the founder of Climax Molybdenum, but when the chips were counted in the prestigious Starlight Roof of the Waldorf Astoria, James Gosnell and his friends had lost, 30 million shares to 1.6 million.

All this lobbying helped make the Alice Arm affair known, but the Canadian Government did not rescind the permit. Fisheries minister Leblanc responded with reluctance to pro-Nishga pressures by authorizing an internal inquiry. Several prominent scientists refused to associate their names with the assignment, but Leblanc finally found a Victoria biologist, John McInerney, to chair his commission. McInerney was in flagrant conflict of interest, since he had been a member of the B.C. Pollution Control Board when that body issued a pollution permit similar to the federal one. His commission had no power of subpoena. His mandate was not to investigate the circumstances of the granting of the permit, but merely to advise the minister about how damage to the fjord could be contained.

The McInerney Commission was boycotted by the Nishga and all their allies. While it was sitting, in May 1981, a cloudy "plume" of denser material was spotted in the fjord, drifting away from AMAX's pipe around seventy metres down. The alarm led to a brief mine shut-down followed by minor modifications in the disposal technique. In July, McInerney produced a spineless report recommending that the pipe discharging the tailings into the ocean be extended to a hundred metres beneath the surface from the original fifty. He did recognize that some forms of life would suffer from the mine, and that levels of lead, zinc, and perhaps also cadmium would be higher than in a normal environment; but on the whole, his report did not seem overly concerned by potential hazards to the Nishga's health.

McInerney's views were not shared by all. On the day following the publication of his report, the Nishga Tribal Council unveiled its rebuttal, written by environment consultant Ross Peterson. Peterson concluded that the data used by the government in assessing AMAX's application were scant, and that the question of the impact of toxic minerals on the food chain and human health had been completely bypassed. Nishga concerns were echoed by other scientists as well. A University of British Columbia oceanographer, Stephen Pond, rejected the claim that the tailings would always stay on the floor of Alice Arm: "There is evidence that heavier, saltier water from outside the inlet flows in, mixing up the water. The prediction made that the material would go down to the bottom and stay there is not likely to hold true." Another scientist, Simon Fraser University biologist Lawrence Albright, warned that the environment of Alice Arm, already polluted by a past spill of polychlorinated biphenol or PCB, was too fragile to tolerate mine tailings.

But the most serious concerns raised had to do with human health. Professor John Sprague, a University of Guelph zoologist, pointed out that none of the thirty-five so-called "technical studies" carried out by AMAX before the opening of the mine dealt with the effects of mineral wastes on the food chain. The problem was to judge not how limpid the water was, but what would happen to the minerals released by the mine, even in small quantities, once they started to concentrate and migrate into algae, shellfish, fish, mammals, and, eventually, humans. A study by the Environmental Health Committee of the British Columbia Medical Association of one of the elements at issue, radium-226, showed how grave the situation was: "About one millionth of a gram (one microgram-Mg) or 35 billionths of an ounce in the body, can cause bone cancer." Moreover, "a great variety of oceanic organisms accumulate radium far in excess of that present in sea water. Some marine micro-organisms (example diatoms) concentrate radium-226 from 1000 to 3000 times sea-water levels."

Even if Ottawa would not reopen the issue of the pollution permit, the Alice Arm controversy forced the federal government to give the Nishga some token satisfaction. In April 1982, the Department of Health and Welfare agreed to conduct a long-term study of blood, urine, and hair samples taken from 540 residents of the Nass Valley. And in July of the same year, the Nishga also obtained a moral victory of a sort. The Standing Joint Committee on Regulations and other Statutory Instruments — a little-known body of the Canadian Parliament, the control of which the ruling Liberals had overlooked — condemned SOR-79-345 from the somewhat dry standpoint of procedure as "an unusual or unexpected use of the powers conferred by the Fisheries Act."

In November 1982, the international collapse of molybdenum prices led to the temporary shut-down of the Kitsault operation. Ten months later, AMAX laid off its employees. The mine is now mothballed pending a resurgence in the world economy. One month before the closing, a study of the fjord's organisms commissioned by the federal government revealed that dramatic changes had occurred after a year and a half of dumping, with benthic life under stress in locations as far as 5.5 and 7 kilometres away from the AMAX pipe.

> Transects CC and DD in Alice Arm had very few species, indicating severe stress at these locations, particularly in the north and middle stations at CC and the middle station at DD. Transect EE [eleven kilometres] had more species but the deep middle station along this transect had numbers comparable to Transects CC and DD. This indicates that mine tailings are beginning to affect the lower section of Alice Arm, and have progressed to the deep middle section of EE. Independent sedimentation data and sediment analyses from other sources agree with these findings.

Here were the results of four million tonnes of effluent. The scientists called for further studies, but they left no doubt as to the nature of the problem: "A variety of fauna may be affected by these tailings due to toxicity of heavy metal concentrations, increased turbidity limiting light penetration and primary production, and smothering of infaunal organisms."

The threat to Nishga health will not materialize immediately. When economic conditions improve and the mine reopens, will the mud eventually move out of Alice Arm? Will the oolichan and salmon runs passing through the fjord be contaminated? Are the sea and land mammals that feed on the marine life going to be affected? How long will it take for toxic substances to concentrate along the food chain and eventually reach man? The validity of expert hypotheses will not be confirmed or contradicted for many years, not until vital statistics eventually reveal abnormal trends. For the Nishga, the conclusion is ominous: they are the guinea pigs in this experiment.

The authorities condoning environmental pollution for the sake of industry operate on the dangerous principle of "acceptable risk." It is a principle as difficult to accept as that of "acceptable losses" on the battlefield. "Acceptable" to whom? At Alice Arm, the people who would have to live with the consequences were not consulted. The risks were taken in the name of a concept of development which was not shared by the population at large. And they were taken in a furtive manner that makes a sham of anything called "democratic process."

Beyond the distressing question of the health of a nation of fishermen lies a new form of violation of Native rights. The reopening of the Kitsault mine will eventually lead to the creation of a white town of a thousand or so inhabitants in the middle of Nishga territory. A new road and a bridge over the Nass River will allow more massive exploitation of the wood and mineral resources on the right bank of the waterway. The timing of order-in-council SOR-79-345 in conjunction with land-claim negotiations gives the lie to Ottawa's public commitment to Native welfare: the process of erosion that began with the first colonists and the first missionaries is to be continued.

The Alice Arm controversy also has broader, international implications. For the multinational corporations, the stakes are high. The dumping methods used by AMAX are claimed as a precedent by other companies beyond the borders of Canada. In the case of the Kitsault mine, the dumping of more than one hundred million tonnes of tailings over twenty-six years means a saving of $23 million, or the cost of installing settling ponds — a solution that is not without risk itself, especially in the event of floods, slides, or spills.

The objective or justification for all this, according to AMAX's figures, is nine million pounds of refined molybdenum over the life of the mine. Fifty kilometres due west, on the other side of the Alaska border, another multinational has plans that are much more grandiose. The U.S. Borax Corporation has notified American authorities of its intention to open a molybdenum mine that will produce sixty thousand tonnes of ore-concentrate per day. The deposits at the Quartz Hill site are estimated at 1.5 billion tonnes of ore or 10 per cent of known world molybdenum reserves; once in operation, the mine should provide 18 per cent of the world's requirements in this precious metal. The method of tailings disposal contemplated by Borax is the same as the one at Kitsault — a pipe dumping waste directly into the sea fifty metres below the surface. Over a seventy-year period, Borax intends to discharge between four hundred million and 1.5 billion tonnes of tailings into two fjords, Wilson Arm and Boca de Quadra. The company cites precedent in its defence: "A similar marine disposal of tailings is currently being practised successfully at Island Copper, British Columbia, and is felt to be a desirable environmental solution to the tailings disposal question."

Island Copper is none other than the copper-molybdenum mine operated by Utah Mines, a subsidiary of General Electric, that has caused the Quatsino Sound Natives to stop fishing in the dirty waters of Rupert Inlet. AMAX, Borax, General Electric — the multinationals are driven by a common strategy and resort to the same sweet euphemisms. Pollution is no longer pollution, but "a desirable environmental solution to the tailings disposal question."

Tactics can change to serve the immutable profit objective. Already, AMAX has absorbed a few lessons from the Kitsault fiasco. In May 1982, the multinational announced its plan to open a $175-million tungsten mine on the border of the Yukon and Northwest territories. The Canadian MacTung site is the largest untapped deposit of its type in the world and has enough tungsten to supply the entire western steel industry for at least twenty years. Yet according to Jim Foreman, president of AMAX Canada, "We are not going to take any decision about MacTung until everyone has looked at it. We can sit down and define the options together. ... And it's not going to be just a government-company arrangement — we need the public in there, too." Conservationists, hunters, Natives — everybody was invited by Mr. Foreman. The new president of AMAX Canada even admitted that he had been embarrassed by the Aice Arm controversy, which he ascribed to "communications failure in the early stages."

Will the Yukon Indians and their neighbours the Dene of the Northwest Territories be pushovers like the Colville tribe? Or will they insist on remaining the masters of their own development, like the Nishga? Whatever the answer, the multinational companies are a new reality in Native life. Their intrusion has profoundly altered the nature of the problem. Until recently, the tormenter of the indigenous peoples of North America had a face, and that face was white. It is no longer possible, however, to assign blame to any specific character — missionary, immigrant, politician, or official. For whites are now increasingly confronted with the same problem the Natives face, a machine nobody seems able to control, a machine that eats the forests and the mountains, floods the valleys and paves the plains, spawning poisons everywhere. This machine — the machine of advanced technology at the sole service of profit — is faceless. In a system where the fate of human beings is shaped by the international eddies of commodities and capital, there is no culprit; there are only victims.

NATIONALISM RISING

The early 1980s have brought the Native land question to public notice again as a result of a tense process that exposed the very bone and sinew of the Canadian beast: the debate on the patriation of the constitution. For well over a hundred years, the fundamental law defining the respective powers of the federal and provincial governments had remained a British statute at the request of the Canadians themselves. By the latter 1970s, the need for complete national status had become more urgent, at least in the opinion of the reigning Liberals, than the delicacy of the federal-provincial balance. The patriation bill finally introduced in 1981 was a countermove against the powerful wave of nationalism that had installed an independentist government in Quebec. And the formula it contained for amending the constitution was designed to prevent any province, and above all Quebec, from blocking unwanted change. For the Québécois, the patriation process was a new phase in the historical trend towards centralization of authority at their expense.

But the constitutional debate was more than the occasion for a power struggle between Ottawa and the provinces. For the Natives, the removal of the last colonial tie came as an opportunity to question the legitimacy of the Canadian political system. Those who already had treaties could not imagine that Britain's relinquishment of her last responsibilities in Canada could happen without a new definition of their relationship with the Canadian state. As for those who, like the Nishga, had never signed any contract with the whites, the process was a time to remind the world that on about half the country's area, the presence of Canadian authority was simply a de facto state of affairs that had never been formally ratified. James Gosnell, president of the Nishga Tribal Council, stressed this before a December 1980 hearing of the joint parliamentary committee on the constitution:

> I have often said this and I will say it now, that the white man should have done a darn good job the first time and killed us all, but because God saw in his wisdom that we should survive and we are now the survivors of this land, the Indian people, the original owners of this land. We are still here today and as long as we are alive our aboriginal title lives with us.

At this early stage, the Trudeau government's constitutional project made only scant reference to Native people. Under clause 24 of the proposed Charter of Rights, "The guarantee in the Charter of certain rights and freedoms shall not be construed as denying the existence of any other rights and freedoms that exist in Canada, including any rights and freedoms that pertain to the native peoples of Canada." The constitutional draft contained no definition of such rights and freedoms; interested Natives were simply referred to the jurisprudence on the subject, that is to say to more than a century of uncertainty and contempt. Many Native people felt that if they did not want to be left at the whim of hostile authorities, they must obtain clear recognition of their rights within the constitution. Gosnell was one leader who made this his goal:

> Our aboriginal title to the Nishga land must be entrenched in the consititution before patriation. That is our position at these hearings. Without the title there can be no negotiation. Without negotiation there cannot be a just settlement of the land question; without a just settlement the Nishga people will have absolutely no economic base upon which to survive.

These Native demands went largely ignored by the government and Parliament of Canada. Land rights were not dealt with in the constitution bill. The resolution passed by the

Commons and Senate at the beginning of 1981 did, however, have some positive features: it dropped all reference to jurisprudence and any restrictive definition of native rights — "rights . . . that exist in Canada" in the previous version. Clause 34(1) of the constitution bill did not close the door to an interpretation in favour of the existence of a Native land title, confirming simply that "the aboriginal and treaty rights of the aboriginal peoples of Canada are hereby recognized and affirmed." The formula was vague enough, but many Natives saw it as holding a promise for the future. Others found the bill unacceptable: Native rights stemmed not from the will of the white power but from an ancestral presence.

The main issue as far as Canadian politicians were concerned was the sharing of powers between Ottawa and the provinces, and the temperature of debate made it really the only issue. In April 1981, eight of the ten provinces, including Quebec, formed a common front to wring an amending formula from the federal government that would have given them a veto over any constitutional change. At a November federal-provincial conference, however, Prime Minister Trudeau managed to turn the situation around by threatening to go to the polls to break the deadlock. Knowing that they would probably lose in a referendum on the question, the English-speaking premiers rallied to his cause, reneged on their agreement with Quebec, and abandoned the French province to a lonely fate. To achieve this, Trudeau had also agreed to certain compromises, among them the scrapping of clause 34 on aboriginal rights. According to paragraph 5 of the 5 November 1981 constitutional agreement:

A constitutional conference as provided for in clause 36 of the Resolution including in its agenda an item respecting constitutional matters that directly affect the Aboriginal peoples of Canada, including the identification of the rights of those peoples to be included in the Constitution of Canada, shall be provided for in the Resolution. The Prime Minister of Canada shall invite representatives of the Aboriginal peoples of Canada to participate in the discussion of that item.

Premier Peter Lougheed of Alberta acknowledged publicly that his province had been one to request the dropping of clause 34. Federal sources let it be known that the delegation of British

Columbia had taken a similar stand in order to eliminate any wording that could pave the way for recognition of Native land rights, though Premier Bennett claimed after his return from Ottawa that he had not been personally aware of the change until the text of the agreement was made public on the last morning of the conference.

The results of the first ministers' efforts were startling, to say the least. The minorities of the country, including the Québécois, the Native nationalities, and women, had been sacrificed on the altar of Canadian unity. In the following weeks, the agreement of the nine English provinces and the federal government attracted strong criticism from these groups. The agitation put the Ottawa Liberals in a bind: they risked losing the unanimity of the Commons' three parties, with the New Democrats threatening to pull out because of the exclusion of Natives and women, and they might also see their resolution turned down by a British Parliament perplexed at the denial of basic human rights that seemed to be its most conspicuous feature.

These considerations led the ten parties to the 5 November agreement to reinstate the rights of women. Meanwhile, Native protest was burgeoning. The Union of B.C. Indian Chiefs was organizing demonstrations at which people could be heard chanting, "We don't want no constitution, we are a nation." This group, whose following was concentrated in the province's southern interior, had rejected the constitution proposal and were taking part in a Native lobby in England against it. Most other Native groups in British Columbia, however, had opted for a different approach from the start of the debate. A coalition had been formed that united the most powerful tribal councils, including the Nishga, Haida, Carrier-Sekani, Nuu-chah-nulth, Haisla, Tsimshian, and Cariboo; the Alliance of B.C. Indian Bands, a group centred on the southern coast; the Native Brotherhood of British Columbia; the Aboriginal Council, a body working to document land claims; and the United Native Nations, a former organization of non-status Indians that had spread to embrace a large tribal following. The coalition and the chiefs' union represented forces that had often clashed in the past on matters of Native politics — government funding, for example, the relative importance of bands and tribal councils, or the relationship between status and non-status Indians — and the constitutional debate was no exception. The coalition saw the patriation process as an opportunity to force the authorities to make concessions and the union did not. Yet beyond differences in strategy, their respective positions started from a common premise — the Native refusal to relinquish title to the land.

On 19 November 1981, Premier Bill Bennett gave in to pressures from Ottawa and Native lobbyists and agreed to the inclusion of a clause on aboriginal rights in the Canadian constitution. His gesture was considerably weakened, however, when he went on to state that from his province's point of view the Native question fell entirely within the federal jurisdiction, and the new constitutional guarantees would imply no obligation on British Columbia's part. Attorney-General Allan Williams added that Victoria would continue to reject the concept of "aboriginal title" and contend that Natives had no valid claim to any part of provincial lands.

Coalition members still thought that they had won a major victory, and they even sent Premier Bennett a letter of congratulations. Their hopes withered a few days later when the nine English provinces and the federal government announced that they had agreed to reintroduce the rights clause, but in a new version that changed the whole scope of the text by the addition of the adjective, "existing." The passage now read: "The existing aboriginal and treaty rights of the aboriginal peoples of Canada are hereby recognized and affirmed." Legal advisors to the Nishga and many other groups argued that this meant they were to have no rights other than those which the Canadian authorities had acknowledged up to the time of patriation in 1982. There would be little likelihood of future judicial decisions in favour of aboriginal rights going beyond what provincial or federal legislators had conceded in the past. It was clear to the Nishga and their allies that the new constitution enshrined a deadlock and obviated any promotion of land claims within the system. What was more, the Canadian government reserved the right to define the meaning of "existing aboriginal and treaty rights" in a subsequent first ministers' conference. At this meeting, the decision-making power would remain with Ottawa and the provinces; it was not to be a negotiation between Native nations and Canada.

At about the same time, Ottawa published a "new" land claims policy which showed how little official thinking had changed. The document, entitled "In all fairness," came as confirmation of the two main aspects of federal strategy: to obtain the final surrender of land rights from Native groups and reject any claim that might conflict with established interests. "Lands selected by Natives for their continuing use," it announced, "should be traditional land that they currently use and occupy; but persons of non-Native origin who have acquired for various purposes, rights in the land in the area claimed, are equally deserving of consideration. Their rights and interests must be dealt with equitably." Thus did the government exlude all claims on regions inhabited by white people or used by industries, limiting any eventual negotiations to marginal areas coveted by no one. And to get settlements, Natives were asked to renounce further claims for ever: "Any land claim settlement will be final. . . . The thrust of this policy is to exchange undefined aboriginal land rights for concrete rights and benefits."

Natives had never expected much from the promises of consideration given them by the governments of the past, but until 1982 they could still believe that the legal system held out the possibility of an amicable solution. Their ancestral rights had not been invalidated by the courts, and the Canadian Supreme Court decision in the Nishga case even showed that land claims had to be taken seriously. The existence of a link with Great Britain, however tenuous, had allowed them to remind Canada of the original conditions of colonization and in particular the 1763 royal proclamation. Now, the patriation process effectively delivered the Native peoples into the hands of their old oppressors, the federal and provincial governments. This operation was conducted with the complicity of the Conservative prime minister of Britain, Margaret Thatcher, who pushed a "Canada Bill" through her Parliament in compliance with the Trudeau government's wishes. Only a few isolated voices, notably those of Labour MPs Bruce George and Stanley Clinton-Davis, dissociated themselves from Britain's abdication of her historic responsibilities.

History will also remember the reaction of the Canadian justice minister Jean Chrétien, who attended the Westminster debate and was reported as having blasted the "instant experts" in London who dared criticize the Ottawa government.

Many British MPs misunderstood the Indian situation in Canada, Chrétien said, and were wrong to portray natives living in appalling poverty throughout the country. If there were poor Indians in Northern Quebec, there were also poor whites, he said. Unemployment was an economic, not a racial problem, and any Indian who felt trapped on a reserve was always free to leave.

Free to leave his reserve, free to disappear into the melting-pot, free to deny his own identity, Chrétien's Native strangely resembled the one of Trudeau's 1969 vision. With its white and anglophone majority, patriated Canada was asserting itself as "one and indivisible." Having dismantled the idea of "two founding nations," French and English, Ottawa was not about to make room now for Native ones.

The constitutional saga was not over. The patriation of 1982 was to be followed by other meetings to deal with the Native question. In British Columbia, the crisis had an unexpected result as rival Native leaders were thrown into a single camp. For regardless of their initial strategy, readiness for dialogue or suspicion of any government, Natives were left with only one avenue — the proclamation as a fundamental principle of the right of all peoples to self-determination.

On 27 January 1982, a General Assembly of the Indians of British Columbia was held in Vancouver. For the first time, the various factions were participating in a joint meeting, with almost all tribal groups represented, in order to define a common position for British Columbia Natives. Because of their historical prestige the Nishga played a leading role in organizing this event, and the president of their tribal council, James Gosnell, was elected as the sole spokesman for all the Natives of British Columbia on constitutional and land questions. Moreover, the assembly adopted as its working position a "Statement on aboriginal rights" submitted by the Nishga Tribal Council:

What do we mean by aboriginal rights? In answering this question, the most important thing that must be borne in mind is that all of our rights flow from our relationship to the land. Our lives, our culture, and our continued existence as a people are completely tied to the land in the area which our ancestors have occupied since time immemorial. That is why our people say that aboriginal rights flow from aboriginal title. This is why our people have indicated that we will never agree to an extinguishment of aboriginal title. We fear that an extinguishment of our title will lead to an extinguishment of our rights, regardless of the words of the Constitution or the words of any land-claim settlement.

Our position is, then, that our rights are those rights which flow from our historical and traditional ownership and occupation of the lands of the Nass Valley. We hold them both collectively and individually. Any attempt to fully define each and every one of these rights would be doomed to failure.

For the Nishga as well as for the other aboriginal nations of British Columbia, Native rights are not a mere collection of specific benefits for activities such as hunting and trapping; they are expressed as a special relationship to the land that cannot be defined by strangers. The assertion that only Native people can define their own rights, the claim to sovereignty and self-government — here are the decisive qualities of true nationalism: "Our aboriginal rights include the right to self-government. We must have the right to determine our collective future as a sovereign people, through an appropriate governmental structure and constitutional relationship with the rest of Canada."

The Nisgha position, adopted unanimously in the general assembly, reflects a basic consensus within the Native movement in spite of its political division. The document's nationalism is shared by all Native nations of the province, including those which, unlike the Nishga, have consistently refused to participate in constitutional dialogue with the authorities. For instance, there are strong echoes of it in the "Elders' position of the Okanagan Nation," presented to the same meeting by a group that is quite different culturally and lives in the populous southern interior region of the province:

The Okanagan Nation is a sovereign nation. This originates from the Creator when he placed us on this island in our territory. We were given instructions under which our people have lived in health for nobody knows how many generations. Those instructions are explained in the teachings of Coyote. No other nation in this world can give us what we already have, our nationhood and our sovereignty.

The 1982 assembly did not lead to any organic fusion among the various Native political groups. Beyond the unavoidable organizational differences, however, a unity of purpose did emerge. Three basic demands were formulated and agreed on: the concept of "aboriginal title" should be entrenched in the Canadian constitution; such a fundamental right should be protected by a consent clause so that politicians could not amend the document without Native approval; and the concrete definition of aboriginal rights should be left to each tribal group. The process outlined by the assembly differed drastically from the official constitutional configuration of a bargaining match between the central and provincial powers. For the Natives, the first step had to be recognition of their right to self-determination, followed by negotiation on the nature of their relationship with the rest of Canada.

The first ministers' constitutional conference on native rights was held at Ottawa in March 1983. Indian, Inuit and Métis leaders were invited, though not as full participants. The meeting had a few results: confirmation that the Métis were indeed one of the aboriginal peoples, a commitment to end sexual discrimination in the Indian Act, and a promise to enshrine any land-claim settlement in the constitution. On the main question of interest to the Nishga, however, that of Native title, no agreement emerged. It was put on the agenda of another conference scheduled for 1984, along with all other unresolved matters.

One reason for this lack of progress lies in the position of some provinces which, like British Columbia, remain hostile to the Native point of view. In a letter of 20 November 1981 to Prime Minister Trudeau, Premier Bennett reiterated his lack of commitment to the settlement of the land question:

> If as a result of the process by which the definition of aboriginal rights is clarified any obligations arise, it will be the clear responsibility of Canada to fully compensate the people and the Province of British Columbia for any participation that Canada may seek from British Columbia in the fulfilment of any treaty or settlement negotiated by Canada with the aboriginal people.

Yet the province, as the historical record shows, was responsible for seizing the Native lands in the first place, while most issues involved in land claims — territory, timber, mineral resources, and so on — are under provincial jurisdiction. These facts did not deter Premier Bennett, however, and the cynicism of his Victoria government became even more apparent when, on the eve of the March 1983 conference, the province's strategy paper was leaked to the press. The bottom line was very simple: as far as British Columbia was concerned, there was nothing to be negotiated.

With regard to the issue of aboriginal rights, it should be noted that British Columbia's position is much tougher than any other government's position on this issue. Very simply, British Columbia's position on aboriginal land claims is that "native title" has never existed in this province, but if it did it was extinguished by pre-Confederation legal actions, and further that even to the extent that any unextinguished title might still remain, it is now the total responsibility of the federal government for settlement.

Due to the fact that British Columbia's position relates to the specific history of this province, our position on this matter is not shared with any other government. At the same time, as it does not appear to recognize the concept of aboriginal title, it is a direct threat to all aboriginal claims in Canada. The position is deeply resented by many native representatives even though it has considerable legal merit. More than any other province, British Columbia can expect direct criticism of its stated policy on the issue of aboriginal title.

Realizing that the province's real position was not going to be particularly popular, the government strategy paper advised the B.C. delegation to be "seen" as receptive and positive:

During the preparatory phase the provincial government should be seen to be genuinely working hard toward the "identification and definition" of aboriginal rights and to be taking this matter seriously as an important constitutional and policy issue.

The provincial government should appear receptive to all statements and proposals of native organizations and should expect that aggressive statements will be made and radical proposals put forward by native organizations. The provincial government should emphasize that it wishes to fully understand the native proposals and their collective aspirations as Canada's aboriginal peoples.

This strategy produced an amazing statement from B.C.'s Attorney-General, Allan Williams, at the conference table:

After you have resolved that with the Nishga [the claim of aboriginal title], and of course it also supports their institutions as well, and when you have reached that with the Nishga then you go to the adjoining Indian nations, the Carrier, the Gitksan, the Tahltans, and on throughout the whole of British Columbia and you find that similar arrangements exist for their self-government based on what they say is their ownership of the land and it is complete. It is the land, what is under it, the rivers, the fish in the rivers, the birds that fly in the sky. They make no distinction.

Therefore, when we talk about constitutional change where we put in the words "aboriginal title," I think there has to be the clearest understanding on our part of what that means to the aboriginal peoples because at some stage, even if we put in the simple words "aboriginal title" there will be a question raised which our courts will determine as to, "What did you mean by title?" and as you said, Mr. Prime Minister, "Is it hunting, fishing, and gathering?" — but Mr. Gosnell says no, it is something much more fundamental to that and it is something upon which their whole nation exists, their whole system . . .

Does their whole system of self-government, including their rights to citizenship, the rights to maintain their institutions, all depend upon the existence of this aboriginal land base, this land base, this ownerhship? I think for British Columbia I could say, yes, it does and that is how enormous the problem is, and in addressing it we have to, as you [the prime minister] said in your opening remarks, see how smoothly we can resolve the aboriginal peoples' concerns, as fundamental as they are, with what the rest of Canada and all the other Canadians see with respect to the land base and resources and so on. That is the enormity of the problem.

At the time of the conference, many listeners believed that the attorney-general was endorsing the concept of aboriginal land ownership. However, this was not what Williams had said. He had used the Native vocabulary to explain their position, not his. The "land," the "fish," the "rivers," and the "birds in the air" were so many images thrown into a convoluted statement to give the impression that the minister was "receptive," but the thrust of his remarks was, on the contrary, to caution governments against accepting the words "aboriginal title" at all.

Chief James Gosnell was more straightforward in his presentation of the B.C. Native position:

If we are going to be talking about our land we have to talk abour our title, because if you do not talk about our title, we are talking about nothing. Without the title, that is why we are here, this is our title, Canada, the whole of Canada is our title and it is subdivided here, there and so on and some of the lands have been negotiated and others haven't. So how do we get the title? . . . The title is held by each family, and I am talking about the Nishga tribe now. Each tribe holds certain sections of the land. As you are aware, we are talking about five thousand square miles and I am using this as an example, it is only a small piece of land in comparison to other tribal claims, but each family has a section of that five thousand square miles and there is a head, a head man in that family. The land is owned not by individuals, but by family ownership. It is one head to each family. So when the head chief dies the next, the successor has to put him away and large amounts of money is spent to put this chief away and so he can rest properly. That is when the deceased's title is then placed on the new chief. That is what we call title. . . . So when you put the whole works together, and I am using the Nishga tribe as an example, but the whole thing becomes our title, and this is what we are talking about . . .

You can't have aboriginal rights without the title, first of all. . . . It is my instructions to put it forward, that aboriginal title is what we are talking about and that it is the B.C. Indians' position, and we are prepared to talk about our title when we are talking about land claims. There is no getting away from this land claims, it must come one way or the other. . . . Putting it in a nutshell, we are the true owners of the land, lock, stock, and barrel, and that is what it means.

Aboriginal title, consent clause, and self-determination — the constitutional position of the B.C. Natives won no positive response from the first ministers. Prime Minister Trudeau was one of the frankest present. While avoiding any direct reference to the traditional federal aim of extinguishment of native title, he displayed marked irritation at the Natives' persistence:

At what point do you stop reading history? Is it only when the white man came, or 30 000 years ago, or somewhere in between? I think we have to realize that if these discussions are going to produce any results, we can all make the historical claims we want, but we will end up having to agree on something which is acceptable to everybody and you can once again make the claim of land which belongs to you time out of mind, but I don't know any part of the world where history isn't constantly rewritten by migrations and immigrations and fights between countries, changing frontiers, and I don't think you can expect North America or the whole of the Western Hemisphere to settle things differently than they have been settled everywhere else, hopefully peacefully here. So, you know, that is the question, are we going to sit down and bargain what your rights are and where your rights are, or are we just going to repeat historical claims?

The deadlock is still with us. The lack of results in the constitutional debate explains the present state of land claims discussions in the Nass Valley. Details of the talks are a well-kept secret, but the reality is obvious: eight years of official negotiation among Ottawa, Victoria, and the Nishga have produced no firm agreement on anything. The land claim has been divided into several areas — forestry, education, social development, and so on — but on only one topic, the fishery, where the province is not directly involved, is there said to be genuine progress. As for the rest, no end is in sight as long as the Victoria government refuses to acknowledge any kind of provincial responsibility for the outcome. Once again, then, the Nishga cause is bogged down. But this time they know that they are not as isolated as in earlier years. The AMAX affair has taught them the value of press and public-opinion campaigns, alliances, lobbying, and even international pressure. They can afford to wait rather than to rush into a bad settlement. As they point out themselves, "We have been patient for over a hundred and fifteen years."

CONCLUSION

The ideas behind land claims — self-government and nation-hood — are no longer dismissed as marginal rhetoric. They have now won legitimacy with the realization by a significant segment of Canada's political elite that the decolonization of the Native question is long overdue. At the 8–9 March 1984 constitutional conference on aboriginal rights, Prime Minister Trudeau acknowledged that his 1969 policy of "integration" had been "paternalistic," and "the other solution" — recognition of aboriginal first nations — had to be given a chance. Endorsing the self-government concept, the departing statesman mused aloud that the old doctrine of extinguishment might even have been wrong. Provincial sabotage, hostility from Trudeau's successors in Ottawa — many are the eventualities that could prevent the new ideas from being translated into lasting reality. Whatever the case, the debate on native decolonization is not going to die away, even if it means, as has already occurred to some aboriginal leaders, attempting to embarrass Canada on the international scene.

This remarkable change of attitude became visible in October 1983 with the publication of an official document which, for the first time in the country's history, supported the Native movement's basic demands. The Special Commons Committee on Indian Self-Government was a group of seven MPs with the task of studying possible improvements in the administration of the reserve system. Some of these politicians already had progressive credentials on Native issues, particularly Warren Allmand, a former Liberal minister of Indian Affairs, and Jim Manly, a New Democrat. The direction of the committee was also strongly influenced by the inclusion of three additional personalities appointed as ex officio or liaison members: Roberta Jamieson from the Assembly of First Nations, Sandra Isaac of the Native Women's Association of Canada, and Bill Wilson, the Kwawkgeulth vice-president of the Native Council of Canada.

The first conclusion the committee reached was that the Indian Act and the Department of Indian Affairs were beyond redemption and had to be scrapped. The MPs decided that the best way to govern the Natives was for the Natives to govern themselves, and recommended that "the federal government establish a new relationship with Indian First Nations and that an essential element of this relationship be recognition of Indian self-government."

"Nations." "Self-government." A new vocabulary had reached the corridors of Parliament. The committee's suggestion was that the federal government claim all the areas of jurisdiction it could, by virtue of its constitutional competence over "Indians, and lands reserved for Indians," and then simply pass these areas on to the first nations as the Natives requested. This could mean, if the bands and nations so wished, Native jurisdiction over local government, justice and law enforcement, land and resource use, education and family relations, revenue raising, and so on.

The Nishga Tribal Council, like most Native organizations, greeted the Penner report with enthusiasm. The committee's document was unquestionably a true manifesto for decolonization, and the federal response of 5 March 1984 was highly positive. Bands or "other groups of Indian people with a common culture, history and language and with a clearly defined territory" would be allowed to opt out of the Indian Act and establish their own governments under certain rules to be spelled out in future legislation. However, Ottawa was not prepared to recognize in the "First Indian Nations" a new level of government enjoying a degree of autonomy comparable with that of provinces. The first step would be little more than an improvement on the existing band structure, with powers limited to "ownership of property, relations with other governments, internal management and administration, financial arrangements and social and economic programs." Further negotiation would be needed for these new institutions to assume control of "land use, environment, public health, education, renewable and non-renewable resources (including wildlife), agriculture, taxation and other financial matters, public order, administration of justice, family law and property law." The Department of Indian Affairs would not necessarily be dismantled, and first nations would have to report to Parliament on the spending of yearly grants from Ottawa.

This official reaction to the Penner report had many progressive features, but one central question remained: on what areas would the first nations exercise their new authority, broken patches of reserve land or true tribal territories? The question was put to the Ottawa conference of first ministers on aboriginal rights that took place in March 1984. Native delegates asked for the creation of a third order of government in Canada which, like the federal and provincial authorities, would have its own sphere of jurisdiction and its own institutions. For its part, the federal government proposed an amendment to the constitution enshrining the principle of tripartite negotiations on first-nation self-government. The proposed amendment was described as "non-justiciable," which meant that it was simply a declaration of good will and not enforceable in a court of law. This did not prevent six of the ten provinces from scuttling it on the spurious grounds that they did not understand its full implications. British Columbia, one of the leading obstructionists, was openly denounced by various Native leaders, but its representatives reasserted blandly under questioning by Rod Robinson of the Nishga that Native land rights were extinct in that province. The constitutional conference ended in great confusion, with no agreement on anything but a commitment to try again the following year.

Without provincial involvement, the principle of self-government will be reduced to an empty shell. Land, resources, health, education, social services, most of the elements of Native daily life fall within provincial jurisdiction. The reason for a province like British Columbia to oppose self-government is the same as the one behind its boycott of the land-claim process: satisfied with the present system of apartheid, it wants nothing to do with the revival of first nations. Even if the federal government kept faith with its recent commitment to Native self-government within however limited a sphere, the result would merely be a glorified reserve system without a Department of Indian Affairs. Such a development would fly in the face of the Penner recommendations, where it was clearly indicated that the report's proposals would be meaningless if the new "Indian self-government" lacked a proper land base. On this point, the Commons committee had supported a concept of land claims which was very close to the Nishga point of view: "The Committee recommends that the doctrine of extinguishment be eliminated from the settlement of claims; settlement agreements should be limited to those matters specifically negotiated."

In spite of Mr. Trudeau's late misgivings on the doctrine of extinguishment, the present position of the Canadian government on the question is far from clear. As the Penner report was being published, the federal government was putting the finishing touches to a major land-claim agreement for the Yukon that was in contradiction with the recommendations of the seven MPs. For four months, the Council for Yukon Indians tried to infuse the new spirit into the settlement, but Ottawa refused steadfastly to depart from its historic doctrine of extinguishment. On 26 January 1984, the C.Y.I. initialled a tentative agreement that had many elements of another James Bay. As requested by the federal government, the six thousand Yukon Natives relinquished title to 95 per cent of the territory in return for $186 million in compensation (in 1982 dollars) over a twenty-year period. The twelve Yukon bands retained control over twenty thousand square kilometres with additional trapping, fishing, and hunting rights over a larger area. The Yukon will be ruled on the one-government principle, and the Council for Yukon Indians will have a minority voice on certain boards and agencies of the territorial bureaucracy. The tentative settlement made no provision for Native control over natural resources and there was some doubt whether Natives would have sub-surface rights on the core twenty thousand square kilometres.

The wind of reform that was supposed to be blowing through the Indian Affairs department had failed to shake loose the old concept of surrender. The minister did promise, however, to ask Cabinet to modify its position on the doctrine of extinguishment, and referred the Yukon Indians to the constitutional forum for a final resolution of the issue. At the same time, a second agreement was initialled with the 2500 Inuit of the Yukon North slope, represented by the Committee for Original

Peoples' Entitlement, after nearly eight years of painful negotiation. This agreement in principle also reflected the "spirit of
James Bay": the Western Inuit had to recognize that their aboriginal rights to the Arctic shores were extinguished, in
exchange for ninety thousand square kilometres of land and
$147 million in compensation.

Native claims are often a puzzle to outsiders. Their constant
reference to the wrongs of the past, their use of such words as
"self-determination" and "sovereignty," their insistence on ownership over immense territories, are all perceived as chimerical
and unreasonable. Opinion-makers tend to dismiss Native goals
as futile since they fail to see "where it all leads, anyway." Just as
persistently, Native nations like the Nishga are deeply convinced of the rightness of a position that has been unchanged
since the first days of white power. No matter how politicians
have tried to justify the seizing of their lands, Native people still
refuse to consider the loss as permanent. The pressures to make
them think otherwise, however, to rush them into surrender,
are tremendous.

The first step in searching for the "real meaning" of land
claims is to understand the nature of contemporary settlements.
Behind each major breakthrough — Alaska, James Bay, and
possibly soon the Yukon and Northwest territories — are powerful forces wanting to open new resources to corporate development: Arctic oil in the case of Alaska, hydro-electricity in
northern Quebec, and oil, gas, and metals in the Yukon and
Northwest territories. The divisions such pressures have created
among U.S. Indians are also present, though less markedly, in
Canada. For their part, the Nishga people have so far maintained their unity. Their tribal council is a fighting entity, deeply
rooted in a tradition of struggle and fully accountable to its
membership. The council was not set up on a white model, and
thus does not share in the ambiguities that plague many other
Native organizations, created *ex nihilo* by government and promoted to the status of valid interlocutors by powers anxious to
strike a deal.

Land claims will no doubt eventually be settled, at least in
regions where massive white immigration has never occurred.
What is not-known is whether they will be settled in ways that
will allow the survival of Native societies or if the settlements will
merely serve the interests of pro-development forces. Large
companies know that a cloud of legal uncertainty hangs over

corporate plans. They have realized that they cannot rely on yesterday's ruthless methods to achieve their aims. Accordingly, they have learned the language of the land claims. A letter of 24 March 1983 from AMAX to Canada's minister of Indian Affairs clearly illustrates this:

> In past discussions with members of the Council for Yukon Indians and the Nishga Tribal Council, we have indicated that AMAX of Canada supports fair and expeditious settlement of native land claims . . .
>
> In view of the continuance of public interest in this matter, I thought it would be appropriate to reaffirm our position in writing to you and other concerned groups as a matter of clarification. We believe that an equitable and timely settlement of native land claims is in the best interest of all Canadians. In particular, we encourage those in the private resource sector who have not already done so, to also support such a settlement. This will facilitate the orderly development of Canada's resources, thus strengthening the country's economic activity for the benefit of all Canadians.

This recent corporate interest in "expeditious" settlements is more than a little suspect. The James Bay precedent and more recent efforts have as a common characteristic the surrender of the land, or most of it, in exchange for an assortment of specific benefits ranging from lump-sum payments to the "granting" of certain trapping, hunting, and fishing rights. The Nishga insistence that the land is theirs has consistently frustrated this approach. The years 1888, 1925, and 1978 are just some of the times when government officials have tried to dissuade them, realizing that if the Nishga were right more than 90 per cent of British Columbia and 40 per cent of the Canadian land mass would still be "Indian."

The Native concept is poorly understood among white Canadians, who sometimes think that Mrs. Smith will lose her summer camp or Mr. McLeod his cattle ranch as a result of land claims. The idea has often been exploited by politicians, most recently during the 1983 British Columbia election campaign, when Premier Bennett held that acceding to Native demands would endanger property rights in the province. Such statements misrepresent the real position. Although three white settlers presently own more land in the Nass Valley than the four thousand Nishga do on their reserves, the tribal council is not calling for the expropriation of any individual citizen. Nor, for that matter, is any other Native organization in Canada. "In principle," as stated in the Nishga position of July 1983, "lands which have been totally alienated to private ownership or industry would not be taken back. We would, however, expect to be compensated for this loss of land and for resources extracted prior to a negotiated settlement. We have always shared our wealth. Thus along with Nishga management and control, we are proposing continued sharing."

Another common prejudice against the claims is that the Natives are "greedy," that they will use the land they expect to receive for purposes of speculation. The Nishga reply is that everything will be taken care of within the frame of Native law, under the traditional ownership system still in place. The Nishga territory is divided into areas called "ango'osk" held by the various chieftains in the name of their respective "houses." Each "ango'osk" includes not only land but all its resources, and is used on a communal basis under the authority of the title-holder.

> Many of our chiefs have certain areas, places where they trap, where they pick berries, and so forth. Certain areas have boundary lines to each tribe. And there are four tribes in the Nass Valley. Now, having come this far to fight for the land the way it has been described, it was necessary to appear as one body of people instead of divided. Suppose there was a settlement in some chief's land. Now he'd be getting a sum of money all by himself, wouldn't he? No, the Nishga, in their wisdom, didn't want that. So we own the land as one people. And so there is no division in the whole land claim area. Everyone shares in every inch of the land that the government has taken away from us.

In North America, the white approach to land has been to carve private properties out of the "public domain," a solution that has always benefited the most affluent and powerful. The Nishga answer is very different. In allocating the lands eventually returned to them, they have decided to extend the communal principle of the "ango'osk" to the whole territory. The real problem is not "greed," then, but whether or not the Canadian state will now accept what it has tried for more than a century to destroy — a Native legal system immune to the concept of private ownership of land and resources.

Another objection to claims like those of the Nishga is that they are in effect an aboriginal version of apartheid and will lead to a multiplicity of small, exclusive nations with citizenship based solely on race. This is probably the ultimate perversion of the Native point of view. The Nishga have adopted several whites into their families, clans, and nation. The only criterion in such cases is the willingness of an individual to integrate into the Nass lifestyle. In the Northwest Territories, the Dene and the Inuit propose the creation of a "Denendah" and a "Nunavut" where outsiders would be granted full citizenship privileges after proof of their commitment to the North such as a minimum stay of some years in the area.

This is not to say that solutions are easy, but racism is certainly not the motive behind the Native movement. More fundamentally, those using the term "apartheid" against Native nationalism conveniently forget to ask the main question: who is in control? The South African "bantustans" and, as presently constituted, the reserves of Canada, have no real power. Power lies outside of Native societies and impedes their development. Thus the emergence of nationalism in indigenous peoples should not be seen as a threat to other ethnic groups, for it is an attempt to restore power to whole societies — an attempt at true democracy, not a new system of oppression.

It is often claimed that the Nishga and other such demands threaten the unity of Canada. To the federal elites, the new wave of Native nationalism is a regressive force that, like Quebec nationalism, could bring about the breakup of the country. It is true that nationalism is not a factor of progress in itself; historically, it has produced catastrophes as states tried to expand and dominate their neighbours. Here again, however, the nationalism of oppressed peoples is clearly different in kind. It is thus misleading to charge that satisfaction of native aspirations would lead to the balkanization of Canada. Recent history tells us that European states such as France and Spain have granted forms of autonomy to their Basques, their Catalans, or their Corsicans, without having to modify the locations of their borders. In America and elsewhere, nationalism stems not only from historical causes, but from a new phenomenon: a reaction by local populations to the general homogenization of lifestyles under the pressure of our monetary society. The Natives are not the only ones in Canada to be faced with a state and a system over which they have no real control. This is why their solution, a model of society in which power would be reappropriated by the people, carries a universal message.

For obvious reasons, the Native movement has always been suspicious of the white world and tried to maintain a safe distance from it. But the nature of its struggle brings it to conclusions that are shared by millions of individuals. The Native fight is the fight of all those trying to regain a sense of owning their own lives, those who are threatened by the "machine": land-deprived peasants of the Third World, citizens of the industrial heartlands refusing atomic plants or nuclear weapons on their doorsteps, fishermen against pollution and the asphyxiation of the sea, workers victimized by inhuman production and investment plans — opponents of all the madness of the present age.

SOURCES

Sources are listed here by page number.

CHAPTER 1

18 Jose Mariano Suarez de Figueroa Moziño, *Noticias de Nutka* (Mexico, 1913), 68

19 Hubert Howe Bancroft, *History of the Northwest Coast* (San Francisco, Bancroft Co., 1884), 251

21 George Vancouver, *A voyage of discovery to the North Pacific and round the world . . . performed 1790–95 with the "Discovery" and the "Chatham" under cap. George Vancouver* (London, 1798), 324

22 Ibid., 327, 330, 340

23 Ibid., 334, 337

24 Ibid., 382, 342

CHAPTER 2

27/8 Thomas Crosby, *Up and down the North Pacific coast by canoe and mission ship* (Toronto, Missionary Society of the Methodist Church, 1914), 209; W.H. Collison, *In the wake of the war canoe* (London, Dutton, 1915), 67, 69

29 Robert Tomlinson, "News from Kincolith" (London, the *Church Missionary Intelligencer*, new series, 1872), 216

30 J.B. McCullagh, "The Indian potlatch" (Toronto Woman's Missionary Society of the Methodist Church, n.d.), 6

31 William Henry Pierce, *From potlatch to pulpit, being the autobiography of the Rev. W.H. Pierce* (Vancouver, Rev. J.P. Hicks, 1933), 125

Robert Tomlinson, "Journal of a tour on the Naas and Skeena Rivers" (London, the *Church Missionary Intelligencer*, 1875), 255

J.B. McCullagh, "Progress among the Nishga Indians" (London, the *Church Missionary Gleaner*, March 1895), 37, 38

CHAPTER 3

36 Jonathan S. Green, *Journal of a tour on the Northwest coast of America in 1829* (New York, C.F. Heartman, 1915), 62, 80

37 Frederic Merck, *Fur trade and Empire: George Simpson's Journal, 1824–25* (Harvard University Press, 1931), 269, 300

38 Ibid.

39 Ibid., 309–11

40 William Fraser Tolmie, *Physician and fur trader* (Vancouver, Mitchell Press, 1963), 290

41 Ibid., 290–1

42 Merck, *Fur trade and Empire*, 324

43 Eugene Stock, *The History of the Church Missionary Society* (London, 1899, part vii), 617

44 Ibid., 618

45 Jean Usher, "William Duncan of Metlakatla: a Victorian missionary in British Columbia" (thesis, University of British Columbia, 1974), 86

CHAPTER 4

48 Collison, *In the wake of the war canoe*, 25; Alexander Begg, "A sketch of the successful missionary work of William Duncan 1858–1901" (Victoria, 1901), 9

49 N.E. Johnson, *Dayspring in the Far West: sketches of missionwork in Northwest America* (London, 1875), 146, 147
    Robert A. Doolan, "Naas-River station" (London, the *Church Missionary Intelligencer*, May 1865), 135

50 Ibid., 139, 140

51 Ibid., 133; R.A. Doolan, "Christian Missions in British Columbia" (London, the *Church Missionary Intelligencer*, August 1867), 248

52 R.A. Doolan, "Pacific Missions" (London, the *Church Missionary Record*, May 1868), 144; Hugh and Carmel McCullum, *Caledonia 100 years ahead* (Toronto, Anglican Book Centre, 1979)

54 "British Columbia: papers connected with the Indian question, 1850–1875" (B.C. Sessional Papers 1876), 230; 223

55 Tomlinson, "News from Kincolith," 213–14

56 Ibid., 216; Tomlinson, *Journal of a tour*, 255

57 Tomlinson, loc. cit.; "News from Kincolith," 215, 216

58 Crosby, *Up and down the North Pacific coast*, 197, 198, 200

59 Alfred E. Green, "New mission to Naas, from the Rev. Alfred E. Green, dated Naas River, B.C., September 21st, 1877" (Toronto, Missionary Notices of the Methodist Church of Canada, February 1878), 272

60 Crosby, 205, 206, 208

CHAPTER 5

62 Pierce, *From potlatch to pulpit*, 37

63 Tomlinson, "Journal of a tour," 287

65 McCullagh, "Progress among the Nishga Indians," 38

65 McCullagh, "In the North Pacific mission, letter from the Rev. J.B. McCullagh" (London, the *Church Missionary Intelligencer*, September 1893), 692, 693

66 McCullagh, "Progress among the Nishga Indians," 36, 37

67 J.W.W. Moeran, *McCullagh of Aiyansh* (London and Edinburgh, Marchall Brothers, 1923) 76

68 Ibid., 80

69 McCullagh, "The Indian potlatch," 3; 8; 5

70 Ibid., 16; 8

71 McCullagh, "A transformed people: the appliances of civilization the result of evangelization, the Rev. J.B. McCullagh's report of the Aiyansh Mission, British Columbia" (London, the *Church Missionary Intelligencer*, July 1896), 511

CHAPTER 6

75 Royal Proclamation of 1763, in Peter A. Cumming and Neil H. Mickenberg, *Native Rights in Canada* (Toronto, Indian-Eskimo Association of Canada, 2 ed., 1972), 291

76 R.A. Fisher, *Contact and conflict: Indian-European relations in British Columbia 1774–1890* (Vancouver, University of British Columbia Press, 1977), 171; R.E. Cail, *Land, man and the law: the disposal of Crown land in British Columbia 1871–1913* (Vancouver, University of British Columbia Press, 1974), Chapter 12

77 Cail, *Land, man and the law*, 198

79 "Letter from the Methodist Missionary Society to the Superintendent General of Indian Affairs respecting British Columbia troubles," with affidavits and declarations (Toronto, May 1889), 14; 15

80 Ibid., 65

81 Peter O'Reilly, "Letter to I.W.W. Powell and to Chief Commissioner of Lands and Works," Victoria, 5 May, 1882, in Indian Affairs black series, Public Archives of Canada, Ottawa; "Report — On Thursday, the 3rd February, 1887, at 11 o'clock in the forenoon, by appointment, a deputation of Indians from Fort Simpson and Naas River was received by the Hon. the Premier at his residence" (B.C. Sessional Papers, 1887), 257
Methodist Missionary Society "Letter," 71
British Columbia, *Royal Commission on Indian Affairs, evidence submitted to* (Victoria, vol. 5, 1915), 18; Methodist Missionary Society "Letter," 67

84 Usher, "William Duncan of Metlakatla," 127

86 British Columbia, "Papers relating to the commission appointed to enquire into the condition of the Indians of the North-West coast" (Victoria, B.C. Sessional Papers, 1888), vcii
British Columbia, "Report of Commissioners to the North-West Coast Indians" (Victoria, B.C. Sessional Papers, 1888), 426, 429

88 Ibid., 432

89 Ibid., 434

90 Ibid., 436; 438

91 British Columbia, "Papers relating to the commission," xcviii
"Letter to Lietutenant-Governor of British Columbia," in Indian Affairs black series, Public Archives of Canada

92 Victoria *Weekly Colonist*, 2 March 1888, "Letter to the editor from Indian chiefs dated Naas River, February 17, 1888"
Mimasth Scottain, "Letter to Indian Agent, Kitlaktamax, January 7, 1888," in Indian Affairs black series, Public Archives of Canada; Chief Sabasa, "Letter to Indian Agent, Kitwanselth, January 8, 1888," in ibid.; Methodist Missionary Society "Letter," 64

93 Clayduk, Gatcakayas, Victoria, Mountain, Ness Jash, "Letter to Mr. Todd, January 4, 1888," in Indian Affairs black series, Public Archives of Canada
Department of Indian Affairs, "Correspondence between Rev. Green and the Department regarding land belonging to the Indians of Naas River, B.C.," in Indian Affairs black series, Public Archives of Canada
Alfred E. Green, "Letter from Rev. A.E. Green, dated Greenville, Naas River, B.C., November 1st, 1887" (Toronto, the *Missionary Outlook*, vol. viii, January 1888), 14–15

94 "Report — On Thursday," 253–9

98 Department of Indian Affairs black series, Public Archives of Canada

99 Ibid.

100 Peter O'Reilly, "Letter to the Hon. the Superintendent of Indian Affairs" (Victoria, 4 October 1888), in Indian Affairs black series, Public Archives of Canada

CHAPTER 7

102 *Royal Commission on Indian Affairs, evidence submitted to* (vol. 5, 1915), 176–84

110 Ibid., 282–8

112 C.E. Cullin, "Report of Inspector of Pre-emptions, Skeena District, January 11th, 1915" (Victoria, B.C. Sessional Papers, 1915), D 28

113 Department of Indian Affairs, "Fisheries of Upper Nass villages, B.C., 1881–83" in Indian Affairs black series, Public Archives of Canada

114 John McNab, "Skeena and Naas Rivers, report of Fishery Guardian" (Victoria, B.C. Sessional Papers, 1889), 249; Cail, *Land, man and the law*, 172

115 V.H.E. Giraud, "The Indian food fishery of British Columbia," historical record prepared for the Department of Fisheries of Canada, 1975, 29, 5

116 Ibid., 28

117 *Royal Commission on Indian Affairs, evidence submitted to* (vol. 5, 1915), 190, 191

118 Ibid., 192; Canada and British Columbia, "Royal commission on Indian Affairs for the Province of British Columbia — confidential report" (Victoria, 1916), Public Archives of British Columbia, 15, 17

119 Giraud, "The Indian food fishery," 35

120 Ibid., 35; 33
Native Brotherhood of British Columbia, "Submission to the Commission on Pacific Fisheries Policy, volume II" (Vancouver, 24 July 1981), 22; 27

CHAPTER 8

121 Forrest E. Laviolette, *The struggle for survival, Indian cultures and the Protestant ethic in British Columbia* (Toronto, University of Toronto Press, 1961), 51

122 Ibid., 52, 68

123 New Westminster *Daily Columbian*, 26 February 1896, and the Victoria *Colonist*, 23 February 1896

124 Laviolette, *The struggle for survival*, 72, 79; Collison, *In the wake of the war canoe*, 344
125 Ibid., 345; Moeran, *McCullagh of Aiyansh*, 148
McCullagh, *The Valley of Eternal Bloom or the wonderful story of Aiyansh* (London, the Church Missionary Society, 1913), 27; 30
126 Newcombe Papers, 1870–1955, in the Public Archives of British Columbia; C.F. Newcombe, "Report on the proposed removal of a totem pole from the Nass River to the Museum of the American Indian, New York City," n.d., in the Newcombe Papers
127 Ibid.

CHAPTER 9

130 Moeran, *McCullagh of Aiyansh*, 157
131 *Royal Commission on Indian Affairs, evidence submitted to*, (vol. 18)
132 Ibid., 262
135 Friends of the Indians of British Columbia, "The B.C. land question from a Canadian point of view ... " (Victoria, 1914), Public Archives of British Columbia, 13; Cail, *Land, man and the law*, 233
136 "The Nishga Petition to His Majesty's Privy Council; a record of interviews with the government of Canada, with related documents" (Victoria, 1915), 4
137 Ibid., 5; 7
138 Privy Council of Canada, "Certified copy of a report of the Committee of the Privy Council approved by His Royal Highness the Governor General on the 20th June, 1914" (Ottawa, 1914)
139 Ibid.
140 Cail, *Land, man and the law*, 242
"Report of the special committee of the Senate and the House of Commons to inquire into the claims of the Allied Indian Tribes of British Columbia" (Ottawa, Journals of the Senate, 1926–27), appendix, ix; xi
141 An Act respecting Indians ..., c.I.98 s.141, 1927
142 Daisy Sewid-Smith, "Prosecution or Persecution" (Cape Mudge, B.C., Nu-Yum-Balees Society, 1979), 1

CHAPTER 10

146 Joint Committee of the Senate and the House of Commons on Indian Affairs, *Minutes of Proceedings and Evidence* (Ottawa, 1960), 582, 585
147 Ibid., 584
148 Ibid., 587, 584
149 Douglas E. Sanders, "The Nishga case," in *B.C. Studies* (Vancouver, Autumn 1973), 10
150 Cumming and Mickenberg, *Native rights in Canada*, 332
151 "In the Supreme Court of Canada, Calder et al. v. Attorney-General of British Columbia, Case on Appeal," statement of claim, 27 September 1967, 9; statement of defence, 23 January 1968, 14
152 Ibid., 30–3
153 Ibid., 112–17

157 Ibid., 521, 533; 540, reasons for judgement, 7 May 1970
158 Ibid., 555
159 *Calder, Frank, et al., plaintiffs-appellants. In the Supreme Court of Canada, v. Attorney-General of British Columbia* (Ottawa, 1973); Rod Robinson, statement at the World Council of Churches taped in Vancouver, 29 July 1983
160 Sanders, "The Nishga Case," 16; *Calder et al.*, 27; Sanders, 17
161 Department of Indian Affairs, "Response of the federal government to the position paper of the Nishga Tribal Council" (Ottawa, 10 January 1978), 2
162 Hugh and Karmel McCullum, *This land is not for sale* (Toronto, Anglican Book Centre, 1975), 66
163 "Citizen Plus. The Nishga people of the Naas River Valley in Northwestern British Columbia. Nishga land is not for sale" (Toronto, Project North, rev. ed. 1980), 27; 17
164 Ibid.; British Columbia, "Response of the Government of British Columbia to the position paper of the Nishga Tribal Council" (Victoria, 10 January 1978), 2
165 "Response of the federal government," 4
166 Ibid., 9; "Nishga Declaration," New Aiyansh, 1976
Nishga Tribal Council, "Position paper of the Nishga Tribal Council: future directions of the negotiations, prepared for a joint federal-provincial negotiation session to be held in Vancouver on April 27th, 1976," 4; 1; 3

CHAPTER 11

167 Thomas Berger, "The B.C. Indian land question and the rights of the Indian people," speech to the ninth annual convention of the Nishga Tribal Council, Port Edwards, B.C., 1 November 1966, 3
168 Harry Nyce, interview, Vancouver, April 1983; An Act respecting Indians, R.S.C. 1970 c.I-6 s.1, 4250
169 Nyce interview
170 Ibid.; Robinson, "Statement to the World Council of Churches"
171 Percy Tait, "Statement to World Council of Churches," Vancouver, 29 July 1983; Nyce interview
172 Noel V. Starblanket, "National Indian Brotherhood's letter to Native leaders" (Ottawa, 17 April 1979), 3; Tait, "Statement . . . "
Special Joint Committee of the Senate and the House of Commons on the constitution of Canada, evidence (Ottawa, 15 December 1980, vol. 25), 26–7
173 Nyce interview
174 Ibid.
175 Larry Still, "Drug-addicted infant remains for adoption," in the *Vancouver Sun*, 4 August 1983, A15
176 Cumming and Mickenberg, *Native rights in Canada*, 331

CHAPTER 12

181 Columbia Cellulose Ltd. *Annual Report 1960*, 7
182 Bill Horswill, "Canadian National Meziadin Project — Impact study — Sociology" (Terrace, B.C., 1975), 6.4; Bob McMurray, "Government gets Colcel for 'nothing,' " in *The Province*, Vancouver, 3 April 1973, 1

184 J.W. Schwab, "Soil disturbance associated with tractor skidding, access logging, and highlead yarding in the Prince Rupert Forest District." B.C. Forest Service, Prince Rupert Forest District, Smithers, January 1978

186 Richard Overstall, "The Nishga forestry proposal" (Telkwa, B.C., Telkwa Foundation Newsletter, January 1979), 8

188 Transport Canada, "Northwest Transportation Plan 1972" (Ottawa, February 1972), 3

189 W.A.C. Bennett, statement to the Royal Commission on the British Columbia Railway, in the *Vancouver Sun*, 15 September 1977, C12

191 Horswill, "Canadian National Meziadin Project"

CHAPTER 13

196 Jim Fulton, "Excerpts from the House of Commons Debates regarding AMAX" (Ottawa, June 1981), excerpt from 27 October 1980
   Ibid., from 16 January 1981, and private members' motions for papers, 22 October 1981

197 Sunday Morning, "Storm at Alice Arm," CBC radio, 4 July 1982

198 John MacLatchy, "Chronology of the drafting of the Alice Arm tailings deposit regulations," Environmental Protection Service, May 1981, 3: Dr. Cam MacLeod's memorandum to G.M. Cornwall, 11 October 1978
   Geoff Meggs, "Marchand pushed approval — New light shed on AMAX mine affair," *The Fisherman*, Vancouver, 28 February 1983

199 Sunday Morning, "Storm at Alice Arm"

200 Ibid.; D.E.C. Trethewey, "R.S.C.C. Project 133 — Climax Molybdenum Corporation, letter to Mr. R. Hoos, Environmental Protection Service, West Vancouver" (Delta, B.C., 11 December 1978), 1
   Sunday Morning, "Storm at Alice Arm"

205 Chester Benson interview, Canyon City, April 1981; Fulton, "Excerpts," 27 October 1980

206 Aspects Consultants, "The AMAX Molybdenum tailings controversy — Why tailings should not be dumped into Alice Arm — Fact sheet produced for the Nishga Tribal Council" (Vancouver, 13 February 1981), 13

207 Michael Waldichuk, "Memorandum to Dr. I.K. Birtwell — Climax Molybdenum, Kitsault, B.C. Project" (7 November 1978), 3

208 Roméo Leblanc, "Letter to the Honourable John M. Godfrey, Joint Chairman, Standing Joint Committee of the Senate and of the House of Commons on Regulations and other Statutory Instruments" (13 May 1982), in minutes, 3 June 1982, 66:4

210 Fulton, "Excerpts," 27 October 1980

211 Ibid.; Leblanc, "Letter," 66:45
   R.D. Kathman, R.O. Brinkhurst, R.E. Woods, and D.C. Jeffries, "Benthic studies in Alice Arm and Hastings Arm, B.C., in relation to mine tailings disposal" (Sidney, B.C., Institute of Ocean Sciences, Department of Fisheries and Oceans, 1983), 1; 2

213 United States Borax & Chemical Corporation, "Development Concepts for the Quartz Hill molybdenum project, First Judicial District, Alaska," prepared for the United States Department of Agriculture Forest Service, 2–6
   Ron Richardson, "AMAX opens up planning of giant tungsten mine," in *The Province*, Vancouver, 19 May 1982

CHAPTER 14

216 *Special Joint Committee . . . on the constitution . . .* , 26:13, 15

217 Ibid., 26:20

Department of Justice, "Text of the proposed constitutional resolution filed by the Deputy Attorney-General of Canada with the Supreme Court of Canada on April 24, 1981" (Ottawa, 1981) clause 34(1), 10

Vancouver Sun, "Exact text of the constitutional agreement," 5 November 1981, B1

219 *The Canadian constitution 1981 — A resolution adopted by the Parliament of Canada, December, 1981* (Ottawa, 1981), clause 35(1), 11

220 Department of Indian Affairs, "In all fairness, a native claims policy" (Ottawa, 1981), 23; 19

Kerra Lockhard, "Chrétien fumes over attack by Indian lobby, British MPs," in the *Vancouver Sun*, 19 February 1982

221 Nishga Tribal Council, "Nishga Tribal Council Statement on aboriginal rights" (Vancouver, January 1982)

222 "Elders' Position, the Okanagan Nation" (Vancouver, 29 January 1982)

223 W.R. Bennett, letter to Prime Minister Trudeau, 20 November 1981, at 1:00 P.M., as dictated to Mr. Mel Smith by Mr. Gardom over the telephone

224 British Columbia, Ministry of Intergovernmental Relations, "First Ministers' conference on the constitution aboriginal issues, overview paper, a negotiating strategy for the section 37 conference" (Victoria, 17 January 1983), 27, 32

225 Canadian Intergovernmental Conference Secretariat, "Federal-provincial conference of First Ministers on aboriginal constitutional matters, verbatim transcript" (Ottawa, 15–16 March 1983), 121, 118

226 Ibid., 128

227 Nishga Tribal Council, "The Nishga Position, some of your questions with Nishga answers" (New Aiyansh, July 1983)

CONCLUSION

229 House of Commons, "Minutes of Proceedings of the Special Committee on Indian Self-Government . . . including the Second Report to the House" (Ottawa, October 1983), 41

229 Canada, Indian and Northern Affairs, "Response to the Government to the Report of the Special Committee on Indian Self-Government," Ottawa, 5 March 1984, 5

230 Ibid., 115; 116

233 J.H. Foreman, "Letter to the Hon. John C. Munro, Minister of Indian Affairs and Northern Development" (Vancouver, 24 March 1982)

234 "The Nishga Position, some of your questions . . ."
Tait interview